THOUGHT DEVELOPMENTAL PRACTICE

Addressing Cognitive Issues *with* Coping Strategies
12 Modules Of Intensive Brain Training

Harrison S. Mungal, BTh, MCC, MSW, Ph.D, Psy.D
A Comprehensive Manual ©

Thought Developmental Practice

Copyright © Harrison Mungal

All rights reserved. Neither this publication nor any part of this publication may be reproduced or transmitted in any form or by any means, electronic or mechanical, including photocopying, recording or any information storage and retrieval system, without permission in writing from the author.

info@agetoage.ca
www.agetoage.ca
www.harrisonmungal.com
www.harrisonmungalbooks.com
Facebook: Harrison Mungal
Twitter: AgeToAgeInc1
LinkedIn: Harrison Mungal, Ph.D., PsyD
YouTube: Harrison Mungal

ABOUT the AUTHOR

With an extensive background in clinical psychology, Harrison is deeply committed to enhancing the lives of those he counsels. His academic credentials are impressive, boasting dual doctoral degrees in Clinical Psychology and Philosophy in Social Work and two master's degrees in Social Work and Counselling. He also holds a Bachelor's degree in Theology. His areas of expertise encompass mental health, addiction, marital and relationship, family dynamics, and parenting issues.

Recognized as a leading authority in cognitive therapy, Harrison is a sought-after presenter at workshops. His multifaceted role allows him to assist individuals, couples, families, and corporations. Harrison, a global public speaker, has addressed audiences in over 42 countries at various conferences, seminars, and public events. His reach extends to radio and television appearances and he has authored over 30 books. He is widely respected for his profound insights, as well as his engaging sense of humour and enthusiasm for subjects like mental health, addictions, relationships, and parenting.

Harrison's approach to his work is both inventive and grounded in scientific principles. This unique methodology has earned him a sterling reputation, along with multiple awards and accolades from an array of institutions, including law enforcement agencies, municipal governments, community leaders, and corporate executives. He offers training and consultations to a diverse range of community partners, including medical professionals, social workers, first responders, law enforcement officials, and senior management teams.

An active participant in cognitive research, Harrison has led several groundbreaking studies aimed at aiding people with mental health issues like addiction, psychosis, anxiety, and depression. Among these studies are explorations into music therapy for schizophrenia, vaccination protocols for young children, and the role of substance abuse in the food service industry. His work on Thought Developmental Practice (TDP) has been particularly notable for providing alternative treatments for conditions like substance abuse, anxiety, PTSD, and depression under Dr. David Koczerginski, a chief psychiatrist.

With over two decades of professional experience, Harrison has worked with a broad and diverse range of populations. His experience encompasses 17 years in the mental health and psychiatry fields and more than a decade as a practicing clinical psychotherapist. He has provided services to a myriad of communities, including those affected by Acquired Brain Injuries, refugees, victims of warfare, and individuals in crisis across various settings, which include collaborations with police forces, hospitals, community agencies, and inpatient mental health facilities.

In terms of therapeutic approaches, Harrison is well-versed in a wide array of evidence-based treatments. These include, but are not limited to, Cognitive Behavioral Therapy (CBT), Cognitive Processing Therapy (CPT), Dialectical Behavioral Therapy (DBT), and Acceptance and Commitment Therapy (ACT). He is also skilled in Interpersonal Therapy (IPT), Motivational Interviewing Techniques, Grounding Techniques, and various other specialized forms of treatment, such as Humanistic Experiential Therapy and Psychodynamic Therapy.

Author: Harrison S. Mungal.

TABLE *of* CONTENT

ABOUT *THE AUTHOR* 3
TABLE *OF* CONTENT 5
INTRODUCTION 15
WHAT *ARE* THOUGHTS? 19
    THE COMPLEXITY OF THOUGHTS 20
        THE EXPANSION OF THOUGHTS 20
        CONSCIOUS AND UNCONSCIOUS DECISION MAKING 20
        THOUGHT PATTERNS IN MENTAL HEALTH 20
        THE POWER OF WORDS AND THOUGHT RECONDITIONING 20
        STOPPING NEGATIVE THINKING THROUGH DISTRACTION 21
    TAKING CONTROL OF THOUGHTS 21
        ADVERTISING AND CONSUMER BEHAVIOUR: THE IMPACT OF VISUAL TRIGGERS 21
        NIGHTTIME THOUGHTS: BEFORE SLEEP AND THOUGHT MANIPULATION . 22
        THOUGHTS AND DAILY LIFE: EATING HABITS, SLEEPING PATTERNS, AND MORE 22
        A FOUR-STEP APPROACH TO MIND MASTERY 22
    BECOMING CHAMPIONS OF YOUR THOUGHTS 23
        THE MINDSET OF A CHAMPION: VISION, CONFIDENCE, AND INDEPENDENCE 23
        THE CHAMPION WITHIN: A CHOICE AND A PRACTICE 23
        RECONDITIONING THE MIND: TOOLS AND STRATEGIES FOR SUCCESS 23
NEGATIVE THOUGHTS 25

WHAT ARE THOUGHTS?

- DIFFERENTIATING NEGATIVE THINKING 25
- FROM NORMAL WORRIES 25
  - CATASTROPHIZING: THE FEAR OF FAILURE AND DISASTER 25
- STRATEGIES FOR CONQUERING NEGATIVE THOUGHTS 26
- THE COMPLEX INTERPLAY OF NEGATIVE THOUGHTS WITH LIFE 26
  - DWELLING ON PAST MISTAKES 26
  - FINANCIAL INSTABILITY 27
  - LOW SELF-ESTEEM AND LACK OF CONFIDENCE 27
  - UNREALISTIC GOALS AND SELF-BLAME 27
  - THE MIND-BODY CONNECTION 27
- SYMPTOMS AND CONSEQUENCES 27
  - STRATEGIES TO TRANSFORM NEGATIVE THOUGHTS INTO POSITIVE OUTLOOK 27
  - EMBRACE THE JOURNEY 30
  - SEEK PROFESSIONAL HELP IF NEEDED 30

MASTER *YOUR* MIND 31

- THE NATURE OF THOUGHTS 31
- STRATEGIES FOR MASTERING THE MIND 32
- THE JOURNEY TO MASTERY 32
- BREAKING THE BONDAGE OF NEGATIVE THOUGHTS 32
- PRACTICAL STRATEGIES FOR MASTERING THE MIND 33
- THE PATH TO FREEDOM AND FULFILLMENT 33
  - EMBRACING THE HUMAN EXPERIENCE 33
  - BUILDING RESILIENCE THROUGH CONNECTION 34
  - CULTIVATING A GROWTH MINDSET 34
- THE DUAL ROLES OF STUDENT AND TEACHER 34
- THE MIND AS A MIRACLE AND SERVANT 34
- HONOURING THE GUT FEELINGS 35
- CONTROLLING ASSUMPTIONS AND COMMUNICATION CHALLENGES 36
- THE POWER TO CONTROL NEGATIVITY 36
  - RECOGNIZING AND CONFRONTING NEGATIVE THOUGHTS 37
  - LEARNING FROM MISTAKES AND ACCEPTING IMPERFECTIONS 37
  - BUILDING EMOTIONAL INTELLIGENCE 37

- CULTIVATING RESILIENCE AND POSITIVE THINKING 37

THE MESOLIMBIC SYSTEM 39
- THE FUNCTION OF THE MESOLIMBIC PATHWAY 39
- STIMULATION OF THE MESOLIMBIC DOPAMINE SYSTEM 39
- ADDICTIVE BEHAVIOUR FROM A NEUROLOGICAL PERSPECTIVE 40
- THE NEGATIVE IMPACT OF NEUROTRANSMITTERS 41
- BRAIN AREAS AFFECTED AND STRATEGIES FOR HEALING 41

ADDICTION 43
- THE ROLE OF DOPAMINE BEHIND ADDICTIONS 43
- BREAKING THE CYCLE 44
- PHYSICAL ADDICTION 44
- BEHAVIOURAL ADDICTION 44
- IMPULSE CONTROL DISORDERS 45
- EXPLORING THE UNDERLYING CAUSES OF ADDICTION 46
- GENETIC FACTORS AND PEER INFLUENCE IN ADDICTION 46
- THE CYCLE OF ADDICTION AND ITS HEALTH IMPLICATIONS 46
- PSYCHOLOGICAL AND FINANCIAL CONSEQUENCES 47
- THE IMPACT OF ADDICTION ON RELATIONSHIPS 47

ABUSE 49
- TYPES OF ABUSE 49
- RECOGNIZING THE SIGNS 50
- INTERVENTION AND SUPPORT 50
- EXPANDING THE HORIZONS OF ABUSE 50
  - FINANCIAL ABUSE 50
  - SPIRITUAL ABUSE 51
  - NEGLECT 51
  - PSYCHOLOGICAL ABUSE 51
- CAUSES OF ABUSE 52
  - LONG-TERM EFFECTS OF ABUSE 53
  - FINDING HELP AND SUPPORT 53

TRAUMA 55
- CAUSES OF TRAUMA 56
- EFFECTS OF TRAUMA 57

A MULTIFACETED CHALLENGE	58
TYPES OF TRAUMAS	58
ACUTE TRAUMA	58
CHRONIC TRAUMA	59
THE COMPLEX LANDSCAPE OF TRAUMA	59
COMPLEX TRAUMA	59
TREATMENT APPROACHES	60
A COMPREHENSIVE UNDERSTANDING OF TRAUMA	61
POST-TRAUMATIC STRESS DISORDER	62
A COMPREHENSIVE UNDERSTANDING OF TRAUMA	64
PSYCHOSOCIAL STRESSORS	65
SOURCES AND TYPES OF PSYCHOSOCIAL STRESSORS	65
THE IMPACT OF PSYCHOSOCIAL STRESS	66
PERSONAL RESPONSE TO STRESS	67
WORK-RELATED STRESSORS	67
RELATIONSHIP-INDUCED STRESS	67
DAILY STRESSES	68
THE PSYCHOLOGICAL TOLL OF STRESS	68
NAVIGATING STRESS AND FINDING SUPPORT	69
MENTAL ILLNESSES	71
UNDERSTANDING AND OVERCOMING STIGMAS	74
PHYSICAL EFFECTS	74
SOCIAL IMPACT	74
ROAD TO RECOVERY	75
PHYSICAL AND EMOTIONAL MANIFESTATIONS	76
THE CHALLENGE OF HEALING	76
CRITICISMS AND STIGMAS	77
BUILDING A SUPPORTIVE ENVIRONMENT	77
ANXIETY	79
GENERALIZED ANXIETY DISORDER (GAD)	81
SOCIAL ANXIETY DISORDER	82
SELECTIVE MUTISM	82
SEPARATION ANXIETY DISORDER	82

- PANIC ATTACKS 82
- SPECIFIC PHOBIAS 82
- AGORAPHOBIA 82
- DRUG-INDUCED ANXIETY 83
- MEDICAL CONDITIONS AND ANXIETY 83
    - EMOTIONAL AND PHYSICAL HEALTH TRIGGERS 83
    - IMPACT OF CHILDHOOD EXPERIENCES 83
    - LIFESTYLE AND ENVIRONMENTAL FACTORS 84
    - UNPREDICTABLE ONSET AND LONG-TERM EFFECTS 84
- SHORT-TERM AND LONG-TERM CONSEQUENCES 84
    - IMMEDIATE PHYSIOLOGICAL RESPONSES 84
    - PERVASIVE EFFECTS OF CHRONIC ANXIETY 84
    - PHYSICAL AND PSYCHOLOGICAL TOLL 84
    - THERAPEUTIC APPROACHES 85
    - THE IMPORTANCE OF MENTAL RESILIENCE 85
- DEPRESSION 87
    - DISTINGUISHING DEPRESSION FROM SADNESS AND GRIEF 87
    - VARIED SUBTYPES OF DEPRESSION 87
        - BIPOLAR SPECTRUM 88
        - POSTPARTUM DEPRESSION (PPD) 88
        - SEASONAL AFFECTIVE DISORDER (SAD) 89
        - ATYPICAL DEPRESSION 89
    - GENETIC AND BIOCHEMICAL FACTORS 89
    - PHYSICAL AND PSYCHOLOGICAL CONSEQUENCES 90
    - PHYSICAL COMPLAINTS AND COEXISTING MEDICAL CONDITIONS 90
    - SELF-ESTEEM AND RISKY BEHAVIOURS 90
- PSYCHOSIS 93
    - A SPECTRUM OF PSYCHOTIC DISORDERS 93
        - PHYSICAL HEALTH AND ITS RELATIONSHIP TO PSYCHOSIS 94
        - MEDICAL CONDITIONS AS TRIGGER POINTS 94
    - SYMPTOMATOLOGY 94
        - THE SPECTRUM OF SEVERITY 95
        - THE ROLE OF SLEEP DISORDERS 95

WHAT ARE THOUGHTS?

    NUTRITIONAL FACTORS AND THEIR INFLUENCE 95
  THE COMPLEXITY OF PSYCHOTIC DISORDERS 95
    FINANCIAL AND RELATIONAL STRAINS 96
    SOCIAL IMPACT AND SUBSTANCE ABUSE 96
    GRAVE CONSEQUENCES FOR UNTREATED PSYCHOSIS 96
    THE DISINTEGRATION OF REALITY 96
MODULE - 1 101
  THOUGHT REDIRECTION 103
    WHAT IS THOUGHT REDIRECTION? 103
    PURPOSE OF THOUGHTS REDIRECTION 103
  THE START OF MENTAL DOWNFALL 104
    THE GRIP OF NEGATIVE THINKING 104
    REDIRECTING NEGATIVE THOUGHTS INTO POSITIVE THOUGHTS 105
  HOW TO REDIRECT THOUGHTS? 105
    STEPS TO REDIRECT THOUGHTS 106
  ACTIVITIES 106
    TYPES OF THOUGHT REDIRECTION ACTIVITIES 106
    THOUGHT REDIRECTION ACTIVITIES IN GROUP 106
MODULE - 2 117
  THOUGHT PREPARATION 119
    THOUGHT MANAGEMENT STRATEGIES 119
    KEY ELEMENTS OF MODULE-2 119
    FOUNDATIONS OF THOUGHT PREPARATION 120
  ACTIVITIES FOR THOUGHT PREPARATION 120
  GROUP/INDIVIDUAL EXERCISES 121
MODULE – 3 131
  THOUGHT DISTRACTION 133
    THE FUNDAMENTALS OF THOUGHT DISTRACTION 133
    THE IMPORTANCE OF THOUGHT DISTRACTION 134
  A PRACTICAL GUIDE 134
  MASTERING THOUGHT DISTRACTION 135
  GROUP/INDIVIDUAL ACTIVITIES 136
  THOUGHT DIVERSION – HOME ACTIVITIES 140

MODULE – 4 143

THOUGHT ILLUSTRATION 145
THE CONCEPT 145
THE SIGNIFICANCE OF THOUGHT ILLUSTRATION 145
ADVANTAGES OF THOUGHT ILLUSTRATION 146
ACTIVITIES 147
GROUP/INDIVIDUAL ACTIVITIES 148
SPECIAL ACTIVITY 157
IN THIS MODULE, YOU WILL BE DOING A PARTICULAR ACTIVITY THAT COMPRISES ALL THE PREVIOUS MODULES, INCLUDING "THOUGHT REDIRECTION, THOUGHT DISTRACTION, & THOUGHT ILLUSTRATION." THIS SPECIFIC ACTIVITY IS KNOWN AS "GREEN TIME," YOU CAN PERFORM IT DURING GROUP SESSIONS (AS GUIDED BY THE THERAPIST) OR AS HOMEWORK BY YOURSELF. YOU WILL GET CLEAR INSTRUCTIONS ON HOW TO DO THE "GREEN TIME" ACTIVITY FOR BOTH THE GROUP AND HOME SESSIONS." 157

MODULE - 5 161
THOUGHT EXPRESSION 163
UNDERSTANDING THOUGHT EXPRESSION 163
THE INTRICATE LANDSCAPE OF OUR THOUGHTS 164
SUPPRESSING THOUGHTS 164
NAVIGATING THE ART OF THOUGHT EXPRESSION 164
THE SIGNIFICANCE OF THOUGHT EXPRESSION 165
OBJECTIVES OF THOUGHT EXPRESSION 165
AN ESSENTIAL COMPONENT OF A FULFILLING LIFE 166
ACTIVITIES 167
HOME ACTIVITIES 175

MODULE - 6 177
THOUGHT SENSORY 179
THE CONCEPT 179
APPLICATION 179
FIVE SENSES AND THEIR IMPACT 181
VISION AND ITS PROFOUND INFLUENCE ON THOUGHT PROCESSES 181
HEARING: A MULTIFACETED SENSORY EXPERIENCE 182

WHAT ARE THOUGHTS?

    TOUCH: THE MULTIFACETED SENSORY EXPERIENCE 183
    TASTE: A COMPLEX SENSORY EXPERIENCE 184
    SMELL AND ITS PROFOUND INFLUENCE ON THOUGHT PATTERNS 185
STRATEGIES FOR LEVERAGING THE SENSES 186
TO OPTIMIZE THOUGHT PATTERNS 186
EXTEND THE ROLE OF SIGHT AND SOUND 187
THE INTEGRAL ROLE OF SENSORY TECHNIQUES 189
SENSORY ACTIVITIES 189
HOME ACTIVITIES 195

MODULE - 7 197
THOUGHT IMAGINATION 199
THE GATEWAY TO REALITY 199
THE SIGNIFICANCE OF THOUGHT IMAGINATION 199
ACTIVITIES 200

MODULE - 8 209
THOUGHT TRANQUILITY 211
A GATEWAY TO INNER PEACE 211
METHODS 211
CORE MINDFULNESS TRAINING 212
THE THREE-TIERED APPROACH 212
ACTIVITIES 213

MODULE - 9 221
THOUGHT AMPLIFICATION 223
THE SCIENCE AND ART 223
EXPLORING 223
STRATEGIES 224
THOUGHT AMPLIFICATION IN SUBSTANCE ABUSE 224
    THE DOUBLE-EDGED SWORD IN ADDICTION 224
    THE PSYCHOLOGICAL CASCADE 225
    THE NEED FOR POSITIVE AMPLIFICATION 225
EXERCISES FOR THOUGHT AMPLIFICATION 225

MODULE - 10 231
THOUGHT VALIDATION 233

THOUGHT DEVELOPMENTAL PRACTICE

THE ESSENCE OF THOUGHT VALIDATION 233
EXPLORING THE CONCEPT 233
LEVELS OF VALIDATION 234
    LEVEL 1: BE PRESENT 234
    LEVEL 2: ACCURATE REFLECTION 235
    LEVEL 3: GUESSING 236
    LEVEL 4: VALIDATING BY HISTORY 237
    LEVEL 5: NORMALIZING 238
    LEVEL 6: RADICAL GENUINENESS 239
THE CRUCIAL ROLE OF VALIDATION 240
    EMOTIONAL REGULATION THROUGH VALIDATION 240
    IDENTITY FORMATION AND SELF-CLARITY 240
    THE CEMENT OF RELATIONSHIPS 240
    FACILITATING EFFECTIVE COMMUNICATION AND MUTUAL UNDERSTANDING 240
    FOSTERING RESILIENCE AND PERSEVERANCE 241
INVALIDATION 241
CATEGORIES OF INVALIDATION 241
    EMOTIONAL INVALIDATION 241
    VERBAL INVALIDATION 241
    NONVERBAL INVALIDATION 242
METHODS OF INVALIDATION 242
    BLAMING 242
    HOOVERING 242
    JUDGING 242
    DENYING 243
    MINIMIZING 243
EMBRACE VALIDATION OVER INVALIDATION 243
    THE INTERSECTION OF MINDFULNESS AND VALIDATION 243
    EMOTIONAL MANAGEMENT THROUGH VALIDATION 244
    APPLYING LEVELS OF VALIDATION TO SELF-VALIDATION 244
ACTIVITIES 244
MODULE - 11 251

WHAT ARE THOUGHTS?

THOUGHT EXAMINATION 253
COMPONENTS OF MENTAL STATE EXAMINATION 253
    OBSERVATION OF THOUGHT PATTERNS: 254
    IDENTIFYING UNDERLYING THEMES: 254
    UNDERSTANDING EMOTIONAL RESONANCE: 254
    EVALUATING REAL-WORLD IMPACTS: 254
    ASSESSING RATIONALITY AND LOGIC: 254
PRACTICAL STEPS FOR THOUGHT EXAMINATION 254
PRACTICAL APPLICATION IN DAILY LIFE 254
MENTAL STATE EXAMINATION 255
    DOMAINS OF ASSESSMENT 255
ACTIVITIES OF THOUGHT EXAMINATION 258
MODULE - 12 267
THOUGHT EXPECTATIONS 269
UNDERSTANDING THOUGHT EXPECTATIONS 269
ACTIVITIES OF THOUGHT EXPECTATIONS 269
REFERENCES 275

INTRODUCTION

Thought Developmental Practice (TDP) emerged from extensive research and clinical efforts aimed at supporting individuals struggling with mental health challenges, including depression, anxiety, psychosis, and addiction. Mental health is a complex interplay of biological, psychological, and environmental influences, and addressing it requires a thoughtful, multifaceted approach. With a dedicated research team working alongside Chief of Psychiatry Dr. David Koczerginski, twelve comprehensive modules were developed to provide targeted support for individuals dealing with anxiety, depression, and addiction. These modules were designed using clinical expertise, patient-centered methods, and psychological principles to ensure effective intervention strategies. Rather than offering generic solutions, TDP provides structured, evidence-based activities and cognitive exercises to help participants build resilience and foster healthier thought patterns.

Understanding mental health requires recognizing the multiple factors that shape emotional well-being. External pressures, such as trauma, substance use, abuse, psychosocial stressors, medical complications, and family conflict, all contribute to psychological distress. Additionally, genetic predispositions and neurochemical imbalances play a critical role in mood regulation, often influencing symptoms of anxiety, depression, and addictive behaviors. Mental health challenges are not merely isolated conditions but rather dynamic states shaped by internal and external influences. Safeguarding mental well-being requires learning how to regulate thoughts, emotions, and brain chemistry, optimizing the release of neurotransmitters like serotonin and dopamine—key chemicals responsible for mood stability and motivation.

The structured modules within this book focus on activating the brain through cognitive engagement and behavioral interventions. These exercises serve as practical tools for reinforcing positive neural connections, allowing individuals to retrain their minds away from negative thought loops. A foundational concept in this approach is neuroplasticity, which refers to the brain's ability to reorganize and form new pathways based on experiences. This principle demonstrates that mental health is not static—it can be reshaped through intentional practices. By incorporating thought-conditioning techniques, mindfulness exercises, and behavioral modifications, participants can gradually strengthen their psychological resilience, reducing the impact of self-defeating thought patterns.

A key philosophy behind Thought Developmental Practice is the role of cognitive stimulation in emotional healing. Much like childhood activities that promote learning, creativity, and curiosity, adults require similarly immersive experiences that engage the brain while fostering mental well-being. Unfortunately, as individuals transition into adulthood, they often explore mental diversions that may be unhealthy or counterproductive, leading to reinforced maladaptive behaviors. The modules in this book are designed to redirect attention toward enriching activities that cultivate mental strength and emotional balance, replacing harmful coping mechanisms with constructive, self-enhancing strategies.

Psychological resilience is developed through consistent reinforcement of healthy cognitive behaviors. Individuals battling mental health challenges benefit from strategies such as emotion regulation, cognitive restructuring, and behavioral adaptation, which allow them to navigate stressful situations without falling into destructive cycles. By training the mind to process stressors differently, individuals gain control over how they react to emotional triggers, reducing impulsivity and promoting stability. These techniques are embedded within the modules in this book, equipping participants with actionable tools to sustain mental clarity and emotional well-being.

Additionally, TDP emphasizes the physiological aspects of mental health, highlighting the importance of lifestyle habits that optimize brain function. Psychological wellness is deeply connected to nutrition, exercise, sleep patterns, and self-care routines, all of which contribute to cognitive health and emotional regulation. Integrating holistic practices into daily life fosters a balanced mental state, ensuring that individuals can sustain long-term recovery and well-being. The activities presented throughout the modules encourage participants to develop self-awareness and self-compassion, reinforcing the belief that mental health is not merely about managing symptoms but about transforming one's cognitive framework for lasting success.

Ultimately, Thought Developmental Practice serves as a blueprint for personal transformation, allowing individuals to reshape their mental habits and cultivate resilience. Through structured interventions, cognitive reframing techniques, and emotional mastery exercises, participants will gain practical insights into how to regulate their thoughts, maintain psychological balance, and foster a growth-oriented mindset. This book is more than just a collection of strategies—it is a guide to reclaiming control over one's mental health and building a foundation for sustained emotional strength. With each module, individuals progress toward greater self-awareness, emotional intelligence, and cognitive flexibility, ultimately empowering themselves to overcome challenges and thrive in their personal and professional lives.

This workbook is designed to facilitate cognitive and emotional transformation by utilizing structured activities and psychological principles to reshape thought patterns. Research conducted with live patients has demonstrated its effectiveness in improving mental states, enhancing mood, and reducing anxiety. Notably, findings indicate a significant decrease in substance use, particularly cannabis, among individuals with addiction concerns. For some patients, especially those experiencing psychosis, the coping mechanisms introduced in these modules provided an alternative to cannabis use, allowing for healthier behavioral adaptations.

At its core, this workbook serves as a tool to help individuals understand and process their "memory cards"—the stored experiences and cognitive imprints that contribute to anxiety, mood disorders, and addiction. By fostering insight and self-awareness, individuals can identify patterns that may be influencing their emotional well-being. The structured exercises assist in resolving unresolved past experiences and replacing negative memory cards with positive, adaptive ones. The human brain, by nature, tends to reinforce negative experiences, often embedding them deeply within memory. Once formed, negative memories may persist indefinitely, influencing perception, emotional responses, and behaviors. These memories are frequently intertwined with sensory experiences—sounds, sights, smells, tastes, and physical sensations—creating strong neural associations that make them difficult to forget.

Unresolved emotional distress can resurface unexpectedly, particularly during periods of elevated stress. Much like a locked closet filled with forgotten burdens, suppressed emotions may remain hidden until the pressures of life cause the proverbial lock to rust, leading to an overwhelming resurgence of past trauma and anxiety. The objective of Thought Developmental Practice is not to eliminate emotions but to equip individuals with practical, psychologically sound strategies to manage their emotional responses effectively. This approach encourages individuals to utilize existing strengths and cognitive resources to support their well-being and foster constructive behavioral changes.

By engaging with these principles, individuals can uncover the root causes of unhappiness, deconstruct maladaptive habits, and replace harmful thought patterns with value-driven perspectives that reinforce self-worth and resilience. This process involves exploring the origins of emotional distress, analyzing its effects, and implementing strategies for resolution. Many deeply ingrained thoughts and emotions originate in childhood, shaping perceptions and behavioral responses well into adulthood. Painful, unacknowledged feelings can act as dormant psychological triggers, accumulating pressure until they manifest in distressing ways. Recognizing and addressing these underlying emotions before they escalate is essential in preventing psychological crises.

The early signs of emotional distress often resemble the warning signals preceding a volcanic eruption—small yet significant indicators that intervention is needed before overwhelming mental strain sets in. Thought Developmental Practice promotes proactive engagement with emotional challenges, helping individuals confront and process their experiences before they lead to detrimental consequences. Mental health difficulties are not obstacles to endure passively; rather, they are challenges that can be addressed and mitigated through structured intervention.

This workbook offers hope and guidance, empowering individuals to take control of their mental well-being. Thought processes, cognitive restructuring, and emotional expression shape identity, influencing how individuals navigate the world. By applying the strategies outlined in this workbook, individuals can enhance self-awareness, develop emotional intelligence, and build resilience. This journey is not about erasing emotions but about refining thought processes and

WHAT ARE THOUGHTS?

mastering the psychological mechanisms that govern mental well-being. Through dedication and practice, individuals can cultivate a strengthened, enlightened mindset, capable of facing life's complexities with confidence and wisdom.

WHAT *ARE* THOUGHTS?

Thoughts are intrinsic to human existence, accompanying us throughout our waking hours. Inescapable and residing within us, thoughts are shaped by what we see, hear, smell, taste, and touch. Our emotions influence them and derive sustenance from opinions, beliefs, perceptions, and ideas gathered through the five senses.

Thoughts act as a cognitive framework through which individuals interpret their surrounding environment. They provide the cognitive tools to process experiences, including those gathered through sensory perception (Sternberg, 2009). Importantly, thoughts are not static entities; they are dynamic and subject to alteration based on multiple factors such as beliefs, attitudes, environmental context, lived experiences, skill sets, and educational background.

The quality of these thoughts—whether positive or negative—significantly impacts an individual's mental and emotional well-being. For example, negative thoughts can trigger emotional responses like stress, anxiety, and anger, creating a psychological burden that may become increasingly difficult to manage. On the other hand, positive thoughts have the ability to enhance mental and emotional health by mitigating the effects of stress and anxiety (Sternberg, 2009).

Furthermore, humans possess the cognitive ability to manage their thought processes. When a thought arises, an individual has the option to either retain it for future reference or dismiss it if it is deemed irrelevant. If a thought is associated with a past event stored in memory, it has the potential to rekindle the emotions linked to that experience, thereby creating a complex interplay of thoughts and emotions that can be either constructive or destructive.

An illustrative example can illuminate this intricate relationship between thoughts, emotions, and memories. Suppose while walking down the street engrossed in a cell phone, one briefly notices a man wearing a red t-shirt. This observation seems inconsequential, yet a minor domestic issue triggers an unexpected wave of anger at home. Upon psychological assessment, it may be revealed that the sight of the red t-shirt unconsciously resurrected a traumatic childhood memory associated with a similar garment. This triggered memory card unleashed anger, influencing mental and psychological well-being.

The example underscores the need to address unresolved issues, as they may lurk within the mind like time bombs, ready to be activated at any unexpected moment. In simple terms, the complex nature of thoughts and their profound connection to emotions and memories necessitates a conscious effort to understand and manage them. The intricate tapestry of thoughts shapes our interpretation of the world and our emotional landscape, playing a vital role in our overall well-being. The mastery of thoughts, then, is not merely a cognitive exercise but a fundamental aspect of human existence, with far-reaching implications for mental health and personal fulfillment.

THE COMPLEXITY OF THOUGHTS

The Expansion of Thoughts

Thoughts are dynamic and often interconnected, revolving around a central idea or theme. They grow and develop based on the amount of attention bestowed upon them. A singular thought can blossom into multiple interconnected thoughts if not carefully managed. This expansion is fueled by sensory input, with thoughts deriving energy from whatever is connected to the five senses that resonate with our cognitive processes. In many ways, the dominant thought seeks to remain at the center, justifying every associated idea to maintain control and sustenance.

Conscious and Unconscious Decision Making

Decision-making is a complex process that occurs both consciously and subconsciously. Impulsive reactions can arise when provoked, leading to defensive or rude responses. Reflecting on the importance of pausing to process thoughts before responding, mainly when triggered, can prevent regrets and mistakes. Recognizing human imperfections and how they manifest through thought processes and verbalizing issues can lead to more thoughtful and practical resolutions. Taking time to analyze, dissect, and conclude feelings about what is heard or experienced can reduce stress and contribute to more enlightened outcomes.

Thought Patterns in Mental Health

For individuals grappling with mental health conditions, addictions, or psychological traumas, the mind can become a tumultuous landscape filled with conflicting and reinforcing thoughts. Addiction, for example, may be characterized by repeated justifications, often centred around the deceiving notion of "this will be the last time." Anxiety might stem from a thought triggered by a past abusive relationship or trauma. Those with psychosis may feel trapped by a thought pressured to act, especially if driven by hallucinations.

The Power of Words and Thought Reconditioning

Words profoundly impact the mind, sometimes triggering unfavourable memories or forming negative sentences. The brain's ability to search for words that connect to statements or experiences can lead to negative thought patterns. However, reconditioning the mind offers the opportunity to flush out negative words and experiences, replacing them with positivity. For those battling depression or mood disorders, the perception of darkness and pessimism can lead to feelings of hopelessness. But by changing thought processes and embracing positive words, individuals can activate an 'optimism switch.' Finding this metaphorical light switch in a dark room symbolizes the transformative power of positive thinking.

Stopping Negative Thinking Through Distraction

Everyone possesses the ability to halt negative thinking, often through simple distractions. Even a brief thirty-second diversion can shift focus. For example, a casual conversation with a colleague on the way to the washroom can momentarily replace an immediate need with a different subject of thought. Such examples illustrate how the mind's focus can be redirected, albeit temporarily.

The exploration of thoughts reveals a complex and multifaceted landscape where thoughts expand, intertwine, and influence decision-making, mental health, and overall well-being. The intricate relationship between thoughts, words, and emotions underscores the necessity for self-awareness and conscious control. Whether recognizing and managing the expansion of thoughts, making more deliberate decisions, understanding thought patterns in mental health conditions, reconditioning thoughts, or utilizing distraction to break negative thinking, the mastery of thoughts is an essential aspect of human psychology. The insights provided in this discussion illuminate the nature of thoughts and offer practical strategies for fostering positive thinking and emotional resilience. The journey through the mind's maze of thoughts is challenging and enlightening, offering pathways to personal growth, healing, and empowerment.

TAKING CONTROL OF THOUGHTS

The human mind is highly receptive to sensory triggers. A simple drive down the street, with the aroma of food wafting through the air, can awaken the brain, stimulating urges or cravings even if a meal was consumed earlier. These sensory cues, whether sight, smell, or taste, can lead to desires. Witnessing someone enjoying ice cream, coffee, or a burger can activate the senses and spark cravings. While often benign, unchecked and unhealthy urges can escalate into more significant problems. Hence, developing the ability to momentarily distract thoughts, even for as brief as thirty seconds, can become a transformative habit for rewiring the brain.

Advertising and Consumer Behaviour: The Impact of Visual Triggers

The power of visual cues in shaping desires is evident in daily life. Watching a television commercial for a coconut cream pie, fried chicken, cars, trucks, clothes, or any other product can create immediate desire. For those with a tendency toward impulsive buying, such advertisements can prompt online purchases or trips to physical stores to satisfy cravings. Window shopping, celebrity endorsements, and popular brands can also influence purchasing behaviour, illustrating the pervasive role of visual triggers in shaping thoughts and actions.

Nighttime Thoughts: Before Sleep and Thought Manipulation

Interestingly, thoughts often become more prominent just before falling asleep. Depending on their nature, thoughts can become fixed or even race uncontrollably. Like a movie playing in the mind, thoughts accumulated during disagreements or regrets throughout the day can take center stage. The ability to manipulate these thoughts, create distractions, or divert them to more positive channels is a skill that this workbook aims to impart.

Thoughts and Daily Life: Eating Habits, Sleeping Patterns, and More

The influence of thoughts extends to various aspects of daily life, including eating habits, sleeping patterns, concentration, memory, and overall emotional well-being. Left unchecked, negative thoughts can spiral into depression and anxiety. In the quest for quick coping strategies, individuals may resort to negative solutions such as gambling, alcohol, street drugs, misuse of prescription medications, or self-harm. This workbook emphasizes positive and healthy alternatives, teaching readers how to leverage disadvantages and implement strategies to gain control over thoughts rather than being led by them.

A Four-Step Approach to Mind Mastery

1. **Taking Control of Thoughts:** The initial step in strengthening the mind involves recognizing and taking control of thoughts, laying the foundation for retraining thinking patterns.

2. **Positive Thinking and Reconditioning:** Embracing positivity and optimism, even amidst life's challenges, constitutes the second step in reconditioning the mind.

3. **Re-phrasing and Restructuring Thoughts:** The third phase transforms how thoughts are framed, contributing to emotional healing.

4. **Living for Fruitful Goals:** The final step emphasizes pursuing meaningful and rewarding goals, empowering individuals to become champions over their thoughts.

The exploration of thought triggers, distractions, and reconditioning provides valuable insights into the complex interplay between the mind, sensory cues, daily habits, and overall well-being. From understanding sensory influences and consumer behaviour to nighttime thoughts and daily life, the ability to take control of thoughts emerges as a vital skill. Through a thoughtful and structured approach, individuals can learn to master their minds, fostering positivity, resilience, and empowerment. The journey towards thought mastery is multifaceted but achievable, offering a pathway to a more fulfilled and balanced life.

BECOMING CHAMPIONS OF YOUR THOUGHTS

Champions are not born; they are meticulously crafted. It is a pursuit of mastery over thoughts that enables one to conquer challenges such as addictions, anxieties, and depression. Champions transform their weaknesses into strengths and use regrets, mistakes, and hurts as nourishing soil to cultivate a flourishing future. They push relentlessly to overcome frailties, strive to win, and are not easily distracted. A champion's determination is a beacon that pierces the darkness, illuminating the path to triumph.

The Mindset of a Champion: Vision, Confidence, and Independence

A champion's mindset is characterized by an ability to see the bigger picture of life. They visualize where they want to be, where they can be, and what it takes to get there. Champions recognize that life's situations could always be worse and use this perspective to fuel their ambition. They embrace self-acceptance, feeling comfortable with who they are, even "dating" themselves and falling in love with their reflection in the mirror. They are not co-dependent and don't rely on others to add value or worth to their lives. Their confidence stems from the belief that life offers abundant opportunities if they take the necessary steps to reach their goals. Champion has vision and knows where they are going. They have confidence, and they don't rely on others to boost their ego so they can stay on track.

The Champion Within: A Choice and a Practice

We all have the potential to be champions if we choose to be. It requires deliberate practice to gain control, train yourself to excel, think positively, and maintain optimism about life. Champions are selective with their thoughts, not wasting time on those that bear no fruit. Negative thoughts such as "I feel like a failure" or "What's the purpose of my life anyway?" must be supplanted with affirmations like "I am not a failure," "My life has purpose and value," and "I have a bright future waiting for discovery."

Reconditioning the Mind: Tools and Strategies for Success

The journey to become a champion over thoughts involves reconditioning the mind. By infusing the mind with positive affirmations and embracing the tools and techniques outlined in this workbook, individuals can learn to recognize their inherent value and worth. Distracting and diverting the mind from unfruitful thoughts is essential in seeing oneself as valuable and worthy.

Becoming champions of our thoughts is more than a metaphorical aspiration; it's a tangible goal that can be achieved through dedication, self-awareness, and a positive mindset. Individuals can rise above their challenges by transcending weaknesses, embracing the vision of a fulfilling future, choosing to be champions, and employing tools to recondition the mind. The transformation from feeling low and depressed to a state of empowerment and self-love is a journey that requires perseverance, but the rewards are profound. Through this process, everyone has the potential to

WHAT ARE THOUGHTS?

discover the champion within, seize control of their thoughts, and chart a path to a life filled with purpose, joy, and fulfillment.

NEGATIVE THOUGHTS

Negative thoughts are a normal aspect of human thinking, stemming from our brain's hardwired tendency to lean toward negativity. As we mature, we learn to regulate our thoughts. Still, failure to control negative thinking can lead to both physical and mental misery, even triggering psychological illnesses like depression and anxiety. Seemingly insignificant at first, these pessimistic patterns can become deeply entrenched, affecting not only mental health but also physical well-being.

DIFFERENTIATING NEGATIVE THINKING FROM NORMAL WORRIES

It is vital to distinguish detrimental negative thinking from everyday life's natural stress and worries. Negative thoughts are characterized by demotivation and a depressive attitude towards oneself and others. While feelings of anger or sadness are normal responses to stressors, they become problematic when they overwhelm the mind and persist long after the triggering situation has passed.

Negative thinking can arise from various sources, including unnoticed or unmanageable stress, faults in brain chemistry, childhood traumas, and genetics. These thoughts can severely hinder performance at work or school and impair interpersonal interactions. A constant barrage of negative thinking can initiate a vicious cycle, deteriorating overall health and well-being.

Catastrophizing: The Fear of Failure and Disaster

One of the manifestations of negative thinking is "catastrophizing," where individuals expect failure and disaster, leading to an overwhelming fear of the unknown and anxiety about the future. This anticipation of negativity can render even small tasks daunting, eroding determination, confidence, and willpower.

The key to confronting and overcoming negative thoughts lies in acknowledging their presence and understanding their limitations. Recognizing that there is a boundary to what we can change about the future and learning to focus on the present is essential in breaking free from the grip of negative thinking.

STRATEGIES FOR CONQUERING NEGATIVE THOUGHTS

1. **Identify and Acknowledge**: Recognize the negative thoughts and accept them without judgment. Understand that they are a part of human experience but not an unchangeable reality.

2. **Seek Professional Help if Needed**: If negative thinking becomes chronic and debilitating, professional intervention, such as therapy or counselling, may be required.

3. **Practice Mindfulness and Meditation**: Embracing mindfulness techniques and meditation can help in grounding oneself in the present reducing the influence of negative thoughts.

4. **Build Positive Affirmations**: Create and repeat positive affirmations that counteract specific negative thoughts. This practice can rewire the brain to embrace positivity.

5. **Avoid Catastrophizing**: Teach yourself to avoid expecting the worst. Focus on what you can control and let go of unnecessary fears and anticipations.

Negative thoughts are not merely inconvenient; they can severely impede personal growth, happiness, and health if left unchecked. Understanding their nature, origins, and manifestations is the first step in confronting and overcoming them. Through conscious effort, mindfulness, positive affirmations, and professional help when needed, individuals can break the cycle of negativity and foster a more optimistic and fulfilling life. The journey may be challenging, but the transformation from being enslaved by negative thoughts to championing them is a rewarding pursuit that leads to empowerment, resilience, and a deeper appreciation of life's potential.

The Complex Interplay of Negative Thoughts with Life

Negative thoughts extend beyond sporadic moments of doubt or fear; they constitute a complex network interacting with multiple facets of our lives. This includes our interpretations of past errors, financial security, the setting of goals, self-blame, and even implications for our physical health (Kross, Ayduk, & Mischel, 2005). Recognizing the intricacies of this relationship is crucial for disentangling the pervasive influence of negative thoughts and redirecting oneself toward a more balanced and fulfilling life.

Dwelling on Past Mistakes

People with a negative mindset often fixate on past errors, mistakes, regrets, weaknesses, and failures, overshadowing their achievements and growth. The positive approach to mistakes is recognizing them, learning from them, and developing strategies to prevent repetition. It's about adopting a constructive perspective, akin to learning from a spilled glass of milk rather than succumbing to anger and frustration.

Financial Instability

Financial instability, whether due to unemployment, overspending, or lack of resources, can breed self-doubt and fear about the future. This often spirals into a loop of negative thoughts, further eroding mental and physical health. Learning from financial missteps and striving for stability is essential to breaking this cycle.

Low Self-Esteem and Lack of Confidence

Doubting one's skills and potential can lead to low self-esteem and a lack of confidence. Negative energies occupy the mind, fostering overthinking, worry, and fear. Continuous and destructive overthinking can become a hard-to-break habit, leading to mental health issues, including substance abuse and addictions, depression and anxiety. Unhealthy coping strategies can include the use of alcohol, cannabis, illicit drugs, misuse of prescription medications, suicidal thoughts and self-harm.

Unrealistic Goals and Self-Blame

Setting unrealistic or unachievable goals can place an undue burden on the mind. Failure to reach these goals often leads to a loss of self-confidence and self-blame, which fuels negative thoughts. Acknowledging and accepting mistakes, rather than playing the blame game, is vital for moving forward.

The Mind-Body Connection

The interplay between mind and body is profound. Physical ailments can lead to depressive and negative thoughts, while pent-up emotions, particularly fear or negativity, can drain mental energy and affect physical health. Recognizing and expressing emotions without judgment is critical to maintaining a healthy balance.

Symptoms and Consequences

Negative thoughts manifest in various psychological and physical symptoms, including disruptive sleep patterns, eating habit changes, restlessness, concentration difficulties, memory problems, anxiety, social isolation, digestive issues, fatigue, headaches, dizziness, suicidal ideation, and more. The influence of negative thoughts extends to relationships, academic performance, work lives, and overall happiness and success (Papageorgiou & Wells, 2003).

Strategies to Transform Negative Thoughts into Positive Outlook

NEGATIVE THOUGHTS

Negative thoughts are not immutable; they can be reshaped and redirected. This transformation requires conscious effort, self-awareness, and the application of scientifically proven methods. Here, we explore various strategies to help us change our negative thinking into an optimistic approach.

Identifying and Replacing Sources of Negativity

1. **Analyzing the Environment**: Identify the sources of negativity in your life, be it relationships, work, school, social media, or entertainment. Recognize how these factors influence your thoughts.

2. **Write down the negative thoughts along with positive thoughts:** Make sure you have more positive thoughts than negatives. You want your brain to acknowledge you are more positive than negative.

3. **Finding Positive Replacements**: Be creative in exploring ways to replace these negative influences with positive ones. Seek out uplifting music, constructive relationships, and inspiring content.

Embracing Physical Activity

1. **Exercise Regularly**: Engage in at least 30 minutes of physical activity daily. It doesn't have to be strenuous; even a simple walk can profoundly relieve stress and anxiety.

2. **Pick a game**: There are many games that do not require you to become exhausted. Find one you like.

3. **Try aerobics, jumping jacks, skipping and other physical activities**. Find some childhood games that can keep you physically active.

Connecting with Others

1. **Talk to Someone**: Conversing with someone close can divert negative thoughts and encourage a positive outlook. Try to talk with five people a week you have not spoken to for a while or never spoken to: strangers.

2. **Help Others**: Connecting and aiding others brings peace and positivity to your life and helps you realize that you're not alone in your struggles.

3. **Volunteer**: Find something you like to do where you can volunteer your time, like a food kitchen or a shelter in a nursing home. You can talk to others and connect.

4. **Join a club or a hobby**. You can find like-minded people with whom you can connect.

5. **Join a sports team or a group**. Finding a community group can help connect.

Cultivating Gratitude

1. **Recognize the Positives**: Focus on the positive aspects of your life and surroundings and express gratitude for them. This can shift the focus away from negativity.

2. **Get a jar**. Write down your gratitude and place them in a jar. At the end of every week, count them and treat yourself. Train your mind to have an attitude of gratitude.

3. **Send a message**. Get used to sending messages via social media, texting or email to those you are grateful for and express your gratitude.

Writing Down Thoughts

1. **Express Your Feelings**: Write down your thoughts and emotions, especially those that disturb your peace of mind. This can help you understand and control them.

2. **Create a Thought Journal**: Keeping a record of your thoughts and their causes can allow you to regulate and replace negative thoughts with positive ones.

3. **Practice CBT**. It is essential to practice CBT, where you verbally express optimism even if you have no evidence. Write down the best positive scenario when you have a negative thought.

Embracing Mindfulness Techniques

1. **Avoid Suppressing Thoughts**: Locking away negative thoughts can lead to depression or PTSD. Mindfulness techniques can lessen the impact of negative thoughts.

2. **Practice Meditation and Relaxation**: These exercises help control emotional reactions, allowing your mind to control the thought process.

3. **Mindfulness in Everyday Life**: Incorporating mindfulness into daily routines can lead to adaptive thinking and fewer negative thoughts after exposure to negative stimuli.

Developing New Habits

1. **Reconditioning and Restructuring Thoughts**: Continuously replace negative thoughts with positive ones. Develop new, healthy habits that shift attention from harmful to wholesome thinking.

2. **Create a Positive Lifestyle**: Make small, enjoyable changes, like limiting news, using positive affirmations, attending motivational events, and reading self-help books.

3. **Practice the Opposite**: Teaching the less dominant side of your life to be co-equal like your dominant side is essential. If your right hand is dominant, teach your left hand to be the same. Take a new route to your destination. Sleep on the opposite side of the bed. Eat with your less dominant hand.

Embrace the Journey

Transforming negative thoughts into an optimistic approach is a journey that requires patience, dedication, and a multifaceted strategy. It involves understanding the underlying causes of negativity and actively working to replace them with positive influences.

Engaging with supportive friends, family members, or professionals can enhance the process. Sometimes, the insight and encouragement of others can provide the perspective and strength needed to make significant changes.

Seek Professional Help if Needed

If negative thoughts persist and interfere with your daily life, seeking professional assistance from mental health experts can be a crucial step. Therapists can provide personalized strategies and support tailored to individual needs.

Overcoming negative thoughts is not a fleeting task; it is a continuous process of growth and self-discovery. It requires a deliberate and conscious effort to identify, challenge, and replace negativity with positivity. By employing these strategies and embracing a holistic approach, individuals can nurture an optimistic mindset that enhances their overall well-being and quality of life. The journey may be complex, but the rewards of a positive, resilient, and empowered mind are invaluable. Remember, the power to change resides within you, and these strategies are tools to help you unlock your potential, connect with others, and live a fulfilling and joyful life.

MASTER YOUR MIND

The mind, an extraordinary gift, holds a dual potential to be both a blessing and a curse, depending on how we harness its power. The flow of thoughts within our minds shapes our perception, interpretation, and overall mental well-being. The process of mastering the mind is an art that requires focus, skill, and determination. In this chapter, we will explore the various aspects of mastering the mind and delve into strategies that can help us control our thinking patterns, thereby enhancing our lives.

The Nature Of Thoughts

1. **Divergent Thinking**: Allowing thoughts to flow smoothly is essential, but not letting them dominate us is equally crucial. Unbridled thoughts can wreak havoc if not controlled, much like unruly children in a household.

2. **Unwanted Thoughts**: These thoughts can create unproductive and unhealthy thinking patterns. Actively changing our thinking to dispel such thoughts is vital to controlling our behaviours.

3. **Thoughts as Squatters**: Certain thoughts reside in our brains without our conscious permission, taking control of our thinking like a squatter seizing a property. Identifying and expelling these thoughts is essential.

4. **Conglomeration of Childhood Words**: Thoughts stemming from words spoken to us in childhood may linger unnecessarily, often leading to self-doubt and a constant struggle to fulfill others' expectations. Recognizing and discarding these thoughts can free us from their grip.

Strategies for Mastering the Mind

1. **Developing the Skill**: Mastering the mind requires practice and development, akin to mastering a career or hobby. It's a continuous process that accompanies us throughout life.
2. **Reprogramming Our Thinking**: By changing our thoughts, we can influence our feelings, enabling a greater level of peace and rest for the heart.
3. **Replacing or Interrupting Thoughts**: We can either replace our thinking with new thoughts or interrupt our thinking patterns. Both strategies require awareness of impulsivity in our thoughts.
4. **Ceremonious Discarding**: Symbolically discarding thoughts that stem from rejection and betrayal can help us break free from emotional pain. This process could involve placing a representation of negativity in a box and ceremoniously burying or burning it.

The Journey to Mastery

The journey to mastering the mind is not merely about suppression but about conscious control and redirection. It's about recognizing the thoughts that serve us and those that don't and actively choosing which ones to nurture.

The process fosters resilience and empowers us to become architects of our thoughts rather than slaves to them. It promotes a proactive approach to mental well-being rather than a reactive one.

Sometimes, the journey may require professional guidance, especially when dealing with deep-seated thoughts or traumatic experiences. Therapists and mental health professionals can provide tailored strategies to assist this mastery.

Mastering the mind is a profound and transformative journey. It's about taking the helm of the most powerful tool we possess and steering it in a direction that enhances our lives. The strategies and insights shared in this chapter are stepping stones toward that mastery. They equip us with the tools to navigate our thoughts' complexities, replace or interrupt those that don't serve us, and cultivate those that uplift and empower us. The path to mastery is a lifelong endeavour filled with challenges and triumphs, but the rewards are immeasurable. By mastering our minds, we unlock the potential to live more fulfilled, peaceful, and purpose-driven lives. It's a journey worth embarking on, with the promise of becoming not only the master of our thoughts but also the author of our destiny.

Breaking the Bondage of Negative Thoughts

Mastering one's mental landscape extends beyond mere cognitive regulation—it's fundamentally about emotional liberation. This journey necessitates dismantling internal barriers like fear, worry, anger, and frustration that often inhibit us. The process involves recognizing signs of mental entrapment like low motivation, poor self-esteem, insecurity, and emotional disorders.

It also calls for proactive control mechanisms, including self-affirmations and visual reminders. Avoiding self-criticism and transitioning from a victim to an empowered mentality are crucial steps in this transformative journey (Bandura, 1991; Seligman, 1991).

1. **Recognize the Signs**: Signs that you may be in bondage due to your thoughts. This may include a lack of motivation, low self-esteem, insecurity, anxiety, depression, passivity, and even violent behaviours.

2. **Take Control**: Assert yourself by affirming, "I am in control." Visual reminders, such as notes posted in visible places, can reinforce this declaration. Accountability for our thoughts and behaviours starts with us, not with blaming others.

3. **Avoid Self-Beating**: Acknowledge flaws and faults, but don't dwell on self-disappointment. Focus on problem-solving and seeking solutions rather than succumbing to negative thoughts.

4. **Escape the Slave Mentality**: This involves moving away from thoughts that belittle or bully us. The path to mastery consists of a shift from a victim mentality to empowerment.

Practical Strategies for Mastering the Mind

1. **Change Your Attitude**: Adopt a positive attitude towards yourself and others. Acknowledge that you don't have all the answers and that it's not your job to "fix" others. Extend positivity even to your adversaries.

2. **Embrace Opportunities**: Be alert to opportunities and willing to take risks. Failure is a stepping stone, not a roadblock. Each experience enriches your skill set and draws you closer to success.

3. **Accept People as They Are**: Recognize that you cannot change others or make them think like you. Acceptance, without the need for control, reduces anxiety and fosters healthier relationships.

4. **Take Responsibility**: Embrace your flaws, mistakes, regrets and weaknesses. Whether you're 100% right or 10% wrong, focus on solutions rather than blame. This mindset empowers you as the master of your life.

5. **Engage with Others**: We are social beings, and isolation can lead to psychological issues. Engaging with others without succumbing to negative influences demonstrates control and balance.

The Path to Freedom and Fulfillment

Embracing the Human Experience

The journey to mastering the mind is not about achieving perfection. It's about embracing our human experience with all its complexities and contradictions. It's about growing through our failures, learning from our mistakes, and finding strength in our vulnerabilities.

Building Resilience Through Connection

Connecting with others and recognizing the value of diverse perspectives enhances our resilience and enriches our lives. It helps us break free from the bondage of isolation and fear, forging connections that nourish our souls.

Cultivating a Growth Mindset

Adopting a growth mindset enables us to see challenges as opportunities rather than obstacles. It fosters a love for learning and resilience, leading to significant accomplishments.

Mastering the mind is an ongoing journey filled with discovery, growth, and transformation. It involves a conscious effort to break free from negative thought patterns, embrace opportunities, foster positive relationships, and take responsibility for our lives. It requires a shift from fear to empowerment, from isolation to connection, and from blame to accountability.

Following the practical strategies outlined in this chapter, we can pave the path to a life of freedom, fulfillment, and self-mastery. The road may be winding, and the journey may be challenging, but the destination is a place of inner peace, joy, and unbounded potential.

Mastering the mind is an art and a science, a journey that requires constant learning, growing, and adapting. As we continue to explore the strategies and principles for self-mastery, we uncover more profound layers of understanding, wisdom, and potential that empower us to live with intention, clarity, and purpose.

The Dual Roles of Student and Teacher

1. **Embrace the Student Mind**: To master our minds, we must become perpetual students, always willing to learn from others and our mistakes. A "know-it-all" attitude often masks insecurity. Openness to new ideas, continuous learning, and humility bring us closer to mastery. Every day brings new lessons, revelations, and growth opportunities.

2. **Become a Teacher**: Alongside being a student, becoming a teacher encourages us to learn to share knowledge. Preparing lessons, teaching others, and communicating effectively sharpens our skills and helps us control our thoughts. It fosters a sense of responsibility and purpose, aligning our thoughts with positive communication and influence.

The Mind as a Miracle and Servant

1. **The Wondrous Brain**: Our brain is a miraculous organ, holding vast amounts of information and resources. It enables us to recall and perform intricate tasks, like riding a

bike or crafting a beautiful piece of art. Understanding the brain's capacity helps us recognize our potential for mastery.

2. **Servant to Master**: While we are great servants to our minds, transitioning to mastery requires discipline, concentration, and thought filtering. Being mindful of what we allow into our minds through our five senses (seeing, smelling, tasting, touching, hearing) helps us manage our emotions and actions. If something is not beneficial, we must have the courage to eliminate it, like excising a harmful element.

Our thoughts, influenced by our senses, precede our emotions and actions. We can manage our feelings, behaviours, and words by controlling what goes into our minds. This mastery draws us closer to our destinies and inner peace.

Sometimes referred to as intuition, our "gut feeling" is often a warning or guidance system that we should not ignore. Whether it's a decision about visiting a friend or making a significant life choice, being alert to these inner signals helps us make decisions aligned with our values and aspirations. Ignoring this intuitive sense can lead to regret and unnecessary struggles.

Mastering the mind is a profound and multifaceted endeavour that requires ongoing vigilance, practice, and self-awareness. It involves adopting the roles of both student and teacher, recognizing the miracle of our minds, transitioning from servant to master, drawing closer to our destinies, and heeding our inner wisdom.

It's a pursuit that goes beyond mere cognitive control; it encompasses emotional intelligence, ethical decision-making, and a deep connection with our core values. It's about living with integrity, courage, compassion, and purpose.

In the end, the path to mastering the mind is a path to freedom, self-realization, and a life lived with joy, love, and meaning. It's a path that beckons us to walk with courage, curiosity, and conviction, knowing that we are the masters of our minds and, thus, the creators of our destinies.

The complexity of mastering our minds is further illustrated through real-life examples, strategies, and challenges that people face every day. From managing gut feelings to developing emotional intelligence, controlling assumptions, and combating negativity, the path to mastering our minds is filled with intricate details, lessons, and growth opportunities.

Honouring The Gut Feelings

1. **Listening to Intuition**: Many individuals recount their struggles with ignoring their "gut feelings," leading to negative outcomes. Learning to trust this intuitive sense and aligning actions accordingly can prevent falling into traps that stimulate negative thoughts.

2. **Healthy Coping Strategies**: For those battling addictions or social pressures, such as drinking at family events, healthy coping strategies like using club soda as a substitute,

setting limits, or employing distraction and diversion methods can be vital. Creating routines and habits that support healthy coping is a valuable tool in mastering the mind.

3. **Learning to Say "No"**: Sometimes, the desire to say "yes" can lead us down a dangerous path. Learning to say "no" helps us stay focused on our priorities and protects us from unnecessary mental turmoil. Saying "no" is not only acceptable but often necessary for self-preservation.

Controlling Assumptions and Communication Challenges

1. **Avoiding Assumptions**: We often make presumptions about communications, such as texts, emails, or phone calls, without knowing the full context. These assumptions can lead us down a rabbit hole of negative thinking. Ensuring clarity and preferring face-to-face communication can prevent misunderstandings.

2. **Emotional Intelligence in Conversations**: We must be cautious not to dominate conversations or manipulate others by steering them in the desired direction. Recognizing our tendencies to control or provoke others helps us engage in authentic, respectful dialogue. Emotional intelligence enables us to navigate conversations with empathy and awareness.

The Power to Control Negativity

1. **Battling Negative Talk**: Some people use negative talk about others to mask their insecurities. This negativity feeds on joy and creates an unhealthy mental environment. Recognizing this pattern and choosing to walk away from gossip and negativity is vital in mastering the mind.

2. **Fostering Positivity**: Cultivating a mindset that focuses on positive attributes and constructive conversations can transform our mental landscape. It promotes a healthier, more fulfilling life, free from the burdens of negativity.

Mastering the mind is not just about controlling thoughts; it's about nurturing wisdom, compassion, and integrity in every aspect of our lives. It involves listening to our intuition, developing coping strategies, learning to say "no," controlling assumptions, harnessing emotional intelligence, and fostering positivity.

The insights and experiences shared by clients and individuals demonstrate the universality of the struggle to master the mind. Yet, they also highlight the potential for transformation and empowerment. These real-life examples serve as both warnings and inspirations, guiding us on our journey toward mental mastery.

The journey to mastering the mind is ongoing, filled with trials, triumphs, mistakes, and milestones. It requires dedication, self-awareness, empathy, and resilience. But the rewards are profound: a life of clarity, purpose, joy, and fulfillment.

By embracing these strategies and lessons, we empower ourselves to become the architects of our thoughts, the sculptors of our emotions, and the creators of our destinies. We not only master our minds but unlock the doors to a more prosperous, more meaningful existence. The mastery of the mind is not merely a goal; it's a lifelong journey, a beautiful dance, and an invitation to the fullness of life.

As we delve further into the mastery of the mind, we must acknowledge and confront our tendency towards impulsive thoughts and reactions. These automatic responses can lead us to say or do things that might be offensive to others or bring emotional harm to ourselves. How can we manage these automatic thoughts and cultivate a more thoughtful and compassionate response?

Recognizing and Confronting Negative Thoughts

Recognizing the power of negativity is vital in the process of mastering the mind. Those who constantly dwell on negativity drain joy from their hearts. Escaping this trap requires awareness and a decisive shift towards healthier thinking. Walking away from negativity and refocusing on positive thoughts nurtures a healthier mind.

Learning from Mistakes and Accepting Imperfections

We must acknowledge our flaws, regrets, and mistakes but not allow them to define us. Understanding that we can learn from our missteps rather than wallowing in self-disappointment fosters growth. Our imperfections are part of our humanity, and accepting them with grace contributes to the mastery of the mind.

Building Emotional Intelligence

Emotional intelligence is the ability to recognize, understand, and manage our own emotions and influence the emotions of others. It's a key component in our journey towards mind mastery. We must learn to be observant, compassionate, and responsive rather than reactive. Tapping into our emotional intelligence enhances our relationships and personal development.

Cultivating Resilience and Positive Thinking

Resilience is the capacity to bounce back from adversity and maintain a positive outlook. Cultivating resilience involves setting goals, staying focused, and utilizing the power of positive thinking. Recognizing that we are in control of our thoughts enables us to transform our lives and achieve our aspirations.

Mastering the mind is an intricate journey of self-awareness, continuous learning, and personal growth. It involves recognizing and confronting negative thoughts, accepting imperfections, building emotional intelligence, and cultivating resilience. Embracing these principles empowers us to live with purpose and joy. The path to mind mastery is a fulfilling adventure, offering a profound transformation that resonates within us and ripples out into the world. The mastery of the mind is not a destination but a dynamic process, a lifelong exploration that beckons us to become the best versions of ourselves (Dweck, 2006).

THE MESOLIMBIC SYSTEM

The mesolimbic pathway, often dubbed the "reward pathway," is a circuit within the brain that plays a critical role in the experience of pleasure, reward, and motivation. This neural network has profound implications not only for the general understanding of human psychology but also for comprehending various psychiatric conditions, such as addictions, anxiety, depression, and psychosis.

The Function of the Mesolimbic Pathway

The mesolimbic pathway primarily involves the ventral tegmental area (VTA), the nucleus accumbens, and the prefrontal cortex. The neurotransmitter dopamine is centrally important in this system (Schultz, 2015). When the pathway is activated—often by rewarding stimuli like food, sex, or social interaction—dopamine is released, creating a feeling of pleasure and reward. However, this system can be hijacked by artificial stimuli, such as addictive substances or behaviours, leading to an array of mental health issues (Volkow, Koob, & McLellan, 2016).

Stimulation of the Mesolimbic Dopamine System

When artificially stimulated by substances like drugs or alcohol, the mesolimbic system can produce effects that support addictions, anxiety, and depression (Goldstein & Volkow, 2011). In the case of substance abuse, the pleasurable feelings generated by dopamine release can become associated with the substance, leading to addictive behaviours (Hyman, Malenka, & Nestler, 2006). Similarly, disruptions in this system can contribute to anxiety and depression, as the individual may lack the neurochemical support for feeling pleasure or motivation in everyday life.

From a neuroethological standpoint, the mesolimbic system encourages behaviours essential for survival and reproduction. However, this system can easily be exploited in a modern context, leading to maladaptive behaviours. For example, the consumption of high-sugar or high-fat foods, initially an evolutionary advantage, can lead to health issues like obesity when the reward system is overactivated.

Addictive Behaviour from a Neurological Perspective

Understanding addictive behaviour from a neurological standpoint demands a comprehensive examination of the intricacies of the brain's reward system, particularly the mesolimbic pathway. This neural circuitry evolved to encourage behaviours essential for survival and is highly susceptible to being taken over by addictive substances or activities, leading to a range of maladaptive outcomes (Goldstein & Volkow, 2011).

Dopamine, often termed the 'pleasure neurotransmitter,' plays a dual role in addiction. On the one hand, it initiates feelings of pleasure and satisfaction as a reward for pro-survival behaviours like eating and mating (Schultz, 2015). On the other hand, dopamine release can be artificially triggered by addictive substances such as drugs or alcohol or even by addictive behaviours like gambling (Hyman, Malenka, & Nestler, 2006). When these substances or behaviours stimulate dopamine release, they can control the brain's natural reward system.

The phenomenon where addictive substances 'hijack' the reward system is not merely a metaphor but a description of what happens at the neuronal level (Volkow, Koob, & McLellan, 2016). When an addictive substance activates the mesolimbic pathway, the flood of dopamine is often much more intense than what is naturally experienced (Goldstein & Volkow, 2011). This exaggerated dopamine release leads to stronger neuronal connections associated with the substance or behaviour, reinforcing the desire to consume the substance again. Over time, this creates a powerful cycle of craving and consumption, making it increasingly difficult to resist the substance or behaviour.

Compounding the problem of addiction is the brain's ability to adapt. Constant exposure to addictive substances leads to a desensitization of the dopamine receptors (Goldstein & Volkow, 2011). This means that over time, the individual needs more substance to achieve the same level of pleasure, leading to a phenomenon known as tolerance. This is a dangerous stage in addiction, as it often necessitates escalating doses of the substance, increasing the risk of overdose and other health complications.

Apart from tolerance, another neurological aspect to consider is cue sensitization. The brain becomes more sensitive to the substance and cues associated with it (Robinson & Berridge, 2008). This means that places, people, or things that remind the individual of the substance can trigger intense cravings, even if the substance itself is absent. This makes the process of quitting even more challenging, as everyday environments can become filled with triggers (Goldstein & Volkow, 2011).

The good news is that the brain is a highly plastic organ capable of forming new connections and weakening old ones. Treatments like Cognitive Behavioral Therapy (CBT) can help individuals understand the triggers and thought patterns that lead to addictive behaviour. Pharmacological treatments can sometimes assist in reducing cravings and withdrawal symptoms. However, recovery often involves long-term commitment and possibly lifestyle changes to avoid relapse.

The Negative Impact of Neurotransmitters

When the brain is flooded with neurotransmitters like dopamine or serotonin, it can lead to a range of negative impacts, affecting mood levels, contributing to psychosis, and exacerbating anxiety (Howes & Kapur, 2009; Albert & Benkelfat, 2013). For instance, excessive dopamine release has been implicated in psychotic episodes, while imbalances in serotonin can contribute to mood disorders.

Multiple studies indicate that therapy, particularly cognitive-behavioural approaches that target the underlying thought patterns driving these behaviours, has been effective in treating individuals with addictions, anxiety, depression, and even psychosis (Hofmann, Asnaani, Vonk, Sawyer, & Fang, 2012). These therapeutic interventions often aim to correct the maladaptive behaviours and thought patterns that exploit the mesolimbic system (Paulus & Stewart, 2014).

Brain Areas Affected and Strategies for Healing

In addition to the mesolimbic system, other brain areas like the amygdala and hippocampus are implicated in anxiety, depression, and other mental health conditions (McEwen, 2007). Therapeutic interventions, lifestyle changes, and, in some cases, medication can help recalibrate the brain's reward system, aiding in recovery and symptom management (Koob & Volkow, 2010; Nestler & Carlezon, 2006).

In summary, the mesolimbic pathway plays a crucial role in regulating behaviours and emotions, and its dysfunction is central to multiple psychiatric conditions. Understanding this system can help clinicians and researchers develop more effective treatments, offering hope for those afflicted by these disorders (Paulus & Stewart, 2014; Hofmann et al., 2012).

THE MESOLIMBIC SYSTEM

ADDICTION

Addiction is a complex neuropsychological disorder that compels individuals to engage in extreme and continuous patterns of behaviour, often involving the use of substances or participating in activities that offer short-lived euphoria but lead to long-term detrimental effects on both physical and mental well-being. Essentially, addiction manifests as an overwhelming urge or dependency on activities or substances that provide intense bursts of excitement and pleasurable feelings in a brief period. However, once the euphoria dissipates, individuals often find themselves in a state of emotional emptiness, devoid of energy and motivation for any productive engagement. To escape feelings of worthlessness and guilt, they return to their addictive behaviours, seeking the illusionary sensations of happiness, empowerment, and relief from worries and tensions.

While it was traditionally thought that addictions primarily revolved around alcohol and recreational drugs, contemporary understanding recognizes a broader and more potent range of addictive behaviours. These include cyberaddiction, sexual addiction, compulsive shopping, video gaming, gambling, and even disordered eating.

The Role of Dopamine behind Addictions

The inability to control oneself, despite awareness of the harmful and morally questionable nature of the behaviour, is a hallmark of addiction. The overstimulation of dopamine, a powerful neurotransmitter produced by the hypothalamus in the brain, is responsible. Dopamine plays a crucial role in regulating motivation, pleasure, memory, reward, social skills, and cognitive functions. In the context of addiction, dopamine is excessively secreted, leading to heightened pleasure sensations. When the addictive stimulus is removed, normal levels of dopamine are insufficient to induce pleasure, compelling the individual to return to addictive behaviours thus perpetuating a vicious cycle.

Dopamine not only initiates addictive behaviours but also reinforces them. When individuals engage in activities or consume substances that trigger a sharp increase in dopamine, they experience a surge of pleasure and activation of their brain's motivation and reward centers. This drives them to seek similar experiences repeatedly, leading to addiction. Over time, elevated dopamine levels trick the brain into considering this heightened state the new normal. Consequently, in the absence of the addictive stimulus, the brain struggles to meet its recalibrated dopamine requirements, compelling individuals to return to artificial dopamine enhancers. As a result, the brain's ability to derive pleasure from average, initially rewarding activities diminishes, perpetuating the cycle of addiction.

Breaking the Cycle

Interrupting this dopamine-driven cycle is an arduous task, often requiring comprehensive intervention and specialized treatment approaches. As addiction progresses, the brain becomes increasingly resistant to deriving pleasure and motivation from activities once considered rewarding. Thus, breaking free from the grip of addiction becomes a complex, multifaceted challenge, often necessitating a combination of medical, psychological, and lifestyle interventions.

The exploration of addiction reveals a deeply intricate interaction between neuropsychological processes, emotional states, and behavioural patterns. Understanding these mechanisms is crucial for anyone grappling with addiction, as well as for those seeking to support them in their journey toward recovery.

Addiction manifests in various forms, encompassing not just the well-known realms of alcohol, smoking, and drug use but also extending to less traditionally recognized areas such as gaming, shopping, social media, and even emotional dependency on another person. Medical professionals broadly categorize addictions into three main classifications: Physical Addiction, Behavioural Addiction, and Impulse Control Disorders.

Physical Addiction

Also known as substance or chemical addiction, Physical Addiction is characterized by a physiological dependency on a specific substance that induces feelings of euphoria and dissociation from reality. This may include addictions to alcohol, tobacco, cocaine, crystal meth (ice), marijuana, opioids, prescription medications like sedatives and tranquillizers, phencyclidine, inhalants, and hallucinogens.

Behavioural Addiction

While substances like drugs and alcohol often dominate discussions around addiction, a new and equally pervasive category known as "Behavioural Addiction" has gained attention. This form of addiction offers the same dopamine-induced highs that substances do, compelling individuals to lose self-control and submit to activities or behaviours that provide immediate gratification. Behavioural addictions are characterized by persistent and compulsive attitudes that become habitual. Although the individual may appear physically normal, their mind is entangled in a web of destructive behaviours. Compliance with these mental compulsions often leads to adverse outcomes, affecting multiple facets of an individual's life, from physical and psychological well-being to social, financial, and even spiritual aspects. Examples encompass a wide range of activities such as social media usage, gambling, video gaming, pornography, sexual behaviours, food-related disorders, compulsive shopping, exercise fixation, workaholism, self-harm tendencies, and various forms of obsession, including emotional and spiritual.

While not explicitly discussed, Impulse Control Disorders form another critical category in the study of addictive behaviours. These disorders often manifest as an inability to resist urges or impulses, leading to potentially harmful actions that serve immediate needs or desires.

Understanding the intricacies of these categories and their respective examples aids not only in the diagnosis but also in crafting customized treatment plans that address the unique challenges presented by each form of addiction. This comprehensive classification underscores the complexity and diversity of addictive behaviours, calling for nuanced and multifaceted approaches to both understanding and treating this pervasive issue.

Impulse Control Disorders

Impulse Control Disorders represent another specialized subcategory of addictions. These are psychological disorders characterized by an individual's inability to regulate emotions and behaviours that can result in significant harm or destruction. This type of addiction often coexists with other forms, including substance or behavioural addictions. It is further divided into several distinct classifications, including Kleptomania, Trichotillomania, Gambling, Pyromania, and Intermittent Explosive Disorder (IED).

- **Kleptomania**: Individuals with kleptomania experience an overpowering compulsion to steal items, even when these items are not needed or wanted.

- **Trichotillomania**: This disorder involves a compelling, uncontrollable urge to pull out hair from various parts of the body, such as the scalp. It is now categorized under obsessive-compulsive disorder (OCD).

- **Gambling**: Classified under behavioural addictions, gambling involves an irrepressible urge to engage in betting activities, even when it leads to severe financial or personal loss.

- **Pyromania**: This is characterized by an intense, bizarre urge to set fires. Medical professionals believe that pyromania may serve as a coping mechanism for suppressed emotions and anxiety.

- **Intermittent Explosive Disorder (IED)**: This involves sudden, intense outbursts of anger, aggression, or violent behaviour triggered by minor provocations. IED is commonly observed in individuals who come from environments where verbal or physical abuse is prevalent.

Exploring the Underlying Causes of Addiction

The root causes of addiction are complex and not fully understood, but it is generally believed that multiple factors contribute to the onset of addictive behaviours.

- **Mental Health Factors**: Existing mental health conditions, such as depression, anxiety, OCD, and psychosis, can significantly predispose an individual to addiction. When traditional medications fail to replenish depleted levels of "happy hormones," the risk of adopting addictive behaviours to cope with mental distress escalates.

- **Work-Related Stress**: While moderate levels of stress and anxiety are a standard part of professional life, an overwhelming work environment can push individuals toward addictive behaviours as an escape mechanism.

- **Financial Instability**: Economic challenges, such as unemployment, lack of education, overspending, and medical expenses, can contribute to addictive behaviours like heavy drinking, gambling, and drug abuse.

- **Childhood Trauma**: Individuals who have experienced childhood trauma or abuse are more likely to develop addictive behaviours later in life.

- **Relational Strains**: Lack of supportive relationships or emotional bonds with friends and family can also be a potential trigger for addiction.

- **Hereditary**: Individuals who grew up with alcoholic parents, family members and loved ones can develop an addictive behaviour.

Understanding these multiple facets and their intricate relationships provides a more comprehensive perspective on addiction. This nuanced understanding is crucial for developing targeted and effective treatment strategies, thereby addressing the complexities inherent in addictive behaviours.

Genetic Factors and Peer Influence in Addiction

The role of genetics in predisposing individuals to addiction is an area of ongoing research. While empirical evidence is still emerging, some studies have identified specific genetic markers that may be linked to addiction. It is essential to note that environmental factors often act in concert with genetic predispositions to precipitate addiction. A leading external factor is the influence of one's social circle. If you find yourself in the company of individuals who engage in addictive behaviours—be it alcohol, drugs, or gambling—you're more likely to develop similar habits. Your family members, friends, and even colleagues can significantly impact your lifestyle choices, including the development of both beneficial and detrimental habits.

The Cycle of Addiction and Its Health Implications

Addiction frequently exists as a self-reinforcing cycle, often stemming from or exacerbating existing mental health issues. The detrimental impact on health is well-documented, with a range of possible consequences depending on the nature and duration of the addiction. These can range from cardiovascular and lung issues to cognitive impairments and life-threatening conditions like seizures and strokes (Degenhardt & Hall, 2012).

Alarmingly, addiction also poses a significant risk of overdose and death. In the United States alone, it is estimated that approximately 90 people succumb daily to opioid overdoses (Scholl, Seth, Kariisa, Wilson, & Baldwin, 2018). Understanding the multidimensional nature of addiction, including its health implications, is essential for effective intervention and support.

Psychological and Financial Consequences

Beyond its physical toll, addiction has profound psychological repercussions, including increased risk of depression, anxiety, panic attacks, and dependency disorders. In more severe cases, individuals may experience hallucinations, delusions, and psychosis. Rates of self-harm and suicide are also notably higher among those struggling with addiction. Financially, the costs can be devastating. Whether it's losing significant amounts of money through gambling or spending on substances, the financial instability wrought by addiction is another of its destructive consequences.

The Impact of Addiction on Relationships

Finally, addiction takes a heavy toll on interpersonal relationships. The incessant quest for immediate gratification often pushes people with an addiction to neglect their loved ones. Additionally, addictive behaviours can breed impulsivity and aggression, leading to a breakdown in social interactions and family life. This emotional turbulence can manifest as abusive behaviour, violence, and estrangement from friends and family, further deteriorating the quality of social life and intimate relationships.

Understanding addiction requires a multi-faceted approach that considers genetic, environmental, and psychological factors. The first step toward breaking the vicious cycle of addiction is recognizing its complexity and the multitude of ways it impacts various aspects of life, from health and finances to relationships and emotional well-being.

In conclusion, addiction serves as a corrosive force that degrades virtually every dimension of one's life. Its detrimental effects are not confined to the individual alone but radiate outward, impacting public safety, economic stability, and the social fabric of communities. For instance, the increasing rate of road traffic accidents attributable to impaired driving is a chilling testament to how addiction can jeopardize not only the addict's life but also those of innocent bystanders. Academic underachievement and unemployment often plague those entangled in the web of addiction, further diminishing their prospects for a fulfilling life.

Moreover, addiction erodes critical life skills and emotional competencies. A loss of self-control is frequently observed, coupled with diminished communication abilities. Financial woes are almost a given, as resources are squandered in pursuing the next 'high.' The degradation of both physical and mental health follows suit, often culminating in a life marred by chronic illness, emotional turmoil, and reduced life expectancy.

Perhaps the most heart-wrenching outcome is the potential estrangement from loved ones. As addiction takes hold, it can dismantle the most enduring relationships, leaving the individual isolated at a time when a support network is most needed for recovery. The ripple effects of addiction extend beyond the immediate circle, destabilizing families and communities and contributing to broader social issues.

Given the far-reaching consequences, it's imperative to steer clear of even seemingly minor or 'harmless' addictive behaviours. Prevention is undoubtedly the best course of action. However, if you or someone you know is already ensnared by addiction, immediate intervention is crucial. Seeking assistance from loved ones, medical professionals, and support groups can initiate the journey towards recovery. Early treatment is not just advisable; it's vital. It provides the best chance for reclaiming a life derailed by addiction and restoring the physical, emotional, and social well-being that is the right of every individual.

Through comprehensive understanding and proactive measures, it is possible to break the shackles of addiction and reclaim a life of purpose, health, and meaningful relationships. Remember, though steep, the path to recovery is never lonely if undertaken with the proper support and resources.

ABUSE

Abuse is a complex, multifaceted issue that transcends physical violence. It encompasses emotional, psychological, and sexual maltreatment, each capable of leaving emotional scars that last a lifetime. Whether within the family, relationships, workplaces, or communities, abuse can happen to anyone, anywhere, and its impacts are far-reaching and devastating. This chapter aims to shed light on different types of abuse, recognizing the signs and emphasizing the importance of intervention and support.

Types of Abuse

1. **Physical Abuse:** Perhaps the most recognizable form, physical abuse involves intentional acts of violence, such as hitting, punching, choking, and burning. It can leave visible signs like bruises, lacerations, and fractures or more subtle indications like confinement or improper drug use.

2. **Emotional Abuse:** Emotional abuse can be as damaging as physical violence. It encompasses behaviours aimed at humiliating, threatening, or intimidating the victim, leading to feelings of helplessness, withdrawal, and anxiety. It can erode a person's self-esteem and mental well-being over time.

3. **Verbal Abuse:** A subset of emotional abuse, verbal abuse utilizes words to dominate, manipulate, or humiliate. Insults, name-calling, and threats can have a profound impact on a person's mental health.

4. **Sexual Abuse:** Sexual abuse involves forced or coerced sexual acts, ranging from inappropriate touching to forced intercourse. It can leave physical signs like bruises in the genital area or more concealed indications like difficulty sitting or walking.

Recognizing the Signs

Recognizing the signs of abuse is crucial for intervention and support. Early detection can break the cycle of abuse and prevent further harm. Some signs to watch for include:

- **Physical Indicators:** Unexplained bruises, lacerations, or other injuries.
- **Behavioural Changes:** Withdrawal, anxiety, depression, or sudden changes in behaviour.
- **Emotional Cues:** Feelings of helplessness, constant fear, or low self-esteem.
- **Relationship Red Flags:** Dominance, control, or isolation exercised by a partner or family member.

Intervention and Support

If abuse is suspected, speaking up and offering support is vital. While it can be an uncomfortable conversation, victims of abuse often feel isolated and alone. Being there for someone can make a significant difference.

- **Provide a Safe Space:** Encourage open communication, listen without judgment, and ensure confidentiality.
- **Offer Assistance:** Help the victim explore options, such as counselling, legal assistance, or shelter.
- **Encourage Professional Help:** Encourage seeking professional support from therapists, counsellors, or support groups.

Abuse, in all its forms, is a grave and complex issue that can have long-lasting effects on an individual's mental health and overall well-being. It requires comprehensive understanding, compassion, and active intervention. Recognizing the signs of abuse and taking timely action can save lives and foster healing. As a society, we must strive to create a culture of empathy, awareness, and proactive support to ensure that those affected by abuse find the strength and resources to rebuild their lives. No one should suffer in silence, and together, we can make a stand against abuse in all its manifestations.

Expanding the Horizons of Abuse

Abuse, a topic already fraught with pain and suffering, expands even further into aspects of life that might go unnoticed. Financial abuse, spiritual abuse, neglect, and psychological abuse are all equally destructive yet often overlooked or misunderstood. This segment delves into these lesser-known forms of abuse, each with its unique characteristics and devastating impacts.

Financial Abuse

Financial abuse represents a manipulative control over a person's financial resources. Financial abuse can impede a person's ability to achieve financial stability and independence, leading to feelings of entrapment and despair. This type of abuse often intersects with physical or emotional abuse and can manifest in various ways:

- **Denying Access to Finances:** This includes restricting access to bank accounts, credit cards, or other financial resources.
- **Obstructing Employment:** Harassing or physically harming the victim before crucial job-related events, thus affecting their work opportunities.
- **Forcing Financial Dependence:** Creating a situation where the victim becomes financially dependent on the abuser, making escape nearly impossible.

Spiritual Abuse

Spiritual abuse occurs when religion or spirituality is used to manipulate, control, or harm. Spiritual abuse can severely affect a person's spiritual identity and emotional well-being. This can include:

- **Forcing Religious Practices:** Compelling someone to engage in religious activities against their will.
- **Preventing Religious Expression:** Restricting someone from practicing their spiritual beliefs.
- **Justifying Violence:** Using religion to excuse abusive behaviour.

Neglect

Neglect involves the failure to provide essential care and necessities. It primarily affects vulnerable populations such as children, the elderly, and individuals with disabilities. Neglect is a severe problem with long-term physical and emotional consequences.

Signs include:

- **Unsuitable Clothing or Hygiene:** Lack of proper clothing, grooming, or hygiene.
- **Missing Medical Appointments:** Neglecting essential healthcare needs.
- **Developmental Issues:** Especially in children, neglect can lead to developmental delays or disorders.

Psychological Abuse

Psychological abuse focuses on damaging a person's mental or emotional well-being. It can occur in various relationships and is often subtle and difficult to detect. Psychological abuse requires careful observation and support to identify and address. Symptoms may include:

- **Manipulation and Control:** Using words or actions to manipulate or frighten the victim.
- **Emotional Withdrawal or Aggression:** Sudden changes in behaviour, becoming unresponsive or hostile.
- **Chronic Mental Stress:** Leading to anxiety, depression, or other mental health issues.

Abuse transcends physical boundaries, affecting various facets of human life, including financial stability, spiritual beliefs, primary care, and mental well-being. Recognizing these forms of abuse is a critical step toward effective intervention and ultimate healing. The abusive acts, regardless of their nature—financial, spiritual, neglectful, or psychological—share a common intent: to exert control and inflict harm. The lingering impact of these abuses can extend far beyond the cessation of the abusive acts themselves (Follingstad, Rutledge, Berg, Hause, & Polek, 1990; Hamby & Grych, 2013).

Healing and recovery often start with recognizing the signs of abuse and seeking help. Support systems, including friends, family, and professionals, can provide invaluable assistance in this journey. In a society where discussions surrounding abuse often remain muted, raising awareness, fostering empathy, and taking action stand as powerful tools for change (Postmus, Plummer, McMahon, Murshid, & Kim, 2012; Ullman & Peter-Hagene, 2016). Understanding the complex roots and the lingering impacts of abuse is vital for survivors and those who aim to provide them with support.

Causes of Abuse

1. Family Background: Some individuals grow up in environments where violence is normalized. Exposure to abusive behaviour during formative years can significantly shape their attitudes and behaviours, increasing the likelihood of them becoming abusers themselves.

2. Substance Abuse: Dependence on alcohol or drugs can cause individuals to lose control, leading to violent tendencies. Substance abuse often leads to erratic behaviour, impaired judgment, and increased aggression.

3. Cultural Factors: Cultural norms and patriarchal systems in certain societies may view women and children as property, subjecting them to control and abuse. These ingrained beliefs perpetuate a cycle of violence that becomes socially accepted.

4. Addiction in the Family: Living with a family member who has an addiction creates a toxic environment filled with blame, anger, and resentment. The emotional turmoil can later manifest as abusive behaviour.

5. Financial and Social Stressors: Financial difficulties, social pressures, victim blaming, and stigmatization can all contribute to a climate where abuse is more likely to occur.

Long-Term Effects of Abuse

The scars of abuse, whether emotional or physical, often linger, manifesting in various ways:

- **Emotional Trauma:** Emotional abuse can lead to mental health issues such as depression, anxiety, and self-harm. Trust issues may arise, hindering the formation of healthy relationships.

- **Physical Consequences:** Physical abuse can result in PTSD, eating disorders, sleep disturbances, and chronic fatigue. These effects disrupt daily routines and overall well-being.

- **Perpetuation of Abuse:** Children who experience abuse may unconsciously seek out unhealthy relationships later in life, continuing the cycle of abuse.

Finding Help and Support

Recovery from abuse requires time, effort, and a robust support system. Here's how to seek help:

- **Professional Assistance:** Therapists or counsellors specializing in abuse and trauma can provide therapy, coping strategies, and a safe space for open communication.

- **Medication:** If depression or anxiety results from abuse, medication prescribed by mental health professionals may alleviate symptoms.

- **Building a Support System:** Connecting with friends and family who provide emotional support and safety is crucial.

- **Prioritize Safety:** If abuse continues, immediate steps must be taken to ensure safety. This may include leaving the situation, seeking legal aid, or contacting organizations and hotlines dedicated to providing support and shelter.

Abuse, in its many forms, leaves a lasting imprint on the lives of those who endure it. A complex web of factors can contribute to its occurrence, each intertwining and compounding to create a destructive pattern that's often difficult to break.

Yet, there is hope.

Professional help, supportive loved ones, and personal resilience can guide the way toward recovery. Knowledge, empathy, and compassion are powerful tools in this battle against abuse, illuminating the darkness and offering a beacon of hope to those who suffer.

The fight against abuse is not just an individual struggle; it's a collective endeavour that requires societal awareness, understanding, and action. By recognizing the signs, understanding the causes, and actively supporting survivors, we can create a world where no one has to suffer the silent agony of abuse.

ABUSE

Abuse, in all its cruel and insidious forms, leaves deep scars that stretch far beyond the immediate moment of victimization. It infiltrates every aspect of life, undermining self-worth, shattering trust, and often perpetuating a cycle that can span generations. The complexity of abuse demands a comprehensive, compassionate, and societal response that both acknowledges the pain of the victims and actively works to prevent further harm.

While deeply personal and often fraught with obstacles, the healing journey is not a solitary path. It is paved with the care and empathy of professionals, friends, family, and community. Recovery is not an event but a process that requires time, patience, understanding, and the courage to reach out for support. The steps toward healing are as diverse as the individuals who walk them, yet they converge on a universal truth: that the human spirit, with nurturing and care, can triumph over trauma.

However, the onus of addressing abuse extends beyond the healing of the individual victim. It calls for a collective awakening to the ugly reality of abuse, coupled with a resolute commitment to eradicate it. Raising awareness is not a mere slogan but an urgent call to action.

It entails educating ourselves and others, recognizing the signs of abuse, fostering environments of safety and respect, and challenging the norms that enable or trivialize abuse. It's about casting aside judgment, stereotypes, and indifference replacing them with compassion, equality, and vigilance.

Supporting survivors of abuse is a moral imperative that transcends any single organization or person. It is the heartbeat of a compassionate society that sees the inherent dignity in every individual. From offering therapy, legal assistance, and sanctuary to simply lending a listening ear, every act of kindness helps restore the broken pieces of a life marred by abuse.

In the battle against abuse, there is no room for complacency. The stakes are too high, the pain too profound. We must recognize that preventing abuse is not solely the responsibility of professionals or lawmakers; it's a shared responsibility that begins with our attitudes, words, and actions.

Abuse is not a distant problem confined to certain pockets of society; it is a haunting spectre that can touch any life. It is a challenge that demands our attention, empathy, and resolve. As we navigate the complex terrain of understanding, preventing, and healing from abuse, we must do so with the unshakeable belief that change is possible. We can build a world where respect and dignity are not mere ideals but lived realities.

We owe it to ourselves, to each other, to our children, and to future generations to make that world a reality. Let us not merely hope for a world free from violence and abuse; let us work tirelessly to create it. In the words, actions, and hearts of each of us lies the power to transform suffering into healing, despair into hope, and silence into a chorus of voices united against abuse. The time to act is now, and the responsibility is ours.

TRAUMA

Trauma is a profound and complex human experience that defies simple categorization. It reaches into the deepest recesses of the mind, altering how we perceive the world and often reshaping the very fabric of our being. Whether precipitated by a sudden accident, a violent assault, the shock of natural disasters, or the haunting spectres of war, trauma lays bare our vulnerability, our fragility, and our humanity.

The initial impact of a traumatic event might be characterized by shock, disbelief, or an overwhelming sense of grief. But trauma, by its nature, is insidious. Its roots spread, often unnoticed, affecting the very core of an individual's mental and emotional well-being. These effects are not uniform, nor are they predictable. They are as varied and unique as the individuals who experience them.

For some, trauma may manifest in a torrent of emotions: fear, anxiety, anger, sadness, a profound sense of loss, or even numbness and dissociation. These emotional symptoms can feel overwhelming, leading to a turbulent inner world that feels out of control. For others, trauma may express itself through physical ailments: headaches, fatigue, nausea, insomnia, and a host of other somatic complaints that are baffling in their persistence.

In some cases, the aftermath of trauma crystallizes into a more chronic and debilitating condition known as post-traumatic stress disorder (PTSD). PTSD is more than a collection of symptoms; it is a disruption of the normal process of healing, a lingering wound that refuses to mend. Its hallmarks—flashbacks, nightmares, emotional avoidance, and a pervasive sense of impending doom—can become a relentless cycle, trapping the individual in a state of perpetual distress.

But amidst the pain and turmoil, there is hope. Healing from trauma is not a linear path, nor is it without its challenges. But it is possible. It requires courage, resilience, and often the guidance of trained professionals who understand the complex landscape of trauma. Therapies tailored to the individual's needs, support groups, medication, and holistic approaches can all play a vital role in recovery.

Recognizing that trauma is not a sign of weakness but a human response to extraordinary events is pivotal for healing. The act of seeking help should be seen not as an admission of defeat but as a courageous step toward regaining control and finding renewed purpose (Brewin, Andrews, & Valentine, 2000; Herman, 2015).

Understanding trauma also calls for a societal approach that goes beyond individual experience. It necessitates empathy, education, and a commitment to fostering environments—be they workplaces, schools, or broader communities—that are attuned to the needs of those who have undergone trauma (Magruder, Kassam-Adams, Thoresen, & Olff, 2016; Substance Abuse and Mental Health Services Administration, 2014).

Moreover, preventive measures are crucial. This involves creating safe spaces and addressing the root causes that predispose individuals to traumatic experiences, such as violence, inequality, and discrimination (Felitti et al., 1998; Slopen, Shonkoff, Albert, Yoshikawa, Jacobs, Stoltz, & Williams, 2016).

The discourse on trauma highlights our collective vulnerability and collective strength, emphasizing the importance of compassion, understanding, and human resilience. It imbues us with hope and a belief in recovery while reinforcing the need to support those who bear the invisible scars of their past (Tedeschi & Calhoun, 2004; Van der Kolk, 2014).

Causes of Trauma

Chronic Illness in the Family

Children growing up with chronically ill parents face a unique set of challenges that can lead to trauma. The anxiety stemming from the fear of losing a parent, coupled with the burden of assuming parental responsibilities, can create an environment ripe for emotional turmoil. The child's developmental needs may be overshadowed by the demands of caregiving, leading to a sense of abandonment and neglect.

Neglect During Childhood

Neglect is a silent trauma that can leave deep scars. Children who grow up with physically or psychologically absent parents may carry the wounds of abandonment well into adulthood. This intentional or unintentional absence can shape the child's self-perception, creating a void that's hard to fill.

Turbulent or Abusive Parenting

Emotionally turbulent or abusive parents can inflict harm that transcends physical injuries. Verbal assaults, emotional manipulation, and unpredictable behaviour can erode a child's self-esteem, creating a constant state of nervous tension. This emotional maelstrom can lay the groundwork for lifelong trauma.

Systematic Racism and Violence

For people of colour subjected to systematic racism and violence, trauma becomes a shared experience. The relentless threat, humiliation, and injustice create a chronic state of fear and vulnerability that can lead to PTSD. This trauma is not confined to individual incidents but reflects a broader societal failure.

Road Accidents

A sudden road accident can shatter lives in an instant. Beyond the immediate physical injuries, the psychological impact can be profound and enduring. The memories of the accident, the pain, and the potential disabilities can haunt survivors, leading to PTSD.

Work-Related Factors

The workplace, often overlooked as a source of trauma, can be a breeding ground for stress and anxiety. A toxic work environment marked by overload, abuse, demanding supervisors, and inadequate remuneration can erode mental well-being, leading to work-related trauma or even PTSD. First responders, including police officers, firefighters, soldiers and military agents, emergency doctors, nurses, mental health workers and others working in the community, are prone to PTSD.

Effects of Trauma

Loss of Self-Worth and Self-Esteem

Trauma can profoundly affect a person's self-perception, leading to a distorted sense of self-worth. Oscillating between inflated self-importance and feelings of being unclean or unworthy, the trauma survivor grapples with a fragmented self-image that is both confusing and painful.

Loss of Intimacy

Sexual trauma can distort perceptions of intimacy, making sexual relationships a source of anxiety or a tool for validation. This complex relationship with sexuality can hinder the ability to form healthy, fulfilling connections, leading to further isolation.

Dissociation and Physical Disconnect

Dissociation is a common defence mechanism employed during traumatic experiences, creating a mental separation from the event. This coping strategy can persist, leading to feelings of detachment and a physical disconnect from the body. Therapies focusing on biological connection, such as yoga, can be particularly challenging for survivors grappling with this disconnection.

A Multifaceted Challenge

Trauma is a multifaceted challenge that reaches into every aspect of human existence. It's a complex interplay of causes and effects, profoundly shaping lives. The intricate web of trauma's origins, from family dynamics to societal structures, reveals the complexity of human vulnerability. The long shadow it casts on self-perception, relationships, physical health, and daily functioning underscores the urgent need for compassion, understanding, and professional support.

The journey through trauma is fraught with difficulties, but it is not a path that must be walked alone. Professional help, community support, and personal resilience can light the way toward healing. The task is immense, but the hope is accurate, and the commitment to understanding and addressing trauma must be unwavering.

Shame

One of the most debilitating effects of trauma is shame. This emotion can be so overwhelming and unbearable that even a minor error, such as performing an activity incorrectly at school, can trigger shame. Such powerful triggers in childhood may evolve into an adult's inability to tolerate being wrong, fostering a lifelong vulnerability to shame.

Loss of Trust

Trauma can erode trust in others, especially when perpetrated by a close relative or friend. The survivor may become hypersensitive to perceived betrayals, losing the ability to trust even those closest to them. This loss of trust can cast a shadow over relationships, inhibiting the ability to connect and find solace in others.

Re-Enactment of Trauma

Re-enactment is a complex and often misunderstood effect of trauma. Survivors may unconsciously recreate scenarios from their past, seeking a different outcome. This repetitive pattern fails to resolve the underlying trauma and instead entrenches it further. Such re-enactments can perpetuate cycles of suffering and dysfunction in relationships.

Types of Traumas

Acute Trauma

Acute trauma refers to the impact of a single, overwhelming event that triggers the body's threat response. This response can range from reactions to sexual assault to natural disasters. The autonomic nervous system's threat reaction is a normal response that has evolved over thousands of years to protect us from danger. However, acute trauma may persist, leading to PTSD if left untreated.

Symptoms and Treatment: Acute trauma symptoms can vary, some more subtle than others. Treatment options include immediate emotional support, removal from the trauma scene, short-term medication to alleviate distress, natural remedies for insomnia, and short-term therapy to restore a sense of safety. There is no universal approach to treating acute trauma, and self-medication with substances like alcohol or drugs can have detrimental effects.

Chronic Trauma

Chronic trauma results from extended exposure to traumatic events, often occurring in succession. Whether in a combat zone or an abusive relationship, the relentless toll of chronic trauma can lead to PTSD.

Symptoms and Treatment: Chronic trauma may manifest through the loss of family members in a tragic accident, followed by other life-altering events such as a severe illness, job loss, or financial hardship. Treatment typically involves psychotherapy, focusing on understanding symptoms, their impact on life, and developing coping strategies. Specific therapies like exposure therapy and cognitive therapy may be employed to confront traumatic memories and alleviate associated guilt or responsibility.

The Complex Landscape of Trauma

Trauma is a multifaceted and deeply personal experience that can manifest in various forms, each with unique challenges and implications. From the soul-crushing weight of shame to the crippling loss of trust, the effects of trauma reach into the core of human existence. They shape identities, influence relationships, and can lead to repetitive patterns of dysfunction.

Acute and chronic traumas, though different in their nature, both present complex therapeutic challenges. They require tailored interventions that consider individual needs, sensitivities, and the specific nature of the traumatic experiences. The healing journey may be extended and fraught with obstacles, but with the proper support and professional care, survivors can reclaim their lives and sense of self.

Understanding trauma's landscape is not merely an academic exercise; it's a call to empathy, compassion, and action. It recognizes the profound human capacity to endure, heal, and grow, even in the face of overwhelming circumstances. The work of untangling the complex web of trauma's causes and effects is both a professional challenge and a societal responsibility, reflecting our shared commitment to human dignity, well-being, and the pursuit of a life free from the shackles of past suffering.

Complex Trauma

Complex trauma occurs when an individual encounters multiple and often ongoing traumatic events, typically during vital developmental stages such as childhood or adolescence. These experiences can encompass conflicts at home, deprivation of necessities, emotional abuse, and living in unsafe communities. As these negative experiences become routine, they can profoundly hinder a child's ability to develop a positive outlook on life, trust in others, or believe that circumstances can improve.

Treatment Approaches

Treatment for complex trauma necessitates a highly individualized approach, recognizing that each person's experiences and suffering are unique. There is no uniform solution, and therapeutic methods must be flexible, adapting to the individual's changing needs and progress.

Emerging Techniques: With ongoing research, new therapeutic techniques continue to appear to provide a corrective emotional experience essential for recovery. The cornerstone of treating complex trauma lies in fostering a supportive and safe environment, enabling individuals to process their experiences and acquire healthy coping mechanisms to manage their emotions.

Therapeutic Interventions: Trauma, in its various forms, requires specialized therapeutic interventions. Identifying the nature and cause of trauma guides healthcare providers in selecting the most effective treatments. Here is a closer look at some of the widely used therapies:

- **Cognitive-Behavioral Treatment (CBT):** This therapy examines the connections between an individual's beliefs, feelings, and behaviours. By understanding these links, the patient may modify their behaviour patterns, reducing trauma-related symptoms. CBT is often employed to help individuals reframe negative thoughts and develop healthier coping strategies.

- **Cognitive Processing Therapy (CPT):** Primarily used for complex trauma and PTSD, CPT helps individuals recognize factors that provoke symptoms of traumatic events, including depression and anxiety. Through a series of sessions, therapists help patients understand and challenge their dysfunctional thoughts, promoting healing.

- **Eye Movement Desensitization and Reprocessing (EMDR):** EMDR involves guided eye movements that help the brain process traumatic memories. The therapist directs the patient's eye movements while recalling the traumatic event, aiming to change how the memory is stored and reduce its emotional charge.

- **Internal Family Structures (IFS):** This therapy focuses on integrating various elements of personality into one cohesive "Self." Through understanding and healing wounded parts of the self, IFS helps trauma survivors gain self-compassion and acceptance.

- **Somatic Therapy:** Rooted in the connection between the body and mind, somatic therapy educates the body to release the constant preparedness for trauma. Techniques may include mindfulness, movement, and breathwork to reconnect with the body and cultivate self-awareness.

- **Dialectical Behavioral Therapy (DBT):** Particularly beneficial for symptoms coinciding with complex trauma, DBT combines cognitive-behavioural techniques with mindfulness strategies. Patients learn skills like emotional regulation and distress tolerance, which are vital for managing trauma-related symptoms.

- **Grounding Techniques:** These self-administered techniques employ activities to help individuals remain connected to the present. Whether through dancing, deep breathing, or sensory experiences like tasting or touching, these techniques reinforce the idea that the past has passed, focusing on the present moment.

- **Pharmacotherapy:** Medication might be prescribed to alleviate specific symptoms in conjunction with psychotherapy. Antidepressants, mood stabilizers, or anxiety-reducing medications can be part of a comprehensive treatment plan tailored to individual needs.

- **Group Therapy:** Sometimes, being part of a group of individuals who have experienced similar trauma can be healing. Group therapy offers a supportive community, shared experiences, and collective coping strategies.

- **Exposure Therapy:** For some, gradually facing and understanding their trauma helps them reduce avoidance and fear. Exposure therapy is conducted carefully and systematically to help individuals confront their trauma and gain control over their feelings.

- **Holistic Approaches:** Integrating art, music, or animal-assisted therapies can provide additional avenues for expressing and processing emotions. These non-traditional therapies might be particularly helpful for those who find verbal communication challenging.

- **Thought Developmental Practice (TDP):** This approach supports all mental illnesses, particularly anxiety, depression, PTSD and addictions. Its twelve modules have been developed to recondition the mind and restructure your thinking.

These therapeutic interventions, individually tailored, can provide significant relief and healing from the scars of trauma. They may be used in combination, depending on the complexity and individual needs, to ensure a comprehensive approach to recovery. The shared goal across all these therapies is to provide trauma survivors with the tools, understanding, and support to rebuild their lives and move toward a future filled with hope and resilience.

A Comprehensive Understanding of Trauma

Trauma is a multifaceted and deeply personal experience that can have enduring effects on an individual's mental, emotional, and physical well-being. The causes of trauma are varied, encompassing childhood neglect or abuse, domestic violence, natural disasters, accidents, and even pandemic-related stress. The individual nature of trauma means that the impacts manifest differently across individuals, leading to varied symptoms such as loss of self-worth, intimacy loss, dissociation, physical disconnect from the body, shame, loss of trust, and re-enactment.

Understanding the depth and breadth of trauma is not just about recognizing the problem. It's about acknowledging the severity, the profound impact on quality of life, and the urgent need for professional intervention. The journey to recovery from trauma is neither swift nor linear. It requires patience, self-care, supportive loved ones, and professional guidance.

As a society, our role extends beyond mere awareness. It involves active participation in creating a safe and compassionate environment for trauma survivors. This includes advocacy for mental health, reducing stigma, and ensuring access to resources and support services. In acknowledging that trauma transcends age, gender, ethnicity, and socioeconomic status, we pave the way for a more empathetic and resilient society committed to the well-being of all its members.

Post-Traumatic Stress Disorder

Post-Traumatic Stress Disorder (PTSD) is a mental health condition that can develop after exposure to a traumatic event. PTSD is often associated with life-threatening events such as warfare, violent personal assaults, or natural disasters. However, it's important to note that not everyone who experiences a traumatic event will develop PTSD. Individuals with PTSD may have changes in physical and emotional reactions as they become easily startled or frightened—an unexpected loud noise could cause them to jump or scream. They may have difficulty sleeping, frequently waking up throughout the night or having trouble falling asleep due to anxiety or nightmares. Aggressive or self-destructive behaviour can also manifest—a normally calm person might start getting into fights, or someone might start drinking excessively as a coping mechanism, using illicit drugs to cope. Hypervigilance is very common, with the feeling of being highly or abnormally alert. They may feel they are in potential danger or threat, heightened with startle responses.

Victims who have PTSD may experience re-experiencing symptoms, which involve the individual reliving the traumatic event in various forms. These symptoms can be incredibly distressing, causing the person to feel as though the event is happening all over again (Hall et al., 2018). It includes recurring memories that are persistent, disturbing memories of an incident. Intrusive thoughts invade the mind during everyday activities. Nightmares are prevalent from incidents that were visual and auditory. A car accident survivor may experience nightmares about the crash, disrupting their sleep and causing anxiety. Flashbacks are very common, creating anxiety and fear. A victim of assault might suddenly feel they're back in the moment of their attack during a triggered episode. This can happen anytime and can be prompted by sights, sounds, or smells that remind them of the event. Avoidance symptoms in PTSD lead individuals to actively evade reminders of the traumatic event, causing them to change their behaviour and lifestyle to minimize exposure to triggering situations.

Avoiding transportation when involved in an MVA is very common. Someone in a severe car accident may avoid driving or even riding in cars, leading to significant challenges in daily life. They would need therapy to reintegrate into driving or being in a vehicle to avoid anxiety. The same idea applies to someone who experienced trauma in a crowded place. They may prevent busy areas like shopping malls or public events, limiting social interactions and possibly affecting their mental well-being.

PTSD can cause a range of adverse alterations in thoughts and mood, including developing negative beliefs, loss of interest in hobbies, and irrational feelings of guilt or blame. There are adverse changes in thinking, behaviours and mood. Some individuals with PTSD may have a fixed belief that they're a terrible person or that the world is entirely dangerous, leading to anxiety and depression. Some individuals may feel guilt and shame, carrying negative beliefs. Survivors may irrationally blame themselves for being unable to prevent it, even though it was beyond their control. They explore in their minds all the different things they could have done to avoid an accident or any incident that created PTSD.

There may be a loss of interest, where isolation and a decreased quality of life become the new normal. Individuals with PTSD may not want to socialize or be around people, as they may not want to share their trauma stories or be triggered by questions. There may be changes in physical and emotional reactions as PTSD can lead to alterations in physical and emotional responses, making trauma individuals more susceptible to startling stimuli, sleep disturbances, and even aggressive or self-destructive behaviour. Some people living with PTSD can be easily startled by unexpected loud noise. They can become "jumpy, hypervigilant, angry and frustrated, making daily life more stressful. Their neurovegetative state of mind can be altered, affecting their eating habits and sleeping patterns, with difficulty waking throughout the night or trouble falling asleep due to anxiety or nightmares. A normally calm person might start getting into fights. Substance and illicit drug use can become very common, developing addictions.

Major depressive disorder is one of the most common conditions co-occurring with PTSD. The shared symptoms of PTSD and depression, such as difficulty sleeping and concentration problems, can complicate the diagnostic process. Moreover, depression can exacerbate the distress experienced by individuals with PTSD and increase the risk of suicide.

PTSD can co-occur with various anxiety disorders, including generalized anxiety disorder (GAD), panic disorder, and social anxiety disorder. These anxiety disorders can worsen the anxiety symptoms associated with PTSD, making it more difficult for individuals to manage their symptoms. Many individuals with PTSD struggle with substance use disorders. This is often an attempt to self-medicate, as substances may temporarily alleviate some of the distressing symptoms of PTSD. However, substance use can exacerbate PTSD symptoms in the long run and lead to additional problems, including physical health issues and interpersonal problems.

Individuals with PTSD are also at an increased risk of experiencing somatic symptoms, such as chronic pain and gastrointestinal problems. They are also more likely to have medical conditions like heart disease, diabetes, and respiratory disorders. The reasons for this are complex and likely involve a combination of factors, including the physiological stress response, health behaviours, and access to healthcare. Healing from PTSD is a complex and gradual process that often requires professional intervention and ongoing support. The journey toward recovery can be slow, and it's vital to recognize that patience, persistence, and individualized care are often needed.

PTSD is a severe and multifaceted mental health condition, but healing is possible with the proper support and therapeutic interventions. It's essential to approach treatment with compassion and an understanding of the time it may take for an individual to recover truly. Recovery is often not a linear path, and setbacks may occur, but continued support and appropriate therapy can lead to profound healing and a return to a fulfilling life.

A Comprehensive Understanding of Trauma

Trauma is a multifaceted and deeply personal experience that can have enduring effects on an individual's mental, emotional, and physical well-being. The causes of trauma are varied, encompassing childhood neglect or abuse, domestic violence, natural disasters, accidents, and even pandemic-related stress. The individual nature of trauma means that the impacts manifest differently across individuals, leading to varied symptoms such as loss of self-worth, intimacy loss, dissociation, physical disconnect from the body, shame, loss of trust, and re-enactment.

Understanding the depth and breadth of trauma is not just about recognizing the problem. It's about acknowledging the severity, the profound impact on quality of life, and the urgent need for professional intervention. The journey to recovery from trauma is neither swift nor linear. It requires patience, self-care, supportive loved ones, and professional guidance.

As a society, our role extends beyond mere awareness. It involves active participation in creating a safe and compassionate environment for trauma survivors. This includes advocacy for mental health, reducing stigma, and ensuring access to resources and support services. In acknowledging that trauma transcends age, gender, ethnicity, and socioeconomic status, we pave the way for a more empathetic and resilient society committed to the well-being of all its members.

PSYCHOSOCIAL STRESSORS

Stress is a natural human response to various life situations and, to a certain extent, serves a beneficial purpose. Stress ensures our attention and promotes success by keeping us alert to vital matters such as financial obligations or family care. However, when stress escalates to extreme levels, it shifts from a motivator to a detrimental force, causing more harm than benefit.

Sources and Types of Psychosocial Stressors

Psychosocial stressors span an extensive array of life's challenges, from personal relationships to professional pressures. These stressors can manifest in various forms, each contributing to an individual's overall mental and emotional well-being, often leading to feelings of worry, anxiety, depression, or even symptoms of psychosis.

Physiological Stress

Physiological stress is typically related to physical injuries or trauma-related incidents. This type of stress can emerge from accidents, surgeries, chronic illnesses, or any physical harm that disrupts the body's equilibrium. While physiological stress primarily affects the body, it can also have psychological repercussions, such as anxiety or depression, stemming from the physical discomfort or limitations experienced.

Psychosocial Stress

Psychosocial stress, on the other hand, represents a more complex interplay between physical and psychological factors. This category includes stressors arising from past regrets, mistakes, wrong choices, perceived social threats, relationship conflicts, career and education struggles, spiritual concerns, financial burdens, domestic challenges, loss of a loved one, medical and mental illnesses, and other unforeseen and uncontrollable situations. The wide-ranging nature of psychosocial stressors makes them particularly challenging to identify and address, often requiring a multifaceted approach to treatment and management.

The Impact of Psychosocial Stress

Economic and Social Interaction

One's economic stability and social interactions play a crucial role in determining stress levels. Financial uncertainty or struggles with interpersonal relationships can create a constant sense of pressure and anxiety. The inability to meet financial obligations or the challenges of navigating complex social dynamics can lead to feelings of inadequacy, failure, and persistent worry.

Environmental Danger

Local environmental dangers, such as pollution, natural disasters, or community violence, can also contribute to psychosocial stress. Living in an area prone to floods, earthquakes, or crime can create a continuous undercurrent of fear and uncertainty, impacting daily life and overall mental health.

Daily Opportunities and Behaviour

Everyday choices, opportunities, and behaviours are other factors that combine to produce stress. Whether it's the pressure to perform at work, the decision-making involved in parenting, or the demands of maintaining a household, these daily challenges can accumulate, leading to overwhelming stress.

The "Fight or Flight" Response

Such factors may provoke a "fight or flight" response, a natural reaction to perceived threats. This response engages the body's stress reaction, activating cardiovascular, metabolic, immune, and neurological systems. While this reaction is customary and even beneficial in short-term stressful situations, chronic activation can lead to detrimental health effects, including anxiety, depression, and even psychosis.

A Multidimensional Challenge

The sources and impacts of psychosocial stressors are multifaceted and deeply interconnected. From physiological stress stemming from physical harm to the more complex psychosocial stress emerging from a blend of life's challenges, understanding these stressors is essential for mental and emotional well-being. The influence of economic stability, social interaction, environmental dangers, and daily life choices adds layers of complexity to the stress experience. Recognizing these factors and seeking appropriate support and coping strategies can foster resilience and enhance overall well-being in the face of life's inevitable pressures.

Other psychosocial stress forms include perceived threats to social background, acceptance, public image, group approval, self-worth, and uncertainty about future events. These perceived threats are challenging to navigate and result in the secretion of hormones like adrenaline, dopamine, and cortisol. These hormones can further escalate anxiety, depression, and psychosis.

Personal Response to Stress

Our personal relationship with stress varies significantly among individuals. Some may thrive on a fast-paced lifestyle, finding relaxation challenging, while others can adapt to stress with relative ease. Reactions to everyday situations like traffic delays or disputes with friends can differ widely, shaping individual anxiety levels and overall mental health.

Psychosocial stressors are an intricate and multifaceted aspect of human life. While stress serves a functional role in driving our focus and success, it can quickly tip into a destructive force when excessive. The sources of stress are varied, encompassing both physiological and psychological spheres, and their impact on mental and physical well-being is profound. Understanding the nature, sources, and personal responses to stress is pivotal in managing its effects and preserving mental health. Whether turning up the music in traffic or seeking professional help for more profound issues, recognizing and addressing psychosocial stressors is vital for our overall well-being.

Work-Related Stressors

The workplace can be a hotbed for psychosocial stressors. Factors such as an unfavourable work environment, incompetent managers, job insecurity, being underpaid, dealing with uneducated coworkers, and pressure to work excessive hours can accumulate, leading to feeling overwhelmed and struggling to cope. The consequences are often severe, manifesting in reduced creativity and enthusiasm, insecurity, declines in productivity, increased sick days, seclusion, impatience, frustration, and difficulties in personal connections. Recognizing and addressing these work-related stressors is essential to mitigate long-term adverse effects on health and well-being, including anxiety, depression, and even psychosis. Strategies to manage stress in this area may include creating a budget, seeking financial counselling, setting realistic work boundaries, and prioritizing self-care activities.

Relationship-Induced Stress

In our personal lives, relationships with family members, close friends, or coworkers can be sources of significant stress. Toxic people may be present in various aspects of our lives, and the pressure from these connections can have a profound impact on both physical and mental health.

- **Parenting Stress:** For many parents, juggling careers, domestic responsibilities, and child-rearing leads to parental stress. This can become challenging and overwhelming, resulting in frustration, anger, and disruption in the quality of parent-child connections. High stress can affect functionality in various areas, including parenting, and manifest in anxiety, depression, and psychosis. Open communication with spouses and children can alleviate frequent disputes and relationship strains, fostering healthier connections.

- **Personality and Stress Management:** Different personalities respond to stress in distinct ways. Extroverts may thrive on the busyness of life, while introverts may struggle with social anxiety. Respecting individual character, personality, and upbringing can create a more harmonious relationship environment. Recognizing these differences allows us to "agree to disagree" without harming mental health.

- **Perfectionists and Type-A Personalities:** Individuals with perfectionist tendencies or "type-A" personalities may experience excessive stress due to stringent standards. This can lead to more severe mental and physical health repercussions. Understanding and accepting these personality traits can prevent tension and anxiety within relationships.

Daily Stresses

Everyday life presents minor but frequent stressors, such as misplacing keys, being late, or forgetting essential items. While these may seem insignificant, their cumulative effect can lead to worry and a negative impact on daily life. Being mindful of reactions to these minor incidents and conditioning our minds to be proactive and positive rather than hostile and angry can contribute to a more balanced mental state.

Psychosocial stress, whether minor or significant, profoundly impacts our daily lives. It's a critical source of anxiety for many individuals, fundamentally altering their existence by putting their bodies into "fight or flight" mode. This response triggers a cascade of hormonal changes that can be detrimental to physical and mental well-being. The consequences manifest as undesirable emotional symptoms, often channelled into feelings of melancholy or concern. Without proper support, these feelings can escalate into a chronic state of anxiety, disrupting all aspects of life.

The Psychological Toll of Stress

Stress takes a heavy toll on mental health, manifesting in various ways:

- **Anxiety:** Stress-induced anxiety can lead to excessive worrying about others and life events. In some cases, this anxiety progresses to panic attacks or phobias, becoming chronic and pervasive.
- **Depression:** Persistent stress can result in depression, characterized by acute sadness that permeates daily life. Sensory experiences, such as sights, sounds, smells, tastes, or touches, can easily trigger mood disturbances.
- **Interpersonal Challenges:** High-stress levels can negatively impact social interactions, leading to anger, irritation, frequent disputes, or social isolation. Some may exhibit aggression, mood swings, resentment, or restlessness.

- **Attention Deficits:** Stress is also linked to attention-related mental health conditions like anxiety, worry, and attention deficit hyperactivity disorder (ADHD). These often manifest as concentration, energy, and motivation struggles, impacting daily functioning.
- **Physical Symptoms:** Chronic stress manifests physically in muscle tension, stiffness, aches, pains, headaches, migraines, heart problems, and gastrointestinal issues. Over time, these symptoms can lead to more severe health problems.

Navigating Stress and Finding Support

While a resilient individual can survive and even thrive in challenging situations, untreated and prolonged stress can become overwhelming and harmful. Recognizing the various negative consequences of stress is essential to understanding its pervasive effects on our lives.

The landscape of psychosocial stress is complex and multifaceted, affecting mental, emotional, and physical well-being. From anxiety and depression to physical health complications, the effects of stress are far-reaching. A comprehensive approach to stress management, encompassing therapy, mindfulness, grounding techniques, and journaling, can effectively mitigate these impacts. By understanding the nature of stress and actively engaging in coping strategies, individuals can navigate the complexities of stress and foster a healthier, more balanced life. Whether in the workplace, relationships, or daily activities, recognizing and addressing psychosocial stressors is vital to overall health and happiness.

PSYCHOSOCIAL STRESSORS

MENTAL ILLNESSES

Mental illnesses are complex and multifaceted disorders that profoundly impact the lives of millions around the world. They vary in severity and manifestation, affecting our thinking, emotions, and behaviour in diverse ways. Understanding the different types of mental illnesses, their underlying causes, and the effects they have on individuals is paramount in fostering empathy, awareness, and effective treatment. This chapter delves into various mental illnesses, shedding light on their characteristics, biological underpinnings, and the importance of identifying vulnerable populations.

Anxiety Disorders

Anxiety disorders represent a spectrum of conditions characterized by persistent worry, fear, or apprehension. It's an overwhelming feeling of discomfort and uneasiness. Excessive and unrealistic feelings interfere with work, school, recreation and social life. It's a heightened sense of assumed danger. They can take various forms, each with its unique manifestations.

Some of the most common anxiety symptoms include:
- Phobias
- Excessive worry and fear
- Feeling a loss of control
- Fatigue
- Feeling irritated and agitation
- Disruptive sleep pattern
- Changes to eating habits
- Inability to concentrate
- Restlessness

- Dizziness
- Headaches
- Hyperventilation, shortness of breath
- Increased heart rate
- Sweating and clammy hands
- Chest pain
- Stomach-aches
- Numbness in the legs and arms
- Difficulty socializing

The most common forms of anxiety are:

- **Generalized Anxiety Disorder (GAD):** Constant worrying that there is a feeling it cannot be controlled.
- **Obsessive-Compulsive Disorder (OCD):** Disturbing and recurrent intrusive thoughts, images or impulses (obsessions), and repetitive, ritualized behaviours (compulsions).
- **Post-Traumatic Stress Disorder (PTSD):** Events that have been experienced, witnessed or heard (vicarious traumas) from others. Symptoms may include intrusive thoughts, flashbacks, nightmares, hypervigilance and uncontrollable thoughts about the event.
- **Panic Disorder**: Intense, recurring panic attacks without apparent cause. Sometimes, it may feel like a brick on your chest and the desire to hyperventilate.
- **Social Anxiety Disorder**: Intense fear of social interactions.
- **Specific Phobias**: Exaggerated fear of particular objects or situations.

These disorders are often linked to abnormal activity in the amygdala, leading to exaggerated emotional responses. Addressing anxiety disorders requires a comprehensive approach that includes therapy and lifestyle changes. Medication is another option for severe anxiety.

Mood Disorders

Mood disorder is manifested through distorted emotions that are inconsistent, affecting the functionality of a person. There may be extreme sadness, a feeling of emptiness, and irritability (depression). There may be periods of depression alternating with being excessively happy (mania).

Mood disorders include:

- **Depression:** Persistent feelings of hopelessness, sadness, and a lack of interest in daily activities. Major or clinical depression includes symptoms of sadness or hopelessness. It may manifest in Postpartum or Peripartum Depression, Persistent Depressive Disorder, Seasonal Affective Disorder (SAD) or Depression with Psychosis.

- **Bipolar disorder:** Alternating periods of manic episodes and depressive states. When there is an intense shift in energy level, mood, thinking pattern and behaviours, there are four basic types of bipolar disorder, including Bipolar I disorder, Bipolar II disorder, Cyclothymia disorder, and other specified and unspecified bipolar-related disorders.

- **Other mood disorders:** Premenstrual Dysphoric Disorder (PMDD), Disruptive Mood Dysregulation Disorder (DMDD).

The biochemical imbalances involving neurotransmitters like serotonin and dopamine are often implicated in mood disorders. Treatment may include medication, counselling, and support groups.

Personality Disorders

These disorders are enduring patterns of behaviour that deviate markedly from societal expectations. They are classified into three clusters:

- **Cluster A**: Paranoid personality disorder characterized by suspiciousness.
- **Cluster B**: Borderline personality disorder, marked by instability in relationships.
- **Cluster C**: Avoidant personality disorder, reflecting anxiety and fearfulness.

Personality disorders are complex and may be related to brain structure and functionality abnormalities. Treatment often involves long-term therapy and support.

Psychosis

It is a severe condition characterized by a disconnection from reality. Symptoms include paranoia, hallucinations, delusions, and disorganized thinking. Neurotransmitter abnormalities, including dopamine and glutamate, play a role in this condition. Early intervention and ongoing support are crucial for managing psychosis.

Eating Disorders

Eating disorders, such as anorexia nervosa and bulimia nervosa, involve distorted eating patterns that impact physical and mental health. These disorders are tied to abnormalities in brain areas governing reward and self-control. Treatment requires a holistic approach involving nutritional counselling, therapy, and medical monitoring.

Understanding the susceptibility and vulnerabilities of specific individuals to mental illnesses is essential. Tailored prevention, support, and treatment strategies can then be devised to address the unique needs of those affected.

Mental illnesses constitute a complex and multifaceted dimension of human health, impacting millions worldwide. These disorders range from anxiety and mood disorders to more severe conditions such as psychosis and eating disorders. Addressing these challenges necessitates a nuanced and individualized approach, emphasizing prevention, intervention, and ongoing support. The path to mental wellness is a collective endeavour that demands broad awareness, compassion, and unwavering commitment (Corrigan & Watson, 2002; Olfson, Blanco, & Marcus, 2016).

Anxiety, depression, and psychosis are common mental health disorders affecting a diverse population. These conditions are not limited to any particular demographic but can influence individuals irrespective of age, gender, ethnicity, or social background. The implications of these mental health conditions extend beyond emotional health, affecting physical well-being and social functioning (Kessler, Berglund, Demler, Jin, & Walters, 2005; Walker, McGee, & Druss, 2015).

Understanding and Overcoming Stigmas

Societal stigmas and criticisms can further complicate the journey towards healing from anxiety, depression, or psychosis. Misunderstandings and lack of awareness can lead to judgment and isolation, hindering recovery. Education, compassion, and empathy are essential in fostering a supportive environment where individuals can seek help without fear of condemnation.

Physical Effects

The physical ramifications of anxiety, depression, and psychosis are often underestimated. Symptoms can manifest as:

- **Chronic Pain**: Persistent aches that disrupt daily life.
- **Fatigue**: Exhaustion that hinders normal functioning.
- **Digestive Issues**: Gastrointestinal problems that can affect overall health.
- **Increased Risk of Chronic Illnesses**: Such as heart disease and diabetes.

These physical symptoms can further feed into the cycle of mental illness, creating a complex interplay between body and mind.

Social Impact

The social implications of mental health disorders are profound:

- **Trust Issues**: Affecting relationships with friends and family.
- **Isolation**: Withdrawal from social situations due to shame or stigma.
- **Financial Instability**: Inability to work or fulfill social roles, leading to economic challenges.

These social effects can exacerbate mental health symptoms, creating a vicious cycle that can be challenging to break.

Road to Recovery

Recovery from anxiety, depression, and psychosis is a multifaceted process, often requiring:

- **Therapy**: Professional counselling to address underlying issues.
- **Medication**: To manage symptoms and stabilize mood.
- **Support Groups**: Peer support can provide understanding and encouragement.
- **Self-Care**: Emphasizing healthy habits and mindfulness techniques.

Recovery is not a linear path, and setbacks may occur. Yet, with perseverance and the proper support, healing is attainable.

Anxiety, depression, and psychosis are complex mental health disorders that require a nuanced and compassionate approach. The effects are not limited to mental distress but encompass physical health and social well-being. Overcoming these challenges is possible but demands concerted effort from individuals, healthcare providers, and society.

The path to recovery emphasizes empathy, education, and tailored support, affirming that no one is alone in this journey. By fostering understanding and providing appropriate care, we can make strides towards a world where mental health is not a hidden struggle but a shared responsibility. The process of healing is a journey, and every step forward counts.

The nuanced nature of anxiety, depression, and psychosis, as manifested across various settings and scenarios, underlines the complexity of mental health issues in our contemporary world.

Anxiety in the Home: Home is often seen as a haven, but for many, it can be a place where anxiety manifests through panic attacks, OCD, phobias, PTSD, and fears. The ripple effects of this anxiety can be far-reaching. Children, in particular, may carry the scars of such experiences into adulthood, struggling with trust issues, self-esteem, and social relationships.

Anxiety in Schools: The school environment, too, can be a breeding ground for anxiety. Bullying, harassment, and discrimination can lead to long-term mental health challenges, including panic attacks, depression, and PTSD. Tragically, sexual abuse can also occur in educational settings, leaving victims grappling with profound feelings of shame, guilt, and embarrassment, often hampering their ability to seek help.

Anxiety in the Workplace: Workplaces are not immune to the tentacles of anxiety. Harassment, discrimination, or physical harm can give rise to various mental health problems, including hypertension, cardiac issues, and diabetes. Beyond the individual, workplace anxiety can have organizational impacts, leading to decreased productivity and increased absenteeism.

Anxiety in the Community: On a community level, anxiety may manifest through violence, natural disasters, or other traumatic events. These community-wide experiences can create a cycle of panic attacks, depression, and PTSD, leading to broader societal problems like increased crime rates, poverty, and overall reduced quality of life.

Physical and Emotional Manifestations

The intertwining of anxiety, depression, and psychosis with physical abuse adds another layer to the complexity. Impulsive reactions to disagreements may lead to physical harm, causing both physical injuries and emotional trauma. The effects can persist long after the incidents themselves, leading to chronic difficulties in forming and maintaining relationships, trust issues, and emotional instability.

Children, with their still-developing emotional landscapes, are particularly vulnerable. Lack of coping mechanisms to deal with abusive or traumatic events may predispose them to mental health issues later in life. Recognizing signs of abuse or neglect in children and intervening promptly is critical to their long-term well-being.

The social ramifications of mental illnesses are profound and multifaceted. The impacts are wide-ranging, from withdrawal and isolation to financial instability and difficulty enjoying life. Stigmatization and shame often accompany these challenges, further isolating individuals from the support they need.

Mental illnesses like anxiety, depression, and psychosis are intricate, multifaceted issues that permeate every aspect of life—from personal spaces like home and school to broader societal contexts. The long-lasting effects can be devastating, but hope and healing are within reach. Proper support and treatment can enable individuals to rebuild their lives, underscoring the importance of empathy, awareness, and timely intervention. The journey towards mental well-being is a shared responsibility, and every step taken to understand, support, and treat these complex issues brings us closer to a society where mental health is neither stigmatized nor overlooked but a fundamental aspect of our collective human experience.

The journey towards healing and recovery from anxiety, depression, and psychosis is laden with challenges, obstacles, and complexities. The experiences of individuals affected by these mental health issues are deeply personal and profound. Yet, they are often met with criticism and stigmatization that can further hinder the healing process.

The Challenge of Healing

Healing from anxiety, depression, and psychosis is not a linear path. It requires time, effort, support, and understanding. Many resources, including therapy, support groups, and medication, can aid in this journey, helping individuals regain control over their lives and improve their overall quality of life. The path to healing is a journey, often marked by gradual progress rather than immediate transformation. Knowing that one is not alone and that help is available is vital in the healing process.

Criticisms and Stigmas

Unfortunately, the path to recovery is often obstructed by societal criticisms and stigmas. Three main types of criticisms can particularly exacerbate the struggles of those grappling with these mental health issues:

1. **Victim Blaming:** This criticism involves attributing fault to the individual, suggesting that they somehow caused or deserved their mental health challenges. Victim blaming can deepen feelings of shame and guilt, further entrenching the mental health issues rather than aiding recovery.

2. **Minimization of Experiences:** Another harmful reaction is the tendency to downplay or dismiss the severity of an individual's experiences. This depreciation can lead a person to question their feelings and experiences, adding a layer of confusion and self-doubt to an already complex emotional landscape.

3. **The "Get Over It" Mentality:** Perhaps one of the most damaging criticisms is the belief that individuals should simply "get over" their anxiety, depression, or psychosis without needing professional help or support. This view fosters a culture of silence and shame, making individuals feel weak or inadequate for seeking help.

Building a Supportive Environment

Addressing and overcoming these criticisms and stigmas is a collective responsibility. By fostering an environment of empathy, compassion, and understanding, we can dismantle these barriers to healing. Recognizing the courage and resilience it takes to face and overcome mental health challenges is a significant step toward creating a more supportive community.

Anxiety, depression, and psychosis are complex, multifaceted issues that require a compassionate and informed approach. The criticisms and stigmas associated with these mental health challenges are not merely societal issues but deeply personal obstacles that can affect an individual's path to recovery. By actively working to reduce these barriers and offering genuine support, we can create a society where healing is not only possible but encouraged. As we look forward to exploring further stressors contributing to these mental health challenges, let us carry a renewed commitment to empathy, understanding, and compassion. The mental well-being of our communities depends on our collective efforts to foster an environment where every individual feels seen, heard, and supported.

MENTAL ILLNESSES

ANXIETY

Anxiety is more than just a fleeting emotion; it represents a spectrum of feelings characterized by pervasive worry, stress, apprehension, and a sense of unease. Often stemming from the uncertainty surrounding future events, it amplifies the typical concern for what lies ahead into disproportionate levels of nervousness.

While contemplating the future is a natural human tendency and can be advantageous—enabling us to make informed decisions and prepare for various life scenarios—it's important to distinguish this from debilitating anxiety. Mild forms of anxiety can indeed serve as adaptive responses, stimulating the release of stress hormones like cortisol and norepinephrine. These biochemical changes prepare the body to face potential challenges, making anxiety a protective mechanism at its core. For example, feeling nervous before a public speaking engagement or the first day of school is a normal physiological response that can motivate you to prepare adequately and improve your performance. Once the specific event or trigger has passed, most people can transition back to a state of emotional equilibrium.

However, the landscape of anxiety becomes perilous when worry becomes chronic and uncontrollable, colouring one's perspective of life's uncertainties in an overwhelmingly negative light. At this stage, the mind often spirals into a cycle of incessant worrying, leading to the belief that something catastrophic is imminent.

This heightened state of anxiety is often linked to neurotransmitter imbalances in the brain. For instance, fluctuations in dopamine and serotonin levels can influence emotional states. Elevated levels of these neurotransmitters can induce states resembling psychosis, whereas depleted levels are associated with depressive symptoms. The resultant neurochemical shifts can create an exaggerated sense of impending doom, manifesting as overwhelming anxiety or even panic attacks, which can feel as debilitating as a physical ailment.

Anxiety has the capacity to be triggered by both monumental life events—such as marriage, job interviews, or examinations—and seemingly inconsequential occurrences, like receiving an unexpected phone call from a supervisor or attending a social gathering alone. The root issue is that the mind, in a state of heightened anxiety, leans towards negative thought patterns. This negativity bias exacerbates worries, convincing us that disastrous outcomes are almost inevitable.

If such episodes of intense anxiety persist and interfere with daily functioning over an extended period—typically six months or longer—this could warrant a clinical diagnosis of an anxiety disorder. These disorders represent the most prevalent category of emotional disorders and can occur at any life stage. The pervasive nature of anxiety disorders can severely compromise one's quality of life, engendering a perpetual state of fear and doubt. In extreme cases, the debilitating anxiety can become so restrictive that it hinders basic activities like using an elevator, crossing a street, or even stepping out of one's home.

If left unaddressed, chronic anxiety can serve as a gateway to additional mental health conditions, further complicating an individual's emotional well-being. Thus, recognizing and tackling anxiety in its various forms is crucial for maintaining a balanced, fulfilling life.

Personal Odyssey

My journey with anxiety has been a strenuous and protracted one, commencing during my formative school years and persisting into the complex terrain of marital life. As a 14-year-old adolescent, I grappled with social anxiety that relegated me to the status of an introvert, often perceived as asocial. Public speaking was particularly excruciating; my legs would tremble, my voice would become entrapped within my throat, and my cognitive processes would be inundated with a rapid succession of thoughts. The visibility of my anxiety rendered me susceptible to bullying, a social dynamic that only exacerbated my condition.

However, maturation and the advent of marital life instigated a transformative phase. I invested in self-improvement techniques aimed at ameliorating my phobias. With concerted effort and sustained resilience, I eventually surmounted these challenges. Alongside social anxiety, I also contended with Obsessive-Compulsive Disorder (OCD), a condition that intensified post-marriage. Through cognitive restructuring and concerted mental conditioning, I managed to substantially mitigate the triggers associated with both social anxiety and OCD.

Yet, one specific phobia—ophidiophobia, or an intense fear of snakes—continues to be a source of situational anxiety and panic attacks for me. My initial exposure to this phobia occurred during an ostensibly innocuous climb up a coconut tree. An unexpected encounter with a snake gliding over my hand paralyzed me with fear, causing me to nearly plummet from the tree. The physical aftermath was characterized by hyperthermia, profuse perspiration, nausea, and respiratory difficulties. Subsequent snake encounters, coupled with anecdotal narratives from family members about the perils associated with snakes, further solidified this phobia.

In an endeavour to confront this deeply rooted fear, I partook in an exposure therapy exercise in Thailand. Alongside my son, I visited a snake farm, where I allowed a snake to be placed on my shoulder and sat in proximity to multiple cobras. This audacious act considerably attenuated my ophidiophobia, potentially signalling the onset of its dissolution.

The Multifaceted Manifestations of Anxiety Disorders

Anxiety exists as a complex umbrella term that encompasses a diverse range of conditions, such as panic disorders, phobias, OCD, Post-Traumatic Stress Disorder (PTSD), and Generalized Anxiety Disorder (GAD). Though the manifestation of symptoms can vary considerably among individuals, some common indicators necessitate clinical attention and may even warrant emergency intervention.

These commonly observed symptoms include an acute sense of impending doom, restlessness, hyperventilation, and pronounced perspiration. Social anxiety frequently manifests as an aversion to specific situations and social configurations. Additional indicators may include inexplicable fatigue, bodily tremors, and obsessive preoccupations, which could evolve into OCD. Physiological symptoms can extend to gastrointestinal issues, nausea, emesis, cognitive impairments, and speech difficulties. In extreme instances, individuals may experience choking sensations, cardiac palpitations, and even transient loss of consciousness. Such severe manifestations can induce an overwhelming fear of mortality, further perpetuating the cycle of anxiety.

Anxiety is a multifaceted term covering a variety of conditions such as panic disorders, phobias, OCD, PTSD, and GAD. Though symptoms can differ significantly, common indicators like a sense of impending doom, restlessness, hyperventilation, and pronounced perspiration are frequently observed and may require immediate medical intervention (American Psychiatric Association, 2013; Clark & Beck, 2010). Physiological symptoms may extend to gastrointestinal issues, while cognitive and behavioural manifestations can be severe enough to induce a fear of mortality, thus exacerbating the cycle of anxiety (Bandelow & Michaelis, 2015).

Understanding the nuanced symptomatology of anxiety disorders is critical for timely diagnosis and effective treatment, thereby enhancing the quality of life for affected individuals.

Generalized Anxiety Disorder (GAD)

Generalized Anxiety Disorder, commonly abbreviated as GAD, represents one of the most prevalent forms of anxiety. This pervasive disorder is characterized by a constant state of worry and stress that lacks a specific, identifiable cause. The unease infiltrates the most mundane aspects of daily life, disrupting routines and diminishing overall productivity. Symptoms often manifest as a heightened sense of fear and apprehension toward routine activities, accompanied by psychological confusion, impaired concentration, physical tension, and an overemphasis on potential negative outcomes.

Social Anxiety Disorder

Also known as social phobia, social anxiety disorder manifests as an overwhelming sense of apprehension and fear in social settings. Individuals suffering from this disorder are preoccupied with concerns about negative judgment or ridicule from others, often leading to panic attacks and subsequent social withdrawal. It's critical to differentiate social anxiety from introversion or a preference for solitude; the former is a pathological condition that significantly impairs one's ability to function socially.

Selective Mutism

Selective mutism is a specialized form of anxiety that manifests as an inability to speak in specific contexts. For instance, a child who communicates freely at home might find themselves rendered speechless in an educational setting due to extreme nervousness. This form of anxiety serves as a compelling example of how environmental triggers can activate deeply ingrained psychological responses, in this case, inhibiting verbal communication.

Separation Anxiety Disorder

While often associated with childhood, separation anxiety is a condition that can affect individuals of all ages. It's characterized by excessive fear or worry triggered by the physical or emotional separation from a loved one, most commonly a parent. The disorder can manifest in varying degrees of severity, from mild discomfort to extreme distress. For example, a child who becomes inconsolable when a parent leaves the room may be experiencing an acute form of separation anxiety.

Panic Attacks

A panic attack constitutes a sudden surge of debilitating anxiety characterized by symptoms like rapid heart rate, profuse sweating, difficulty breathing, and chest discomfort. Some individuals may even mistake the experience for a heart attack or choking episode. These episodes may seem to occur without a recognizable trigger, but they are often initiated by sensory stimuli or specific thought patterns.

Specific Phobias

Specific phobias represent intense, irrational fears triggered by particular objects or situations. Common examples include acrophobia (fear of heights), aviophobia (fear of flying), and arachnophobia (fear of spiders). The individual's response can be so acute that even moderate exposure to the phobia—such as standing on a low platform—can provoke extreme emotional reactions, such as crying or outright refusal to proceed.

Agoraphobia

Agoraphobia is an anxiety disorder characterized by a fear of being in places where escape might be intricate or help might be unavailable in the event of a panic attack. This can manifest as a reluctance to leave one's home, enter crowded areas, or even step into open spaces. The condition can elicit intense feelings of embarrassment and panic, fueled by the thought that escape would be difficult and assistance unlikely in an emergency situation. This is distinct from claustrophobia, which is a fear of confined spaces.

Understanding these various subtypes of anxiety disorders is crucial for effective diagnosis and treatment, as each presents its own unique set of challenges and requires tailored therapeutic approaches.

Drug-Induced Anxiety

Anxiety can manifest as an unintended consequence of drug use, whether from prescribed medications, recreational substances, or illicit drugs. In some cases, heightened anxiety occurs during the drug's active phase, often described as a "bad trip," where the individual may experience obsessive thoughts or even perceive imminent, life-threatening danger.

Medical Conditions and Anxiety

Certain medical conditions can temporarily induce symptoms of anxiety, which typically subside upon recovery. This transient form of anxiety can be triggered by a range of medications prescribed for various conditions such as thyroid imbalances, epilepsy, Attention Deficit Hyperactivity Disorder (ADHD), asthma, and migraines. Each of these medications has the potential to initiate or amplify symptoms of anxiety disorders.

Emotional and Physical Health Triggers

Anxiety disorders are often the culmination of a complex interplay between emotional triggers and suboptimal physical or mental health. Prominent among these is fear of the unknown, significantly when exacerbated by depression or neurotransmitter imbalances. Poor mental health, manifesting as conditions like depression, psychosis, Obsessive-Compulsive Disorder (OCD), or Post-Traumatic Stress Disorder (PTSD), significantly contributes to the onset of anxiety disorders. Similarly, declining physical health, particularly in the face of chronic or life-threatening illnesses like cancer, serves as a significant catalyst for anxiety disorders. Genetic predispositions, evidenced by family history, can also heighten the risk.

Impact of Childhood Experiences

Experiencing abuse or trauma during childhood can substantially elevate the risk of developing anxiety disorders later in life. Such risk amplifies if the individual has faced parental loss, endured bullying, or suffered from neglect or emotional deprivation. These formative experiences often impair one's ability to cope with life's challenges, making them more susceptible to anxiety and panic attacks in stressful situations.

Lifestyle and Environmental Factors

Various facets of daily life, such as work-related stress, academic pressures, relationship difficulties, financial uncertainties, and fear of unemployment, can fuel anxiety. Even dietary choices, like excessive consumption of junk food or caffeinated beverages, can aggravate anxiety symptoms. The correlation between diet and mental health is akin to how excessive caffeine can escalate stress levels, thereby worsening existing anxiety disorders.

Unpredictable Onset and Long-Term Effects

Anxiety can strike without warning, sometimes triggered by a fleeting thought or memory, leading to a cascade of symptoms like fear, trembling, weakness, and difficulty focusing. If left unaddressed, anxiety can exert a lasting impact, transforming even simple, everyday tasks into Herculean challenges.

Understanding the manifold triggers and manifestations of anxiety is crucial for effective intervention and management. Ignoring or trivializing these symptoms can lead to long-term detrimental effects on one's overall well-being, making early diagnosis and treatment paramount.

Short-Term and Long-Term Consequences

Immediate Physiological Responses

In the short term, anxiety can induce a spectrum of physical symptoms ranging from hyperventilation and breathing difficulties to persistent fatigue. Gastrointestinal upset, body aches, elevated blood pressure, and even urinary incontinence may also ensue. Additionally, a compromised immune system can make one more susceptible to common infections like colds and the flu, while sleep disturbances become increasingly prevalent.

Pervasive Effects of Chronic Anxiety

Chronic anxiety poses a unique challenge as the body misinterprets minor anxiety triggers as substantial threats, leading to the excessive release of hormones like cortisol and noradrenaline. This prepares the body for "fight-or-flight" scenarios, causing an extended state of heightened alertness that can be physically and mentally detrimental. The long-term manifestations of chronic anxiety are diverse and severe, encompassing conditions like depression, Obsessive-Compulsive Disorder (OCD), an impaired immune system, recurrent panic attacks over trivial triggers, insomnia, chronic pain, decreased work performance, and a decline in social interactions.

Physical and Psychological Toll

It's imperative to recognize that the repercussions of anxiety extend beyond mental well-being to erode physical health significantly. While anxiety serves as a protective emotional response to specific triggers, its symptoms escalate into severe concerns when they reach moderate to extreme levels, impairing both physical and psychological functions.

Therapeutic Approaches

To mitigate these severe outcomes, a range of evidence-based treatments is available, tailored to individual needs, whether pharmacological or non-pharmacological. Often, individuals with diagnosed anxiety disorders initially consult primary care providers. A comprehensive treatment plan for managing anxiety disorders involves recognizing the symptoms, conducting screenings for accurate diagnosis, and formulating targeted treatment strategies. When adhered to diligently, these therapeutic regimens can significantly enhance the quality of life for those afflicted.

The Importance of Mental Resilience

Contrary to the restlessness induced by anxiety, achieving a state of inner tranquillity is crucial. Cultivating awareness of our emotional states allows for more effective problem-solving and fosters an optimistic mindset capable of finding light even in the darkest circumstances. This mental resilience not only mitigates symptoms of depression but also contributes to overall mental health and well-being.

Understanding the multi-faceted impact of anxiety, both short-term and long-term is essential for timely intervention and effective management. Neglecting these symptoms can result in chronic conditions that severely compromise one's quality of life, making early diagnosis and sustained treatment critically important.

ANXIETY

DEPRESSION

Depression manifests as a mood disorder marked by pervasive feelings of guilt and diminished self-worth, severely curtailing one's ability to experience joy or engage in activities. Frequent signs accompanying depression encompass a spectrum: feelings of loss or pervasive sadness, reduced self-esteem coupled with heightened self-deprecation, a lack of enthusiasm in customary activities, reduced energy levels, cognitive hesitancy, diminished appetite, and sleep irregularities such as insomnia.

Distinguishing Depression from Sadness and Grief

While sadness and grief are natural emotional responses to specific losses or setbacks, depression is a more debilitating condition, often disproportionate to the precipitating event. Depression shares commonalities with other chronic conditions like heart disease and diabetes, manifesting in various forms with distinct characteristics, including the number, duration, and intensity of symptoms. The condition also exhibits age-related variations in symptomatology.

Varied Subtypes of Depression

Depression exists in several forms, each with its unique features:

- **Major Depressive Disorder (MDD)**: Characterized by a constellation of symptoms persisting for a minimum of two weeks, major depression severely impacts one's ability to function, sleep, eat, and derive pleasure from activities. Symptoms may include disrupted sleep patterns, altered eating habits, and difficulty concentrating. Episodes can recur throughout one's life.
- **Dysthymia (Persistent Depressive Disorder)**: A less acute but more enduring form of depression, dysthymia's symptoms are chronic and, while not debilitating, restrict

individuals from operating at their optimal levels. Dysthymia may co-occur with episodes of major depression, known as "double depression."
- **Bipolar Disorder**: Formerly termed manic-depressive disorder, bipolar disorder encompasses a range of mood disorders marked by mood cycles featuring one or more episodes of mania or hypomania and potential periods of depression. These cycles may be acute and recurrent, with mood changes ranging from gradual to abrupt. During depressive phases, individuals may manifest all the typical symptoms of depressive disorders. Manic episodes often lead to impaired judgment and socially inappropriate behaviours, such as reckless financial or sexual activities.
- **Other Forms**: Additional types of depression include Postpartum Depression, Seasonal Affective Disorder, and Atypical Depression, each with its unique set of symptoms and triggers.

Bipolar Spectrum

Within the realm of bipolar disorders, distinctions exist:

- **Bipolar I**: The classic form, featuring full-blown manic episodes.
- **Bipolar II**: Involves recurrent episodes of depression with hypomanic episodes, a milder form of mania.

Understanding depression requires an acknowledgment of its multifaceted nature, the various subtypes, and the broad spectrum of symptoms that can range from mild to incapacitating. Early diagnosis and targeted treatment strategies are crucial for effectively managing this complex psychological condition, which has pervasive impacts on both mental and physical well-being.

Postpartum Depression (PPD)

Postpartum Depression (PPD) manifests as a significant mood disorder often triggered by the substantial hormonal shifts that accompany pregnancy and childbirth. While it's common for women to experience mood variations or the so-called "baby blues" after giving birth, PPD, now classified as depression with peripartum onset, is far more intense and enduring. Symptoms range from persistent low mood to severe manifestations like panic attacks and suicidal ideation. In extreme cases, postpartum psychosis, characterized by disorientation and hallucinations, may occur (Sit et al., 2015). Treatment typically involves a multidimensional approach, including hormone therapy, psychotherapy, and antidepressants (Yonkers et al., 2014). Symptoms can include persistent low mood, marked mood swings, social withdrawal, difficulties in bonding with the newborn, appetite disturbances, a sense of hopelessness, loss of interest in previously enjoyed activities, feelings of inadequacy, and more severe manifestations like panic attacks, suicidal ideation, or thoughts of harming oneself or the child. In extreme cases, postpartum psychosis may occur, characterized by disorientation, hallucinations, or delusions. Left untreated, the condition can persist for up to a year. Treatment often involves a combination of hormone therapy, psychotherapy, and antidepressants tailored to individual needs.

Seasonal Affective Disorder (SAD)

Also known as major depression with a seasonal pattern, Seasonal Affective Disorder (SAD) is a subtype of depression where individuals experience depressive symptoms, lethargy, and weight gain predominantly during winter months but find relief come spring. The condition is believed to stem from disruptions in the body's natural circadian rhythm, often due to decreased daylight exposure during winter. This lack of light can lead to imbalances in serotonin levels, affecting mood and alterations in melatonin levels, which can disrupt sleep patterns. Although often underdiagnosed, SAD can be managed through various interventions such as light therapy, increased outdoor activities, a balanced diet, and regular physical exercise.

Atypical Depression

Despite its name, Atypical Depression is a frequently encountered form of depression, distinguished by specific symptomatology. Individuals with Atypical Depression often respond more effectively to a class of antidepressants known as Monoamine Oxidase Inhibitors (MAOIs) compared to those with other forms of depression.

Understanding these specialized forms of depression provides valuable insights into their unique triggers, symptoms, and treatment modalities. Early diagnosis and targeted treatment strategies are crucial for managing these complex psychological conditions effectively. They offer a nuanced perspective on the diverse manifestations of depression, underlining the need for individualized treatment plans for optimized patient outcomes.

Depression, often clinically described as a state of intense sadness or low mood, has a history that stretches back to antiquity. The ancient Greek physician Hippocrates termed it 'melancholia,' capturing its essence long before contemporary medical characterization. The course of this mood disorder is remarkably diverse, ranging from mild to severe, and can be either acute or chronic in nature. When left unaddressed, this form of emotional suffering can persist for a duration of four months or longer.

Genetic and Biochemical Factors

The likelihood of experiencing depression is notably elevated if there is a familial predisposition to mood disorders. If you have family members who have battled depression or similar mood-related conditions, you're at a greater risk of developing depressive symptoms yourself. One biochemical explanation points to an imbalance in neurotransmitters, the chemicals essential for mood regulation. Neurotransmitters like dopamine, serotonin, and norepinephrine play pivotal roles in facilitating communication between different brain regions. Clinical depression often manifests when there's a deficiency in these critical neurotransmitters.

An individual's inability to effectively manage stress can also contribute to the onset of depression. The hormone cortisol, which is elevated during stressful episodes, can disrupt serotonin levels, leading to depressive symptoms. Those in mourning often exhibit symptoms that closely resemble clinical depression, including sleep disturbances, poor appetite, and diminished interest in day-to-day activities. While grieving is generally considered a natural response to loss, its symptoms usually lessen over time. However, if these symptoms intensify, it could evolve into a depressive disorder.

Physical and Psychological Consequences

Depression bears a multitude of detrimental impacts on both physical and emotional well-being. Chronic stress, often a by-product of persistent depression, has been linked to hypertension, consequently increasing the risk for cardiovascular complications like heart attacks and strokes. Furthermore, individuals grappling with depression often report a pervasive sense of despair characterized by feelings of hopelessness and helplessness. Such negative emotional states can escalate into suicidal thoughts or actions.

Loss of interest in previously enjoyable activities is another hallmark of depression. Whether engaging in sports, socializing with friends, or even performing well at work or school, the motivation to participate dwindles. People affected by depression describe a general sense of fatigue, listlessness, and a lack of enthusiasm for activities that once seemed effortless, such as making the bed or even eating.

Many people enduring depression exhibit emotional volatility, which could range from irritability to extreme aggression. Another noteworthy symptom is a significant fluctuation in weight triggered by changes in appetite and the stress associated with depression. This symptom is among the criteria healthcare professionals utilize for diagnosing the condition.

Physical Complaints and Coexisting Medical Conditions

Individuals who are navigating the maze of depression often report an array of unexplained physical discomforts. The most frequently cited types include headaches, musculoskeletal pain, and, for women, breast tenderness. Depression's far-reaching impact also extends into the digestive system, manifesting as symptoms like nausea, vomiting, constipation, and even irritable bowel syndrome (IBS).

Moreover, pre-existing health conditions can exacerbate the severity of depression, and conversely, depression can aggravate specific medical issues. This mutual amplification can be partially attributed to the individual's diminished capacity for self-care during depressive episodes.

A decreased libido is a common occurrence in those grappling with depression, and this decline in sexual interest can strain interpersonal relationships. Couples facing this issue are strongly advised to consult professionals for guidance, as ignoring this symptom could perpetuate emotional distress within the relationship.

Self-Esteem and Risky Behaviours

Low self-esteem is a hallmark of depression, often further deteriorating when the individual feels undeserving of love or attention. This emotional abyss can make those who are depressed more susceptible to engaging in detrimental behaviours. These may include substance abuse, gambling, usage of illicit drugs, deliberate self-harm, and, in extreme cases, even suicidal actions as a coping mechanism.

The intricate relationship between physical symptoms, existing medical conditions, interpersonal relationships, and self-destructive behaviours underlines the complexity of depression. Recognizing these facets is crucial for comprehensively understanding and effectively managing this debilitating condition.

DEPRESSION

PSYCHOSIS

Psychosis encompasses a range of symptoms, notably including paranoia, delusions, and both visual and auditory hallucinations. If left untreated, these symptoms can escalate, severely affecting an individual's quality of life. The origins of psychosis can be multifactorial, including drug-induced causes, sleep deprivation, extreme stress, physical injuries, hereditary factors, and more.

The underlying causes of psychosis are manifold and differ from individual to individual. Recreational drug use, for instance, can significantly alter one's perception of reality, emotions, and feelings, sometimes culminating in drug-induced psychosis. Childhood trauma and abuse are also significant predictors of psychosis, and victims are at an elevated risk for functional impairment, addictions, depression, and other psychosis-associated conditions later in life.

A Spectrum of Psychotic Disorders

Several types of psychotic disorders exist, each with its own set of characteristics. These include schizophrenia, drug-induced psychosis, brief psychotic disorder, schizophreniform disorder, and delusional disorder, among others, caused by underlying medical conditions.

- **Schizophrenia**: A chronic mental health disorder affecting a person's cognitive functions, emotional regulation, and interpersonal relationships. While not as prevalent as other severe mental illnesses, schizophrenia can be particularly debilitating, impacting multiple facets of an individual's life, including employment, education, and social interactions.
- **Schizoaffective Disorder**: A unique form of psychosis combining features of schizophrenia with mood disorders such as depression, bipolar disorder, and mania.
- **Drug-Induced Psychosis**: Also known as 'Stimulant Psychosis,' this form of psychosis can arise from the misuse of prescribed medications or illicit substances. Overdosing,

withdrawal, or drug interactions may trigger symptoms like hallucinations, panic attacks, impaired focus, confusion, and paranoia.
- **Brief Psychotic Disorder**: Often precipitated by extreme stress, this type of psychosis is, as its name suggests, of short duration, generally resolving within a month.
- **Schizophreniform Disorder**: Similar in symptomatology to schizophrenia, this disorder is typically of shorter duration, ranging from one to six months.
- **Delusional Disorder**: This disorder is defined by the persistent presence of false beliefs, such as the notion of being stalked, poisoned, or spied upon.

Physical Health and Its Relationship to Psychosis

One cannot underestimate the interplay between physical and mental health. A decline in physical well-being can have a corresponding impact on mental health. Various acute and chronic diseases, including hypoglycemia, AIDS, musculoskeletal disorders, tumours, respiratory infections, and body aches, can act as triggers for psychosis.

Medical Conditions as Trigger Points

Certain other medical conditions can also precipitate psychosis, displaying symptoms like hallucinations, delusions, disorganized thinking and speech, as well as inappropriate behaviours. Conditions such as strokes, migraines, tumours, and specific infections can be potent contributors to psychosis.

Understanding the spectrum of psychotic disorders, their various types, and potential triggers is critical for effective diagnosis and treatment. Therefore, a comprehensive approach that considers all these factors is essential for managing this complex mental health condition.

Psychosis manifests in different ways across individuals. Some may experience a single episode, while others may have periodic episodes throughout their lives. Some may even live in a constant state of psychosis. While a few individuals report having positive experiences during psychotic episodes, the majority often reside in a reality that diverges significantly from the norm. Their beliefs often lack verifiable evidence and stand in contrast to commonly accepted realities.

Psychosis can be a distressing and disorienting experience that profoundly influences behaviour and overall well-being. It often gives rise to feelings of depression, anxiety, fear, and confusion, accompanied by diminished trust in others. Common indicators of psychosis can include a sudden disinterest in previously enjoyable activities, a lack of motivation, social withdrawal, abrupt changes in sleep and eating patterns, difficulties with concentration, restlessness, and memory issues. These symptoms serve as red flags, indicating the onset of psychosis.

Symptomatology

The experience of psychosis is unique to each individual and can have both immediate and gradual onsets. Symptoms of psychosis are generally categorized into "positive" and "negative" types. Positive symptoms are those that add to or distort normal functioning, including delusions, hallucinations, and disorganized speech, thoughts, or behaviours. On the other hand, negative symptoms entail a loss or reduction in everyday functioning. They may include diminished emotional expression, restricted speech output, decreased ability to initiate activities, and social withdrawal, such as disturbed sleep and eating habits.

The Spectrum of Severity

In some instances, psychosis is mild and short-lived, posing minimal disruption to daily life. However, there are cases where psychosis becomes overpowering, leading individuals to inhabit self-constructed 'fantasy worlds.' In such situations, the individual often becomes convinced of the legitimacy of their beliefs, perceiving others as threats or as denying their 'truths,' which can significantly deteriorate their quality of life.

The Role of Sleep Disorders

Sleep disturbances like prolonged sleep deprivation, insomnia, and irregular sleep patterns are also associated with psychosis. These sleep-related issues not only act as triggers but can further exacerbate existing psychotic conditions. Symptoms manifesting from sleep disorders can range from visual and auditory hallucinations to delusions, impaired concentration, confusion, and a palpable disconnect from reality.

Nutritional Factors and Their Influence

Unhealthy eating habits can also contribute to the emergence and progression of psychosis. Poor dietary choices may lead to metabolic imbalances, electrolyte fluctuations, and disruptions in the body's physiological and chemical processes, all of which can be precursors to psychotic symptoms.

Understanding the multi-dimensional nature of psychosis, its varying symptomatology, and its potential triggers is crucial for both diagnosis and treatment. This comprehensive understanding allows healthcare providers to tailor interventions that are most effective for each individual's unique experience with psychosis.

The Complexity of Psychotic Disorders

Psychotic disorders represent a severe class of mental health conditions that significantly impair cognitive functions such as logical thinking, judgment, emotional response, communication, and perception of reality (American Psychiatric Association, 2013). The disruptive nature of these disorders makes it difficult for affected individuals to navigate daily life and sustain a coherent sense of reality. However, it's important to emphasize that even severe forms of psychotic disorders can be treated effectively (McGrath, Saha, Chant, & Welham, 2008).

Financial and Relational Strains

A noticeable fallout of experiencing psychotic episodes is financial instability. The compromised cognitive functions often lead to underperformance in professional settings, putting individuals at risk of unemployment. The condition also affects financial decision-making abilities, such as budgeting and saving, often leading to unsustainable spending habits. Beyond the realm of work and finances, chronic psychosis frequently gives rise to relationship difficulties. The disorder's symptoms can place immense strain on personal interactions, often leading to fractured relationships.

Social Impact and Substance Abuse

The social implications of psychosis are significant. The disorder often fosters a distorted view of others, leading to fears of betrayal, hatred, or abandonment. This anxiety typically results in social withdrawal and a life of self-imposed isolation. While substance abuse is a leading cause of psychosis, it is also a coping mechanism for some individuals already suffering from the condition. While substances might provide temporary relief from symptoms, their long-term use exacerbates mental health deterioration and may lead to more severe psychotic states.

Grave Consequences for Untreated Psychosis

Untreated psychosis poses severe risks, including the potential for irreversible brain damage if episodes are prolonged and untreated. Perhaps the most alarming consequence is the heightened risk of self-harm and suicidality. Among those with psychotic disorders, the rate of suicide is alarmingly high, underscoring the critical need for timely intervention and treatment.

The Disintegration of Reality

In essence, psychosis acts as a corrosive force on the tether connecting an individual to reality. Afflicted individuals come to accept bizarre and erroneous beliefs as truth, experience hallucinations, and often surrender to delusional thinking. An understanding of the intricate and multi-faceted nature of psychosis is essential for providing adequate support and treatment for those suffering from this debilitating mental health condition.

Recognizing the various dimensions of psychosis, from its impact on cognitive functions and social life to its potential for severe, life-altering consequences, is pivotal for both clinical diagnosis and the formulation of individualized treatment plans.

In summary, psychosis is a complex and severe mental health disorder that profoundly disrupts an individual's cognitive functions, emotional stability, and social interactions. Its far-reaching impacts extend from professional life and financial management to personal relationships and self-perception. While the disorder's symptoms can be deeply distressing and socially isolating, it is crucial to remember that even severe forms of psychosis are treatable. Early diagnosis, timely intervention, and a comprehensive treatment approach can significantly improve those affected's prognosis and quality of life. Given the potential for dire consequences, including self-harm and suicidality, a nuanced understanding of psychosis is indispensable for effective clinical management. With advancing medical research and evolving therapeutic strategies, hope remains for those grappling with this challenging condition.

PSYCHOSIS

THOUGHT DEVELOPMENTAL PRACTICE

MODULES and -ACTIVITIES -

MODULE - 1

MODULE-1
THOUGHT REDIRECTION

This module aims to equip individuals with the skills needed to redirect negative thoughts and thought processes towards more positive trajectories. By identifying and understanding negative thoughts, individuals are empowered to sidestep these unproductive patterns, concentrating instead on positive, productive, and beneficial thoughts.

WHAT IS THOUGHT REDIRECTION?

Thought redirection is a method employed to shift focus and attention from negative and stress-inducing thoughts to positive and productive ones. This technique is the foundational step to clear the path for constructive thinking and eradicate negativity. In straightforward terms, "redirection" denotes a change in direction, a shift in focus, or an alteration in the path that may lead to negativity. It is a vital component of mental rehabilitation and is integral to therapeutic treatment plans.

PURPOSE OF THOUGHTS REDIRECTION

Thought redirection serves as a remedy for self-sabotage. Many individuals are trapped in self-criticism, lacking positive self-affirmation, with confidence levels plummeting alongside diminished self-esteem. Focus often fixates on personal weaknesses and the accomplishments of others rather than pursuing personal goals. This outlook can dampen family dynamics, affecting relationships with children, spouses, family, and friends, leading to withdrawal from social engagement due to perceived inadequacies.

Conversely, some individuals may exhibit excessive confidence, perceiving themselves as superior and incomparable. These individuals may harbour illusions of invincibility and uniqueness.

Thought redirection is pertinent for both these groups, as each is ensnared in a distorted reality. One group undervalues their potential, while the other overestimates their abilities. Both are thus encouraged to recalibrate their thoughts, focusing on truth rather than the deceptive realities constructed by their minds. Thought redirection emphasizes positivity and learning from past mistakes to avoid repetition. Many individuals allow their past to dictate their future, ensnared in a mire of regret and negative thinking. Emphasis must be placed on the realization that it is never too late to make positive choices and reshape one's life. The goal is to transform negative patterns into fruitful thoughts.

Moreover, thought redirection is essential for understanding mental disorders and their consequences. Mental challenges like depression, anxiety, PTSD or addiction may be misconstrued as escapes from life's pressures, seemingly alleviating failure and pain. In truth, these disorders can lead to significant life failures and irreparable damage if left unattended. Thought redirection stands as an initial and potent step towards protection from mental afflictions and the promotion of healing.

But the purpose of thought redirection extends beyond mere healing; it aims to instill the ability to triumph over adversity, face failure with resilience, manage daily anxieties and adeptly navigate life's challenges. Thought redirection is not about forcibly negating or altering negative thoughts to positive ones; instead, it involves recognizing and understanding the sources of negativity, actively working on them, and refocusing the mind to embrace and practice positivity. This nuanced approach ensures a comprehensive and authentic transformation of thought patterns, fostering a mindset that is not only resilient but also flourishing and harmonious.

THE START OF MENTAL DOWNFALL

Emotions and reactions are mirrored in thoughts, and since the human brain has a predisposition toward negativity, negative thoughts often predominate and exert a significant influence on emotions. Recognizing and understanding negative thinking is essential, as these thoughts can lead to failure even when success is attainable. They are unproductive and persistent, creating a pathway to mental downfall. It's crucial to remind oneself that happiness is a choice and that obsession with a fixed negative belief or thought, although detrimental to joy, is something that can be overcome.

THE GRIP OF NEGATIVE THINKING

Some individuals may cling to material possessions for a sense of contentment, acquiring large homes, new cars, expensive clothing, and other luxurious items. While these may offer temporary satisfaction, they often leave an underlying emptiness, fostering a friendship with the negative thoughts circulating in the mind.

Others may find comfort in a world of discontent, embracing complaining as a way of life. This attitude can encompass all aspects of life, from jobs, salaries, and relationships to doctors, counsellors, family, and friends. Persistent negativity is not only unproductive and unhealthy for the individual but also for those who are exposed to it.

The effects of negative thinking can also manifest in physical health, with worry and anxiety leading to disturbances in eating and sleeping patterns. This negativity can spiral into a mental health diagnosis, with expectations of failure permeating all aspects of life, from career and education to relationships, friendships, and social interactions. Living in a passive-aggressive world with low self-esteem can tear at the fabric of well-being. Negative thinking is indeed a precursor to many mental health problems, and to halt this downward spiral, it is vital to cultivate positivity and redirect thoughts toward a healthy and practical approach.

REDIRECTING NEGATIVE THOUGHTS INTO POSITIVE THOUGHTS

Negative thinking often arises from universal issues such as guilt, procrastination, past mistakes, or uncertainty about the future. Recognizing that the past cannot be changed, but the future can be shaped through thoughtful choices can bring peace of mind. The redirection of negative thoughts towards positive ones involves focusing on both short-term and long-term goals, teaching the mind to think positively by taking time to understand the broader context rather than impulsively reacting or relying on assumptions.

The transformation from a negative to a positive mindset requires refraining from projecting hopelessness. Problems will not vanish unless addressed; the sooner they are confronted, the quicker solutions can be found. Some individuals may become obsessive with negative thinking, extracting pessimistic messages from every conversation and replaying them repeatedly. In these situations, it's valuable to visualize the negative thought, associating it with the person who expressed it and then reframing it with positivity. Understanding the intent behind negative statements and recognizing that they may not have been deliberate can also help restructure thoughts.

Negative thinking is something everyone may experience, but it can be controlled and redirected. Becoming conscious of thought patterns and actively steering them towards positivity is essential. Sometimes, thoughts may seem like a broken record playing on a loop, but they can be stopped and the direction of thinking purposefully changed. Embracing this capacity to change and redirect thought patterns is a vital step in overcoming the mental downfall initiated by negative thinking. It is a path towards mental integrity, resilience, and a positive, fulfilling life.

HOW TO REDIRECT THOUGHTS?

MODULE - 1

The primary objective of this chapter is to impart the techniques for redirecting thoughts and focusing on positivity. The process begins with simple, scientifically-backed steps to shift attention and restructure thinking patterns.

STEPS TO REDIRECT THOUGHTS

1. **Recognize Your Thoughts**: Identify the causes of particular thoughts. Documenting thoughts and events that disrupt inner peace can be illuminating. Though circumstances may not always be controllable, refocusing thoughts is achievable.
2. **Understand Positive Thoughts**: In addition to negative thoughts, pinpoint those that motivate and uplift, even in challenging times. Identify events, stimuli, habits, or actions that fuel persistence.
3. **Differentiate Between Thoughts**: Recognize that not all negative thoughts are harmful; some may lead to solutions or help in appreciating positivity. Separate thoughts into positive, negative, and 'useless' categories, discarding the latter two.
4. **Strengthen Positive Thoughts**: Focus on moments that inspire, motivate, and enhance mood. Writing these thoughts and feelings down can be a powerful tool to understand and control them.
5. **Learn About Self-Talk**: Since much self-talk tends to be negative, understanding its impact can lead to effective redirection towards positivity, shifting from a pessimistic to an optimistic approach to life.
6. **Refocus Your Thoughts**: Understanding the distinctions between thought types and cultivating positivity, despite challenges, enables a shift towards a brighter perspective. Though not an instant transformation, the magic of positivity can be unlocked with effort and adherence to the above steps.

ACTIVITIES

After grasping the principles of thought redirection, engaging in specific activities can reinforce the ability to focus on positivity, solve problems, and alleviate mental stress.

TYPES OF THOUGHT REDIRECTION ACTIVITIES

A wide array of activities can assist in redirecting thoughts and concentrating on positive aspects. Selecting activities that appeal to individual preferences and that can be performed even during periods of low mood is essential. These activities can be executed in groups, under professional guidance, or individually at home.

THOUGHT REDIRECTION ACTIVITIES IN GROUP

The following activities offer substantial relief from depression, anxiety, panic attacks, negative thinking, and addiction. These group exercises should be conducted under the supervision of a mental health professional.

1. **Group Discussions**: Facilitating discussions about positive experiences, personal growth, and shared goals can foster a supportive environment.
2. **Creative Expression**: Engaging in collaborative art projects or writing workshops allows for positive emotional expression and connection.
3. **Mindfulness Practices**: Guided group meditation or yoga sessions promote awareness and control over thoughts, emphasizing presence and acceptance.
4. **Role-Playing**: Acting out scenarios that demand positive thinking and problem-solving skills can build confidence and perspective.
5. **Team Building Exercises**: Activities that require cooperation, communication, and mutual support encourage positive interaction and trust.
6. **Outdoor Activities**: Group hikes, nature walks, or community gardening foster a connection with nature and others, reinforcing positivity.

Redirecting thoughts is a dynamic process that requires understanding, differentiation, strengthening, learning, and refocusing. The blend of theoretical insights and practical activities paves the way for a resilient, optimistic approach to life. Whether through individual reflection or group activities, thought redirection equips individuals with the tools to navigate life's complexities with grace and positivity. The journey from recognizing negativity to embracing a brighter perspective is filled with growth, healing, and empowerment. It is a path that leads not merely to coping but to thriving.

ACTIVITY 1

Log Down Your Thoughts: Positives And Negatives

___
___
___
___

IMPLEMENTATION

Use a notebook to write down your thoughts. Separate the notebook into two parts: The front of the notebook starts with the number 1 and continues on a sequential number with POSITIVE THOUGHTS, and somewhere in the middle of the book, write down NEGATIVE THOUGHTS beginning with number one. The goal is to flush out negative thoughts with positive thoughts. There should always be more positive thoughts than negative thoughts.

The goal is to redirect the past traumas, abuse, and adverse incidents and focus on moving ahead with the future.

___
___

MODULE - 1

OUTCOME

Put closure to your past and negative thoughts, burn them, make a jet plane with them and shoot them off, or make a boat and see it float away. The goal is to create a new memory card that is positive to the mind. Detaching the negative thoughts with positive ones is essential. Creating a new memory card as a reminder of how and when you got rid of the past negative thoughts.

Redirect the past to closure and focus on the future.

ACTIVITY 2

What If Statements

IMPLEMENTATION

Write "What if" statements on a piece of paper. The statements should be reflective of the negative thoughts. Get the mind to expose the negative thoughts so they can be redirected to something positive. The goal is not to act on impulsive thoughts but on second thoughts.

EXAMPLE:

What if I didn't graduate from high school?

Think about changing the negatives of the what-if to a more favourable solution.

THOUGHT DEVELOPMENTAL PRACTICE

Example:

Q: "What if I haven't graduated high school when I'm 25."

Solution: "I will be the CEO of my own company."

Or

"I will be an adult student."

_____
_____
_____

OUTCOME

Condition the mind to think outside the box.

Think of positive outcomes until this becomes the normal pattern. Constantly redirecting the negatives into positives.

_____
_____
_____
_____

ACTIVITY 3

The Pig Personality Test

_____
_____
_____

IMPLEMENTATION

Sketch a pig on the paper, aiming for as much detail as possible. After completing your drawing, evaluate it using the following criteria to gain insights into your personality traits and tendencies:

- **Positioned at the Top of the Paper**: This suggests a generally optimistic and positive outlook on life.
- **Centred on the Paper**: This placement points to a realistic worldview.
- **Located at the Bottom**: A tendency toward a pessimistic mindset and potentially negative behaviour may be indicated.

MODULE - 1

- **Facing Left**: This could mean you value tradition and friendliness. You may also have a knack for remembering important dates.
- **Facing Right**: This implies a propensity for innovation and activity. However, you might not be great at remembering dates and may not prioritize family ties as much.
- **Facing Forward**: This suggests that you are straightforward and may relish taking on the role of devil's advocate. You are also likely unafraid of contentious discussions.
- **Highly Detailed**: A detailed drawing indicates an analytical mindset. However, you might be overly cautious, to the point of having trust issues.
- **Lacking Detail**: This could mean you are more emotionally driven and focus on the big picture over the minutiae. You might also be inclined to take significant risks, occasionally acting recklessly or impulsively.
- **Fewer than Four Legs Visible**: This could signify that you are currently undergoing significant life changes and may be dealing with insecurities.
- **Four Legs Visible**: Indicates a sense of security and a commitment to your ideals, although some might perceive you as stubborn.
- **Large Ears**: The size of the ears serves as an indicator of your listening skills—the more significant, the better.
- **Long Tail**: A longer tail suggests higher intelligence levels.

(Author Unknown)

Use this analysis as a fun and insightful way to understand yourself better.

_____
_____
_____

OUTCOME

Redirect the thoughts and think that everything you score on the pig test is positive.

_____
_____
_____

ACTIVITY 4

Green space grounding techniques

_____
_____
_____

THOUGHT DEVELOPMENTAL PRACTICE

IMPLEMENTATION

Stand on the green grass and try to ground yourself, tapping into your sensory nerves: smelling, touching, seeing. You can use a green rug and implement the same principle of grounding.

OUTCOME

Redirect the thoughts to sensory nerves and ground oneself in the present. Redirect the mind to being in a safe place.

ACTIVITY 5

Meditation

IMPLEMENTATION

Get the brain to focus only on one thought or statement. Redirecting the mind to stay at peace. Focus on candlelight for 3 seconds, see the flame while your eyes are closed, listen to soft music, feel the ground where you are sitting and keep the flame in your mind as you see all the negative thoughts leaving your mind. Try to stay focused for 3-5 minutes. Imagine an eraser cleaning the mind that is dark. Then, place a positive word or phrase in the mind.

OUTCOME

Calm down the mind and redirect your thoughts.

MODULE - 1

ACTIVITY 6

Thought focused

IMPLEMENTATION

Have a list of things to do when going for a walk to redirect the thoughts to stay focused

EXAMPLE

- count how many dogs you see
- count the number of different types of trees you can find

Or

- count how many people you see

OUTCOME

Train the brain to focus on one thing at a time.

ACTIVITY 7

THOUGHT DEVELOPMENTAL PRACTICE

Negative/Positive thought jar

_____
_____
_____
_____

IMPLEMENTATION

Add to each jar positive and negative thoughts as they come to mind. The goal is to have more positive than negative thoughts to reward yourself.

_____
_____
_____
_____

OUTCOME

Condition the mind with the distraction of emptying the brain. Redirect the mind to become more positive in thinking.

_____
_____
_____
_____

ACTIVITY 8

Chain of independent thoughts

_____
_____
_____
_____

IMPLEMENTATION

Cut a strip from the coloured construction paper. Write something positive about yourself on the paper. Create a ring with the construction paper and staple it together. Write a positive/ encouraging message to yourself and attach it to the previous link to make a chain. Each colour of construction paper has a different meaning.

The colour that best describes your feelings for that day will be the one you write on and attach to the chain. Here is what each colour means:

- Green = positivity
- Red = power

MODULE - 1

- Blue = motivation
- Yellow = accomplishment
- Orange = courage
- Pink = strength

OUTCOME

Distract the mind to think positively with visual accomplishments and redirect the thoughts to positivity.

ACTIVITY 9

Positive Green Poster

IMPLEMENTATION

Write a positive message to yourself on the green construction paper. The message can either be a very personal or vague one.

EXAMPLE

- "I am in control," "Every day is a second chance," "Respect yourself and your body," or "Don't lose hope."

OUTCOME

Recondition the mind towards the thoughts that will empower the individual. Redirect the mind to who you are, valuing the "you" and the worth you carry.

_____
_____
_____
_____

PRACTICAL THOUGHT REDIRECTION ACTIVITIES

The following thought redirection activities are highly recommended whenever you feel down or want to change the direction of your thoughts.

- Cook your favourite meal
- Clean your house
- Organize your wardrobe
- Play video games
- Watch TV/movies
- Internet Surfing
- Call your loved ones
- Groom yourself
- Read, Sketch, Color
- Write a journal
- Yoga & Meditation
- Relaxation exercises

MODULE - 1

MODULE – 2

MODULE - 2
THOUGHT PREPARATION

This module aims to equip participants with the skills necessary to reframe their thought patterns. This transformative process encourages a more hopeful perspective when encountering life's hurdles, thereby enabling practical solutions to everyday challenges as opposed to succumbing to depression, anxiety, or addiction. In essence, this module serves as a guide for individuals to master their cognitive processes for an enhanced quality of life.

THOUGHT MANAGEMENT STRATEGIES

When facilitated these sessions, the feedback was overwhelmingly positive. A remarkable 92% of participants were fully engaged, taking the modules to heart. They demonstrated keen interest, arriving prepared with all necessary materials for each session. Conversely, the remaining 8% displayed a lack of engagement and minimal participation. This subset of participants appeared disinterested in the activities and displayed a laissez-faire attitude toward self-improvement, seemingly indifferent to their future well-being.

KEY ELEMENTS OF MODULE-2

The first step toward improved mental resilience involves thought redirection—shifting focus toward the positive even in challenging times. The subsequent, equally crucial step involves thought preparation. This entails becoming aware of the cognitive strategies needed to eliminate negative thinking, acknowledging life's challenges, and identifying potential solutions. In simpler terms, thought preparation involves mental readiness for executing actions or performances in various life scenarios, such as preparing for job interviews, studying for exams, or devising a stress-free plan for problem-solving. Like thought redirection, the practice of thought preparation offers pragmatic solutions to life's numerous setbacks while serving as a safeguard against depression, addiction, and other mental health issues.

FOUNDATIONS OF THOUGHT PREPARATION

It's a natural human response to feel despondent and entertain negative thoughts when faced with adversity. However, it's crucial to note that people often lose control in these situations, spiralling into an endless loop of negativity that may culminate in depression, anxiety disorders, and substance abuse. Mastering thought preparation is essential to break this cycle and maintain mental equilibrium. Understand that challenges are ubiquitous, affecting everyone somehow and potentially undermining their belief systems. However, those with mental fortitude don't let life's obstacles overwhelm them; instead, they are adept at preparing their thoughts to face any situation and rebound effectively. The concept of thought preparation is rooted in activities and mindsets that guide you toward the most suitable and actionable solutions to your challenges. To implement this, it's imperative to confront your problems rather than ignore them. Compile a list of issues causing stress and anxiety, then outline actionable steps or resources needed to mitigate or resolve these challenges, irrespective of their magnitude or complexity.

The guiding principle of "Utilize Your Past to Cultivate Your Future" is the cornerstone of a healthy mental framework. Everyone has a history replete with uplifting and challenging experiences, moments of euphoria, and periods of sorrow. The silver lining is that positive and negative memories can be leveraged to sculpt a better future. Favourable memories can instill a sense of optimism and fuel your ambition for a more fulfilling life. Conversely, adverse memories are invaluable life lessons, offering the experiential wisdom necessary for future success. These challenging memories also function as cautionary tales, encouraging prudent decision-making in future endeavours. To truly harness the power of your past, it's vital to consciously reflect on the memories that can positively inform your future, enabling you to live a life devoid of regret, guilt, and undue stress.

To make the concept of thought preparation tangible and actionable, consider assembling a "Cognitive Toolkit." Just as a carpenter wouldn't arrive at a job without the essential tools for any given task, large or small, you too can curate a mental toolkit. This could be an internal mental list or a written compilation for more effective results. This cognitive toolkit will serve as a quick reference guide, helping you to assess life situations rapidly and tailor your thoughts accordingly. In essence, this toolkit equips you to adaptively respond to various challenges that arise in your daily life, providing you with strategies to address them effectively.

ACTIVITIES FOR THOUGHT PREPARATION

The thought preparation module is organized into two activity categories: "Under Therapist Supervision" and "Home Activities." The therapist-supervised exercises can be conducted either in a group setting or individually. Each session commences with a review of the previous session's material, followed by an introduction to the current module and its associated activities and a gathering of any required materials. Before initiating the session, you will be provided with two distinct handouts: the SMART Goals Template and a compendium of Inspirational Quotes for Thought Preparation. Detailed explanations of these handouts are provided at the module's conclusion.

GROUP/INDIVIDUAL EXERCISES

The activities designed for "Thought Preparation" are as follows:

ACTIVITY 1

Create Alertness

IMPLEMENTATION

The therapist or facilitator will accidentally drop the papers on the floor and ask the participants to help in picking up the papers. Papers are numbered from 1 to 16, and once the helper picks up all the pages from the floor, the therapist will stick the papers to the whiteboard using tape.

EXAMPLE

For example, the therapist will begin the warm-up session by doing this:

"Welcome everyone to our... oops! (Drops the bundle) "Can someone please help me to gather these papers? I have them in a certain order, numbered on the back."

OUTCOME

The therapist will intentionally drop the bundle of papers on the floor to alert the participants. When the facilitator asks for help, everyone will automatically become conscious of their environment and achieve the alertness they need to begin the session. This is a simple yet highly effective technique that creates alertness and warm-up the group members

MODULE - 2

ACTIVITY 2

Anger Ball-Toss

IMPLEMENTATION

Find a softball and tell the class to stand in a circle. Begin by completing the sentence, "I feel angry when ..." Ask a volunteer willing to restate what the therapist said. Toss that participant the ball. That participant summarizes what the therapist said and then completes the sentence for themselves. They then toss the ball to someone else, who repeats what they said, completes the sentence themselves, and so on.

OUTCOME

This activity will help to declutter the mind by releasing frustrations, negative feelings, and anger. People will learn not to hold back the emotions that are bothersome and are causing unnecessary stress.

ACTIVITY 3

"I Got What I Wanted"

IMPLEMENTATION

Let the participants complete the following sentence: "A time I got something I wanted was when ..."

OUTCOME

It is based on gratitude. Participants will recall good times when their wishes were fulfilled, what they did to get what they wanted, and how they felt then. They will teach them that life is not always unfair; it is a matter of time and effort!

ACTIVITY 4

Standing Up

IMPLEMENTATION

Now, tell the group members to describe a time they felt they were being taken advantage of, and they stood up for themselves.

OUTCOME

Through this activity, the group members will be able to recognize their strengths and weaknesses. They will understand how people would target their weaknesses to gain an advantage and how they could tackle this attack by standing up for themselves and how they do so.

MODULE - 2

ACTIVITY 5

What Color is Conflict?

IMPLEMENTATION

Cut a large piece of 4x4 construction paper into squares in various colours. Be sure to have plenty of red, black, brown, and gray. Ask each student to choose a colour or group of colours that they think represents conflict. In the large or smaller groups of five or six, have participants share the colours they chose and why they chose them. In the case of small groups, gather the participants at the end and let the volunteers share with the whole group which colours they chose and why.

OUTCOME

This task enables the participants to identify the source of the conflict. They will learn to promote good relationships through mutual respect and courteous behaviour and keep the problem separate from the person while addressing the real issues. For this, you must pay attention to each person's interests, listen carefully and respectfully, and be open to exploring all options to resolve conflicts.

ACTIVITY 6

Wrap-up activity

IMPLEMENTATION

Wrap-up activities will involve asking some reflective questions, such as:
- Can you think of a time when being prepared helped you to function better in your situation?
- Can you think of a time when you were not prepared for any situation and had to suffer because of this?
- Today, which activity excites you and makes you curious?

The therapist can ask any reflective question, either it is general or related to the sessions

OUTCOME

Reflective questions offer self-recognition and self-analysis. Also, these questions predict what participants have learned through the activities and what is their area of interest. Reflective questions enable the teachers to know the deficiencies and what they can do for improvement.

THOUGHT PREPARATION – HOME ACTIVITIES

All participants are given handouts of the SMART template and preparation quotes as homework. Besides, participants are instructed to practice decluttering and other activities assigned as homework. The purpose of the "Take Home Activities" is to keep track of the progress of all the group activities. Moreover, it is also important to keep you busy and active at home and protect you from negative thoughts, depression, and the dangers of addictions.

ACTIVITY 1

Mock Start-up

IMPLEMENTATION

MODULE - 2

Begin with outlines of the following:

Idea: Related to something you enjoy, e.g., a restaurant with seafood as the main course, writing a book or a novel, learning the French language, etc.

Name: It could be any name you like to give to your mission, or it could be similar to your business idea

Logo: Show as much creativity as you can according to the name and nature of your idea.

Mission Statement: It is an action-based brief that will include the purpose of your idea and how it can help you and others

Steps: After finalizing the main parts, move towards the steps required to make it a dream come true. For the best outcomes, write down all parts, especially the steps you are going to follow.

_____
_____
_____
_____

OUTCOME

This activity consists of visualizing an idea or project you would like to do or planning to do in the near future. By doing this, you can stimulate your thinking mechanism and prepare your mind to make better decisions

_____
_____
_____
_____

ACTIVITY 2

SMART goal

_____
_____
_____
_____

IMPLEMENTATION

List a few new skills you'd like to learn and create a S.M.A.R.T. goal for each (minimum of 3 skills)

_____
_____
_____
_____

OUTCOME

This will keep you busy with productive things and focused on moving ahead. It will prepare your thoughts to achieve and accomplish what your dreams are.

_____
_____
_____
_____

ACTIVITY 3

The SMART goal for two weeks

_____
_____
_____
_____

IMPLEMENTATION

Create a S.M.A.R.T. goal of something you would like to achieve in the next two weeks, and create a schedule that will allow you to accomplish this goal.

_____
_____
_____
_____

OUTCOME

You will get closer to your goals, and it will become easier to achieve them. You will pursue your life with positive thoughts and reduce procrastination from manifesting itself in your life.

_____
_____
_____
_____

ACTIVITY 4

Bucket list

_____
_____

MODULE - 2

IMPLEMENTATION

Create a bucket list and outline how you will accomplish the things on your bucket list

OUTCOME

This activity will help you to recognize your inner desires and accomplish them

ACTIVITY 5

De-Cluttering

IMPLEMENTATION

Empty your mind to stay calm and relaxed. Consider the following:

- Take care of your hygiene
- Change your appearance
- Give yourself a 'me' time
- Be disciplined
- Avoid unhealthy habits, e.g., smoking, procrastination
- Invest in what you love
- Learn self-love
- Try to have proper sleep
- Learn to 'Let go' when needed
- Make a 'To-do List'
- Do important chores first
- Show gratitude
- Walk daily and eat healthily
- Never stop learning

THOUGHT DEVELOPMENTAL PRACTICE

OUTCOME

De-cluttering can help you eliminate junk inside your mind and achieve mental peace and relaxation.

HANDOUTS

Before the beginning of the session, you will be provided with two types of handouts:

1. SMART goal template
2. Preparation quotes handout

1) S.M.A.R.T GOALS

A SMART goal is a template for setting goals and taking practical, timely, and specific steps to achieve these goals. SMART is a mnemonic for:

S - Specific, significant, stretching
M - Measurable, meaningful, motivational
A - Agreed upon, attainable, achievable, acceptable, action-oriented
R - Realistic, relevant, reasonable, rewarding, results-oriented
T - Time-based, time-bound, timely, tangible, trackable

SMART goals provide you with the steps through which you can achieve your goals by utilizing the available resources in a definite period.

2) PREPARATION QUOTES

A handout with quotes from famous people will be provided. This will help you to stay motivated, focused, and prepared for different phases of life. For example,

- "People who ask confidently get more than those who are hesitant and uncertain. When you've figured out what you want to ask for, do it with certainty, boldness, and confidence. Don't be shy or feel intimidated by the experience. You may face some unexpected criticism, but be prepared for it with confidence". ~ **Jack Canfield**

- "If you believe you can accomplish everything by "cramming" at the eleventh hour, by all means, don't lift a finger now. But you may think twice about beginning to build your ark once it has already started raining" ~ **Max Brooks, *The Zombie Survival Guide: Complete Protection from the Living Dead***

- "Another way to be prepared is to think negatively. Yes, I'm a great optimist. But, when trying to make a decision, I often think of the worst-case scenario. I call it 'the eaten-by-wolves factor.' If I do something, what's the most terrible thing that could happen? Would I be eaten by wolves? One thing that makes it possible to be an optimist is that you have a contingency plan for when all hell breaks loose. There are many things I don't worry about because I have a plan in place if they do." ~ **Randy Pausch, *The Last Lecture***

- "Forewarned, forearmed; to be prepared is half the victory." ~ **Miguel de Cervantes**

- "In the future, instead of striving to be right at a high cost, it will be more appropriate to be flexible and plural at a lower cost. If you cannot accurately predict the future, you must flexibly be prepared to deal with various possible futures." ~ **Edward de Bono**

- "Life belongs to the living, and he who lives must be prepared for changes." ~ **Johann Wolfgang von Goethe**

- "Give me six hours to chop down a tree, and I will spend the first four sharpening the axe." ~**Abraham Lincoln**

- "Clearly outline your plans, acknowledge God, and he will direct them for you. If you can have it planned, you can achieve it; if you have it planned big, you will achieve it big. Make your choice!" ~ **Israelmore Ayivor, *Dream Big!: See Your Bigger Picture!***

MODULE – 3

MODULE – 3
THOUGHT DISTRACTION

The aim of this module is to introduce you to the concept of thought distraction, a technique aimed at interrupting negative emotional cycles by immersing yourself in an activity that captures your full attention and interest. While the relief offered by thought distraction is temporary, it provides a valuable mental respite by shifting your focus away from stress-inducing thoughts. Over time, this practice will cultivate greater mental resilience, enabling you to tackle negative thoughts and emotional challenges in the future more effectively.

THE FUNDAMENTALS OF THOUGHT DISTRACTION

The concept of thought distraction is rooted in intentionally redirecting mental focus from emotionally burdensome or stress-inducing thoughts toward pleasurable and cognitively absorbing activities. This shift in focus is not to be mistaken for evasion or denial; instead, it serves as a psychological buffer, providing an immediate yet temporary respite from the emotional weight you might be carrying. The aim is to lift you out of the emotional quagmire, even if it's just for a short period, thereby offering much-needed mental relaxation and a renewed readiness to tackle such thoughts more constructively in the future.

The mechanics of thought distraction revolve around the brain's capacity to concentrate on one thing at a time, making it exceedingly difficult to dwell on a stressor when fully engaged in an alternate activity. By purposefully choosing activities demanding enough to require your full attention, you create a sort of mental 'interference' that disrupts the cycle of negative or obsessive thoughts. This 'interference' acts like a circuit breaker in an electrical system, halting the flow of negativity just long enough for you to regain your emotional balance.

To further illustrate the potency of thought distraction, consider another example. Suppose you are anxiously waiting for a medical test result. Your mind might be a whirlpool of worst-case scenarios, amplifying your stress levels. If you engage in a challenging puzzle game or immerse yourself in a captivating book during this waiting period, you're likely to find that your anxiety diminishes, at least temporarily. The act of focusing on the puzzle or the storyline acts as a mental barrier, preventing your mind from diving further into anxiety-provoking thoughts.

Understanding the limitations of thought distraction is also crucial. While it is an effective technique for immediate relief, it is not a long-term solution for deep-rooted emotional or psychological issues. It is most effective when used as a component of a broader emotional regulation strategy, which might include techniques like mindfulness, cognitive restructuring, and problem-solving. Think of thought distraction as a first-aid measure—highly effective for immediate relief but not a substitute for more comprehensive mental health treatments.

In summary, thought distraction offers a versatile and accessible tool for anyone looking to break free, even momentarily, from the clutch of overwhelming or intrusive thoughts. This temporary relief can sometimes make all the difference, providing you with the emotional breathing room to approach your challenges with a clearer, more focused mind.

THE IMPORTANCE OF THOUGHT DISTRACTION

The utility of thought distraction lies in its ability to act as a circuit breaker for negative emotional spirals. It provides a mental timeout, reducing the intensity of negative emotions and offering a pause to regather your thoughts. This pause is invaluable; most emotional upheavals last only a few hours. By delaying your reaction to them, you allow time for alternative solutions to present themselves, solutions that may not be apparent when you're in the emotional thick of it.

Thought distraction serves as a conscious effort to safeguard your emotional well-being. It requires self-awareness to recognize you're experiencing distress and then make the deliberate choice to focus your attention elsewhere until the emotional intensity subsides. This strategy stands in stark contrast to unhealthy distractions like substance abuse, which serve only to numb the senses and cloud judgment.

When negative thoughts and beliefs assault you, practicing thought distraction allows you to momentarily disengage, regain emotional equilibrium, and take control of these intrusive thoughts. Although the relief is temporary, it offers you the mental space to think and act more skillfully, creatively, and logically.

A PRACTICAL GUIDE

Opting to divert your attention from an emotional trigger or a craving is an intricate process, especially when compared to the automatic, almost reflexive response associated with substance use or other unhealthy coping mechanisms. Initially, you must become conscious of the emotional turbulence or craving you're experiencing. Subsequently, you should acknowledge that such experiences are a typical facet of the recovery or emotional regulation journey, resisting the urge to react impulsively. The next step is to construct a targeted distraction strategy and implement it. As you're strategizing, your innate reflexes might counteract your efforts, urging you towards anxiety, depression, or undesirable behaviours like substance abuse. Here are some practical examples of thought distraction techniques:

- Immerse yourself in a magazine, allowing your focus to get absorbed in captivating visuals or an engaging article.
- Investigate a subject that intrigues you, whether planning a future holiday, exploring local attractions, delving into a topic you're passionate about, or catching up on the latest films.
- Draft a task list or jot down the shopping items you need, offering your mind an organizational task to focus on.
- Indulge in a shower or bath. Research substantiates that the simple act of splashing cold water on your face can diminish emotional volatility, particularly anxiety. Tune into the sensory experience—the temperature shifts, the aroma of your soap, and its texture.
- Engage in physical activity. Whether running, brisk walking, or even performing jumping jacks in your living room, movement elevates mindfulness related to physiological sensations, steering your focus away from emotional turmoil.
- Browse the internet, but exercise caution to avoid content that might exacerbate your emotional state—such as platforms or sites that may trigger self-doubt or anxiety. Opt for reading news articles, searching for uplifting quotes, or exploring a new blog that resonates with you.
- Organize your environment. Choose a specific area—your desk or a corner of your room—that needs tidying and concentrate on making it more orderly.
- Engage in gaming. Whether it's on your phone, a Sudoku puzzle, a video game, or a card game, the objective is to center your attention on the here and now.
- Strike up a conversation with someone, but refrain from projecting your anxieties onto them. Instead, inquire about their well-being and, if possible, offer your assistance in resolving an issue they might be grappling with. This act of helping can effectively shift your mental focus.

By employing these techniques, you're not just evading the issue but providing your mind with a constructive recess, allowing you to return to your challenges with renewed clarity and emotional equilibrium.

MASTERING THOUGHT DISTRACTION

The significance of thought distraction activities is particularly pronounced for individuals at risk of succumbing to addiction or depression due to excessive mental strain. It's important to understand that addictive substances and behaviours trigger an abnormal release of dopamine in the brain, which in turn stimulates the brain's reward and pleasure centers. This cascade of neurotransmitter release engenders a vicious cycle, compelling the individual to seek out the

MODULE – 3

addictive stimulus repeatedly. The challenge for mental health professionals, therefore, lies in replicating these dopamine-induced brain responses through natural, wholesome activities.

The foundational premise of thought distraction revolves around the notion of deriving a sense of reward, gratification, and achievement without resorting to substances like drugs or alcohol. This makes the skill of effective thought distraction a monumental stride toward mental well-being or a recuperative journey from psychological challenges. Like its preceding modules, the activities within the "Thought Distraction" module are bifurcated into two primary categories: Group Activities and Home Activities.

The Thought Distraction module commences with a recapitulation of the previous session's key takeaways, followed by an introduction to the current module and its slated activities. Necessary materials are assembled prior to the session's onset, with particular emphasis on acquiring a 200-piece puzzle and the Mad Gab game. This meticulous preparation ensures that participants are fully equipped to engage in the activities, optimizing the chances of successfully employing thought distraction as a tool for mental resilience.

GROUP/INDIVIDUAL ACTIVITIES

The "Thought Distraction" activities are given below:

ACTIVITY 1

Reverse Videoing

_____
_____
_____
_____

IMPLEMENTATION

Use 'Reverse Videoing' to warm up the class before the main activity. There is a large number of such videos available online, preferably on YouTube. This warm-up activity can also be used before the 'introduction' part. After the videos, ask participants for reviews regarding this warm-up activity, i.e., Do you feel relaxed/ satisfied? What are your thoughts on the video you just watched?

_____
_____
_____
_____

OUTCOME

Many reverse video therapy clips on the internet are said to be calming and relaxing. Showing participants these videos will hopefully catch their attention and make them feel as comfortable as possible.

ACTIVITY 2

Jigsaw Puzzle

IMPLEMENTATION

Scatter the puzzle pieces on the table and help the participants flip all the pieces. Let the participants work on trying to solve the puzzle, and then begin the discussion phase. Once the activity is completed, the therapist will initiate the discussion by asking questions like, "Did you feel a sense of ongoing satisfaction as you started working on solving the puzzle? Did you feel that your attention was completely engaged in the puzzle? Did you enjoy this task? How are you feeling now?" etc.

OUTCOME

Puzzles are a great distraction that fully engages people who wish to solve them. After completing the puzzle or successfully placing one piece, the brain releases dopamine, which induces pleasure

MODULE – 3

and increases learning and memory. This is a cost-effective, fun activity you can also do at home. Solving puzzles also helps in decluttering the brain.

ACTIVITY 3

Walk around and Find distractions

IMPLEMENTATION

Take participants on a walk around the hospital, school, office, or any place possible (route to be decided on during mock week) and ask them to list 20 things they found distracting along the walk. If the participants list more than 20, that is also fine. After finishing the task, start the general discussion by asking questions like, "What were some of the distractions you found on the walk? Compare your list with others if you feel comfortable in doing so?"

OUTCOME

Walking has a significant impact on improving mental health. Not only can it help alleviate anxiety and depression symptoms, but it can also help with controlling addiction. Exercising releases dopamine into the brain, which makes them de-prioritize substance abuse (in the short term). As participants may not be prepared or don't want to exercise, the purpose of the walk around the hospital is to help introduce the concept of how exercising for a short period of time every couple of days can benefit one's health.

THOUGHT DEVELOPMENTAL PRACTICE

ACTIVITY 4

Mad Gab

IMPLEMENTATION

Set the deck of questions on the table and ask one of the participants to select a card. The participant will read both sides of the card and show the other players only the question side of the card. The participant who selected the card will know the answer to the question on the card, and the other participants will try to guess the correct answer. The correct answer is located on the back of the card.

OUTCOME

Mad Gab is a game where cards have a phrase of confusing words that, when said with proper timing and emphasis, a well-organized and commonly used phrase is formed. The goal of the game is to guess the correct phrase from the confusing arrangement of words

MODULE – 3

ACTIVITY 5

Flowers/Herbs

_____
_____
_____
_____

IMPLEMENTATION

Participants may choose from various seeds, including different herbs or flowers, and will also get their small pot to put it in. Growing these herbs will help them feel a sense of accomplishment and hopefully promote cooking after harvest. Initiate the discussion session by asking these questions, "By planting the seed yourself, does it give you more incentive to take care of the plant? Do you think you will try and grow more plants like these in the future? Will you consider making an herb garden?

_____
_____
_____
_____

OUTCOME

Gardening has been proven to help recover from mental fatigue, cope with stress, and improve productivity, outlook on life, and life satisfaction. Simply looking at plants has been shown to reduce fear, anger, muscle tension, and blood pressure. The harvesting of fruits, vegetables, and herbs also releases dopamine, activating the reward center of the brain.

_____
_____
_____
_____

THOUGHT DIVERSION – HOME ACTIVITIES

Supplemental materials will be distributed to participants, offering a curated selection of thought diversion techniques. These handouts aim to stimulate creative thinking, encouraging individuals to partake in activities aligned with their personal preferences. Participants are encouraged to follow the techniques outlined in the supplemental materials or explore other suitable distraction methods. These handouts and associated tasks serve dual purposes: they engage participants in their home settings while steering their focus away from unproductive stressors toward more fulfilling activities, thereby offering immediate relief from anxiety and fortifying coping mechanisms.

Engaging in a home-based distraction activity is not an intricate undertaking. It can be as simple as doing something you genuinely enjoy. The primary objective of these homework assignments is to shift your attention from the burdensome stress and pressures of daily life to activities that not only pacify your mind but also equip you with the mental clarity to tackle everyday challenges. To offer some suggestions for thought-diverting activities, the homework will include specific notes and guidelines. All participants will receive tracking sheets and handouts comprising various distraction activities. These sheets provide a concrete roadmap for allocating time and a mechanism to monitor your progress.

Below are a few examples of activities conducive to thought diversion that can be undertaken at home:

- Engaging with Television Shows or Movies
- Participating in Recreational Games
- Web Browsing for Constructive Content
- Acquiring a New Skill or Hobby
- Sewing or Knitting Crafts
- Envisioning and Planning Your Dream Home
- Musical Instrument Practice
- Reading, Sketching, or Coloring Activities
- Listening to Podcasts for Enlightenment or Entertainment
- Horticultural Activities or Gardening
- Organizational and Productivity Tasks

By partaking in such activities, you can effectively redirect your focus, making your domestic environment a sanctuary for mental rejuvenation and constructive thought processes.

MODULE – 3

MODULE – 4

MODULE – 4
THOUGHT ILLUSTRATION

The objective of this module is to rekindle the dormant creative faculties in individuals who find themselves ensnared in the rigours of daily stress, thereby losing touch with their innate artistic sensibilities. Through 'Thought Illustration,' you will learn practical strategies to dispel negative thoughts and cultivate an optimistic outlook. Moreover, you will be introduced to a repertoire of engaging and imaginative activities designed to bolster self-esteem, regulate emotions, manage stress, mitigate the risk of mental disorders such as depression, anxiety, and panic disorders, and build resilience against addictive behaviours.

THE CONCEPT

Thought Illustration serves as a universal lexicon that harnesses your creative potential for achieving mental equilibrium and life balance. Within us all lies an intrinsic creative impulse. For some, this impulse is already an active participant in their daily lives, aiding them in navigating life's complexities. For others, however, this creativity is in a latent state, awaiting activation.

This dormant creativity holds the potential to be a powerful coping mechanism, making it an avenue worth exploring. You may be asking yourself, "If I am inherently creative, why doesn't that automatically make me artistic?" The answer is simple: while you may possess raw creativity, channelling it into artistic expression necessitates specific techniques and practices, and it is here that the role of Thought Illustration is pivotal.

This module encompasses a gamut of carefully curated activities that focus your attention on creative tasks, offering you a resourceful toolkit for confronting life's challenges.

THE SIGNIFICANCE OF THOUGHT ILLUSTRATION

According to www.healthybrains.org, "Your brain is a three-pound universe that processes 70,000 thoughts daily using 100 billion neurons that connect at more than 500 trillion points through synapses that travel 300 miles/hour." Thought Illustration offers a mechanism to sift through this expansive mental chatter, isolating and leveraging positive thoughts to create a more fulfilling and productive life.

Moreover, the act of illustration enhances neural connectivity and plasticity, facilitating improved communication between disparate regions of the brain. As empirical evidence suggests, engaging in illustrative activities amplifies psychological resilience and fortifies your resistance to stress. Translating thoughts into illustrations serves as an external outlet for the potent emotions you might have otherwise internalized. The complexity of these illustrated thoughts can range from the simplistic to the intricate, contingent on the thought being represented and your capacity for artistic expression.

For instance, conveying the concept of 'red' could be as elementary as utilizing a red pencil, ink, or paint to jot down a letter or word. However, composing lyrics for a song or crafting a poem demands a more extensive cognitive process to articulate thoughts into verbal language. The encouraging aspect is that proficiency in thought illustration improves with practice.

The more you invest in articulating your thoughts, the more effortless it becomes, explaining why some individuals can compose captivating books within a week or pen emotionally resonant lyrics within just a few days.

ADVANTAGES OF THOUGHT ILLUSTRATION

Thought Illustration, although intricate in its process compared to other modules, serves as a cornerstone for enhancing mental well-being. Its myriad benefits manifest in numerous ways:

- Thought Illustration serves as a mental respite, offering a diversion from the habitual thoughts that occupy your daily consciousness.
- Engaging in art nurtures creative faculties, encouraging you to devise original solutions. It also elevates self-esteem and engenders a sense of fulfillment.
- Innovative thinking catalyzes the growth of new neurons, enriching your cognitive functions.
- The act of creating art releases dopamine, commonly termed the 'motivation molecule,' which augments focus, drive, and concentration. This neurotransmitter fortifies your ability to plan and control impulses, thereby aiding you in attaining your objectives.
- Dopamine also promotes neural genesis, preparing your brain for enhanced learning.
- The practice of art fortifies neural connectivity and plasticity, serving as a conduit for communication between disparate brain regions. Consequently, art bolsters psychological resilience and reduces susceptibility to stress.

- Artistic engagement nurtures social and ethical values, cultivating empathy, tolerance, and emotional warmth. Merely viewing art can elicit pleasure, akin to the sensation of falling in love, as evidenced by dopamine surges in the brain's emotional centers.
- Artistic practices sharpen cognitive capabilities, improve memory, and diminish stress by reducing cortisol levels.
- Art encourages a positive life outlook, fostering attributes such as autonomy, self-reliance, and self-sufficiency.
- Through art and illustration, individuals acquire robust coping mechanisms, alleviate emotional distress, and cultivate self-awareness.
- The practice can normalize physiological metrics like heart rate and blood pressure.
- Art profoundly influences behavioural and cognitive patterns. By externalizing potent internalized emotions through art, one gains a therapeutic emotional outlet.

ACTIVITIES

Mastering the transformative technique of Thought Illustration is accessible through a compendium of practical activities delineated in this module. These activities aim to awaken your creative prowess, offering you the tools to articulate your thoughts and gain mastery over your mental landscape. Activities in this module are categorized into two subsets: "Under Therapist Supervision" and "Home Activities." The module commences with a recapitulation of the previous session, an introduction to the current 'Thought Illustration' session and its activities, and a compilation of essential materials required for the session. These materials include:

- Paint & Paint Brushes
- Thick Paper
- Cups (filled with water)
- Q-tips (cotton ball swabs)
- Writing Paper & Pencils
- Colouring Crayons
- Napkins
- Plastic Zip-lock Bags
- Popsicle Sticks
- Sharpie Markers (Black)
- Pages from Books

This module aims to provide a holistic experience through these activities and materials, empowering you to harness your creativity for enhanced mental well-being.

MODULE – 4

GROUP/INDIVIDUAL ACTIVITIES

The "Thought Illustration" activities are given below:

ACTIVITY 1

Scribble Swab

___

IMPLEMENTATION

Draw a quick scribble on your paper. Now, pass your scribble to the person next to you. Take the scribble that you received and develop it into a picture.

___

DISCUSSION

Discuss this activity with the whole group by asking, " What was it like to develop the scribble? What was it like to work with something you didn't necessarily want or expect? (since you had to use someone else's scribble) How do you usually respond to unexpected events in your own life, and is your reaction similar or different from how you responded in the art? What if you change your attitude to unforeseen situations and try something new and a more positive approach to the ups and downs of your life?

___

OUTCOME

This warm-up activity aims to induce sensory regulation, stimulate creative instinct, and encourage listening to one's intuition. The scribbling back and forth across the page can be suitable for sensory-based regulation, the challenge of developing the scribble into an art piece can stimulate creativity, and the focus on the art can facilitate mindfulness and relaxation.

_____

_____

_____

_____

ACTIVITY 2

Advertisement Illustrations/ Famous Illustrations

_____

_____

_____

_____

IMPLEMENTATION

Discuss how people and companies use illustrations to attract individuals and persuade them to purchase their materials or products. Why do specific pictures and art pieces attract the mind?

Discuss how art and illustrations become famous. How do these pieces get so much attention? Who are the people who created the pieces? What thought were they trying to express through their illustrations?

_____

_____

_____

_____

EXAMPLES

Some examples of masterpieces are discussed below:

- **Mona Lisa:** Leonardo da Vinci's Mona Lisa is the most famous painting in the world. Sitting behind bullet-proof glass at the Musée du Louvre in Paris, the miniature portrait attracts

MODULE – 4

around six million visitors annually. People all around the world still do not know who the woman in the image is; was it Vinci's mother, lover, or just his imagination?

- **Starry Night:** Van Gogh struggled with mental illness and remained poor and virtually unknown throughout his life. Starry Night depicts the view from the east-facing window of his asylum room, just before sunrise, with the addition of an idealized village. Van Gogh struggled with his mental health and committed suicide in his mid-30s.
- **Creation of Adam:** The Creation of Adam differs from typical Creation scenes painted up until that time. Here, two figures dominate the scene: God on the right and Adam on the left. Discuss how art and illustrations become famous. How do these pieces get so much attention? Who are the people who created the pieces? What thought were they trying to express through their illustrations?

_____
_____
_____
_____

OUTCOME

This activity will teach you how to illustrate your thoughts and express them with utmost clarity. You will also learn to channel your attention to one point and control your focus. Moreover, going deep into the details of famous art pieces is a direct way to awaken your artistic self and gain control over your mental state

_____
_____
_____
_____

ACTIVITY 3

Picture activity

_____
_____

IMPLEMENTATION

For the main activity, provide participants with 12 different pictures and ask their thoughts regarding the pictures. Tell participants to write their thoughts on the board. To make this activity easy and interesting, briefly explain the views of the artist regarding each picture. To complete this activity, review the following sets of images and their description, and then let the participants present their views.

Image #1: Cat & Mouse: The artist wanted viewers to see how society is so caught up in media. Instead of saving the other mouse from the cat, the mouse is taking photos of their kind getting eaten by the cat.

Image #2: Voting & Sheep: This image portrays how politicians and other individuals may act like shepherds directing the community and people to where they should vote. People are looked at as sheep following the shepherd's command.

Image #3: Fountain: In this illustration, the man in the fountain represents a person preaching good things but not allowing others to drink from the fountain. So, he is telling others to be good people but not following a good path and acting like a hypocrite.

Image #4: Facebook & Ego: This illustrates how society focuses on Facebook and how many likes they get. Here, the cereal box represents Facebook, and the food represents the like by which we are trying to satisfy our ego.

Image #5: Men in Suits: This illustrates how someone is always above you, pointing the finger. If one person makes a mistake, the other person above gets in trouble.

Image #6: Beach & Cellphones: This illustrates how much people use cell phones. When they decide to go swimming, you can see a tan mark on their chest showing a hand holding a cell phone because they are always on their cell phones.

Image #7: Facebook Dogs: This image illustrates how people are always into other people's businesses through Facebook. Portraying society as dogs sniffing other people's behind is illustrated as Facebook.

MODULE – 4

Image #8: Facebook & Priest: This image portrays someone going to a church to confess their sins; however, a speaker above them is illustrated as Facebook. People are so into Facebook that they put everything on there, sharing all their problems, guilts, and sins.

Image#9: Games Vs. Chores: This image portrays how children are getting increasingly into video games and staying away from helping their parents with chores.

Image #10: Death Vs. Art: This illustrates how people are interested more in the art rather than the artists who painted it and the reason why he created the art.

Image#11: Heaven & Cellphones: This image illustrates how people are so into their cell phones that when they go to a place without cellphones, they don't know what to do, and they just stare at their hands, thinking they are still holding their phones.

Image#12: Snow White Selfie Stick: This image shows how society is so into technology, using their cell phones rather than a mirror and comparing who has the better profile picture.

OUTCOME

The picture activity is designed to directly target the illustrating skill of the participants. This activity will stimulate your creative thinking process and activate problem-solving elements of your mind. Also, engaging in such activity will calm your mind and boost confidence by interacting with each other and sharing your views.

ACTIVITY 4

Tree Of Affirmation

THOUGHT DEVELOPMENTAL PRACTICE

IMPLEMENTATION

This activity is performed during the group training session in two ways.

Option 1: Give participants an Affirmation tree outline and get them to compare their lives to the tree. The branches are positive affirmations of what they think of themselves and what others think of them, which are of a positive characteristic. The trunk is their backbone, what is holding them together. Their roots are the qualities that ground them without falling apart. And the leaves are negative time plots to record and discuss. It's the only part of the tree with negative words or incidents in the participant's life.

Option 2: Pass around the affirmation tree and get participants to write on the tree. Inform them this is something that will be kept posted on the wall throughout the modules/weeks.

OUTCOME

Affirmations are the most effective way to manifest positivity. Through this activity, participants can illustrate their optimistic views and achieve more.

ACTIVITY 5

Imagery Poetry

MODULE – 4

IMPLEMENTATION

Give each participant a page from a book along with some markers and coloured crayons. Find words that form a mini-story or poem and use a marker to cover the rest of the words. Feel free to be creative, use different colour markers and crayons, and create images or shapes if possible. Display participants' work on the table and let all participants view others' work.

Proceed ahead by asking questions like;

"What inspired you to draw or colour the way you did to block out the words? Why did you choose those particular words? What were you thinking about when forming your poem/ story?"

OUTCOME

Like all other activities of thought illustration, this activity is also beneficial in stimulating the artistic instinct of the participants. The group discussion will promote confidence and a friendly environment among participants.

ACTIVITY 6

Heart Mapping

IMPLEMENTATION

Draw a picture of your heart – Divide it into nine segments or rooms that look like a map. One room or segment would be the junk room with all the negative things, and the other eight rooms are all the things that mean a lot to you. The expected time for this activity is 10 minutes.

_____
_____
_____
_____

OUTCOME

Write what you feel after the activity.

_____
_____
_____
_____

ACTIVITY 7

Plastic Bag Painting

_____
_____
_____
_____

IMPLEMENTATION

Paint a pattern, design, or whatever you like on the plastic bag using a paintbrush. Feel free to use different colours. Now, take the painted bag and press it against the paper. Use a Popsicle stick to push down on the plastic bag. Remove the bag and continue painting on it different designs and patterns. Repeat. After some tries, you are expected to write down your experience and views regarding the activity, for example, why you selected a specific colour. Why do you create such

MODULE – 4

designs or patterns? What are your thoughts while painting and drawing? What do you feel after this activity?

**** This activity can also be done during group sessions. All participants display their work on the table with their names or initials during a group session. Other members will walk around and look at each other's work. Initiate discussion by asking questions like, "What was that experience like for everyone? What made you decide to use certain colours and objects? What kind of thoughts did you experience while painting?"

The expected time for this activity is 30 minutes.

___

OUTCOME

Write what you feel after the activity.

___

ACTIVITY 8

Body painting

___

IMPLEMENTATION

Option 1: Paint your body reflecting a thought you have.

Option 2: Lay on a painted canvas on the floor and allow the paint to fall on you from a bucket with holes. Feel the paint as it falls on you with clothes or without being fully dressed. Use paint that is not sensitive to your skin. Focus on your senses of smell, touch, sight and sound, maybe taste.

Option 3: Use your different body parts to paint on a canvas or the wall. Use your hands, feet, face and other parts of your body.

___
___
___
___

OUTCOME

Write what you feel after the activity.

___
___
___
___

SPECIAL ACTIVITY

In this module, you will be doing a particular activity that comprises all the previous modules, including "Thought Redirection, Thought Distraction, & Thought Illustration." This specific activity is known as "Green Time," you can perform it during group sessions (as guided by the therapist) or as homework by yourself. You will get clear instructions on how to do the "Green time" activity for both the group and home sessions."

To get a better understanding of this activity, consider the following details:

MODULE 1

Thought Redirection

___
___
___
___

MODULE – 4

IMPLEMENTATION

Go to a park or any place with greenery

OUTCOME

Going to a park for green time is a redirection.

MODULE 2

Thought Distraction

IMPLEMENTATION

Observe people talking, dogs running, ducks swimming, cars passing by, or anything related

---

OUTCOME

All these or other things at the park will distract your thoughts

---

THOUGHT DEVELOPMENTAL PRACTICE

MODULE 3

Thought Illustration

IMPLEMENTATION

To touch your artistic self where you feel most alive, visit parks, buildings, and other artifacts such as monuments, fountains, or playground structures.

OUTCOME

Parks illustrate a sense of relaxation and calmness, a place to enjoy nature and fresh air, where humans, animals, and other life forms reside in the same space. In short, where you can enjoy and feel relaxation

MODULE – 4

MODULE – 5

MODULE – 5
THOUGHT EXPRESSION

The objective of this module is to instruct individuals in effectively articulating their thoughts, feelings, and emotions. By engaging in a range of activities delineated in this module, you will acquire the skills needed to express your emotional and psychological states cogently and clearly. Furthermore, these activities will guide you in refining your thought patterns to be more constructive and optimistic.

UNDERSTANDING THOUGHT EXPRESSION

Thought Expression encapsulates the skill of articulating your internal thought processes and emotional states in a manner that is understandable to yourself and others. By mastering thought expression, you gain a clearer understanding of your cognitive patterns and enable others to grasp the sentiments and ideas you aim to communicate.

Thought expression is particularly pivotal for those grappling with mental health challenges like addiction, anxiety, PTSD or depression, as they often find it taxing to convey their experiences in a way that others can understand. Thus, the module aims to equip individuals with techniques for effectively constructing coherent dialogues that marry their thoughts with words.

For many, expressing one's thoughts can be a daunting experience, particularly when the mind is awash with numerous conflicting ideas. The struggle to verbally articulate one's emotions can lead to anxiety, stammering, or even complete silence.

In such instances, people often prefer a more passive approach, suppressing their urge to speak. This module offers a remedy for such quandaries by imparting techniques and strategies designed to manage and channel your thoughts productively.

MODULE – 5

THE INTRICATE LANDSCAPE OF OUR THOUGHTS

Our thoughts are universal experiences, transcending ethnic and national boundaries; they reside inherently within us. We choose to express these thoughts through various means—verbal communication, non-verbal cues, written words, music, dance, and other creative outlets. Unfortunately, the realm of negative thinking often revolves around toxic elements like sarcasm, cynicism, and derogatory remarks. Such negative thought patterns cultivate an environment of pessimism, clouding one's emotional state and obstructing the path to truth.

Some individuals, consumed by anger, employ it as an emotional outlet, while others resort to gossip as a false sense of emotional gratification. Both approaches culminate in nothing more than a perpetuation of negative emotional states. Then there are those who oscillate between positive and negative thoughts, navigating life in a constant state of emotional imbalance due to their inability to express these conflicting thoughts effectively.

This module aims to address these issues, guiding you through the labyrinth of your thoughts, helping you articulate them effectively, and empowering you to master your mental and emotional landscapes.

SUPPRESSING THOUGHTS

While there may be some temporary benefits to suppressing your thoughts, it's crucial to understand that this approach doesn't offer a lasting solution to the emotional challenges that often lead to addiction, anxiety, PTSD or depression. On the positive side, thought suppression can serve as a defensive mechanism, preventing you from outwardly displaying anger or frustration. Over time, these suppressed thoughts may fade, giving you a false sense of resolution. Often, this suppression normalizes the challenges, abuses or traumas we face, masking them as acceptable. However, the downside is much more concerning. Suppressed thoughts accumulate internally, creating emotional pressure akin to a volcano on the brink of eruption. This internal turmoil manifests as feelings of depression and low self-worth, fostering a mindset of inadequacy and a lack of confidence. You may start to feel misunderstood and disregarded, leading you to lose sight of your life's purpose and engage in internal dialogues only you can comprehend.

NAVIGATING THE ART OF THOUGHT EXPRESSION

In the content of this lesson, the myriad ways people choose to express themselves were considered. Some find expression through their grooming habits; others opt for clothing that ranges from eye-catching to understated. Some people are vocally expressive, while others are more reserved. Some prefer to dance, others to remain seated; some seek attention, while others are indifferent. Expression is an inherent liberty encompassing various facets of our being—our spirit, character, personality, emotions, reactions, and attitudes.

Unfortunately, people often default to negative forms of expression, particularly when angered. Insults and derogatory comments are flung in heated moments, escalating into emotional abuse. Such individuals can become increasingly agitated, even violent, causing harm both to themselves and others. Conversely, those who opt for positive verbal expression tend to elevate their emotional state and those around them. This module aims to guide you in exploring various methods of expression, enabling you to channel your emotions in a constructive manner. You can effectively dispel lingering emotional burdens by learning to articulate your thoughts positively.

THE SIGNIFICANCE OF THOUGHT EXPRESSION

The thoughts we harbour wield immense power in shaping our lives and our destinies. Often, people devote excessive time contemplating what they don't desire, adversely affecting their emotional well-being and overall lifestyle. Learning how to liberate ourselves by processing and articulating our thoughts can pave the way to achieving our deepest aspirations. When we master the art of thought expression, we become architects of our reality. Recognizing the need to distinguish between achievable goals and mere fantasy, thought expression offers a practical toolkit. To conclude, the importance of thought expression is encapsulated in the following key points:

- Thought expression allows you to scrutinize your cognitive patterns, enabling you to replace undesirable elements in your life and mind and aligning you closer with attainable objectives.
- It facilitates a better understanding of your thoughts, offering a platform to share and nurture your ideas with trusted individuals.
- The practice empowers you to gain better control over your actions and maintain your integrity. It sharpens your ability to articulate thoughts clearly, bolstering self-confidence and self-esteem.
- It enables you to navigate your emotions effectively, transforming negative tendencies into positive behavioural outcomes.
- Thought expression serves as a catalyst in shifting your focus from negative to constructive thought patterns.

Ideally, our thoughts should center around education, career, health, spirituality, family, healthy relationships, passion, finances, and hobbies rather than being clouded by guilt, regrets, mistakes, weaknesses, flaws, jealousy, envy, and negativity.

OBJECTIVES OF THOUGHT EXPRESSION

The primary goal of this 'Thought Expression' module is to dismantle the barriers that inhibit your ability to articulate your thoughts freely. The module aims to equip individuals with the skills necessary to authentically convey their thoughts, emphasizing the significance of expressing their image, character, and personality. Upon close observation of the world around us, it's evident that life offers countless learning opportunities. To reap the maximum benefits, one must be willing to liberate one's emotions and give voice to their thoughts.

Moreover, the module targets eradicating self-imposed limitations, guiding you to express your feelings through audible, visual, or physical avenues. This requires acknowledging any hesitancy or weaknesses in conveying your emotions. It's essential to understand that not everyone will agree with you, and that's perfectly okay. In thought expression, perspectives aren't merely binary; they're multi-dimensional, urging you to consider issues from various angles.

Ultimately, the module seeks to instill the skill of transforming negative thought patterns into positive ones without resorting to self-criticism. Learning from past conversations and adapting for future interactions will propel you forward, reinforcing that differing opinions are not threats but mirrors reflecting aspects of ourselves. This module aims to imbue the notion that everyone should possess the freedom to articulate their thoughts authentically.

AN ESSENTIAL COMPONENT OF A FULFILLING LIFE

Often, we encase our thoughts within the fortress of our minds, unwilling to let them escape—even when they're wreaking havoc on our inner peace, diminishing our mental well-being, and undermining our productivity. This reluctance may stem from a fear of being perceived as vulnerable, a lack of practical communication skills, or perhaps even a misunderstanding of our thoughts. It is precisely in such situations that mastering the art of thought expression becomes indispensable for a more prosperous, happier life.

People who are overly self-conscious or perpetually concerned about others' perceptions of them often find themselves ensnared in a web of negative thinking. They cultivate poor self-images, continually doubting their worth and questioning their right to happiness. This damaging mindset can have cascading repercussions across various life sectors—be it relationships, career, education, or health—ultimately funnelling individuals into the trenches of depression, anxiety, and addiction.

The silver lining, however, is this downward spiral that is not inescapable. Understanding your thought patterns and learning the skills to articulate them can halt this negative cascade and steer your life toward a more fulfilling existence. Every day, our minds are a battleground of countless thoughts. The challenge lies in sifting through this mental chatter, separating the wheat from the chaff, and nurturing positivity. It's crucial to assess whether these thoughts align with your identity, core beliefs, culture, traditions, and values. Equally important is recognizing how these thoughts influence your emotional state and how adept you are at expressing these emotions.

In essence, your thoughts wield enormous power over your life experience. Since you spend so much time within the confines of your mind, it's imperative to cultivate an inner environment that is harmonious, peaceful, and conducive to well-being. Achieving this involves letting your thoughts flow freely and articulating your feelings, irrespective of their positive or negative nature. It's undeniable that a mix of emotions often populates our minds—be it confusion, joy, sadness, guilt, anger, stress, or fear. However, it's crucial to remember that you hold the reins of your thoughts and possess the capability to shift your mindset from negative to positive.

By acquiring the invaluable skill of thought expression, you're essentially charting a course toward happiness and freedom—much like a bird soaring freely through life's endless sky. This enables you to become a herald of much-needed virtues such as love, kindness, gentleness, patience, mercy, peace, joy, truth, purpose, strength, and empowerment. All it takes is mastering the transformative technique of thought expression.

ACTIVITIES

In this module, we aim to cultivate authentic emotional expression as a means to foster a more positive life experience. We will focus on reframing life's challenges positively, emphasizing constructive rather than destructive thought processes. Our objective is to identify the kernels of positivity in each thought that crosses our mind and to make conscious decisions on whether to nurture or eliminate these thoughts. Thought expression isn't merely a skill—it's a way of life manifested through various activities like singing, dancing, spinning, and jumping. The ultimate goal is not to suppress or repress your thoughts and emotions but to express them freely and creatively.

Suppressing or repressing thoughts often leads to emotional turmoil. Suppressing involves holding in your thoughts in the hope they will disappear while repressing involves actively denying the thoughts or emotions you're experiencing. Learning to effectively express your thoughts and feelings liberates your mind and ushers in a sense of peace and joy.

To facilitate the journey towards practical thought expression, we've structured this module into two types of activities: those conducted "Under Therapist Supervision" and those categorized as "Home Activities." The session will begin with a review of the previous module, followed by an introduction to the current module's activities. To ensure that you are fully equipped for the session, the following materials are required:

- Tree pictures: To serve as a metaphor for growing positive thoughts
- Music playlist: For auditory expression and emotional regulation
- Paper and pens: For written expression and introspective activities
- Dance video: To guide bodily expression and liberate pent-up emotions
- Foam roller: For physical relaxation and emotional release
- Mirror: To practice facial expressions and become aware of non-verbal cues
- Pencil or chopstick: To assist in fine motor activities that promote thought expression

MODULE – 5

By engaging in these activities, you'll not only learn to express your thoughts and emotions. Still, you will also develop the skills needed to transform your life experience into positivity, peace, and freedom.

THOUGHT EXPRESSION – GROUP/INDIVIDUAL ACTIVITIES

The "Thought Expression" activities are given below:

ACTIVITY 1

The Tree

_____
_____
_____
_____

IMPLEMENTATION

Look at the picture of the tree, and pick a character you feel resembles you and your life at this current moment. Now discuss: What made you choose that specific character on the tree? How do you think it resembles you or your life? Does anyone feel the same as others? How do you think you can reach the top of the tree? What will your life look like up there?

_____
_____
_____
_____

OUTCOME

The picture is used as a way for the participants to express how they are feeling in their lives. It is a way for participants to open up, connect and get to know other individuals.

_____
_____
_____
_____

ACTIVITY 2

Music Expression

_____
_____
_____
_____

THOUGHT DEVELOPMENTAL PRACTICE

IMPLEMENTATION

Listen carefully to the few songs played. Write down what message each song gives you, what emotions you feel (makes you feel happy, sad, angry), or what thoughts come to mind when listening to each song. Using childhood music may trigger more applicable.

_____
_____
_____
_____

OUTCOME

Listening to music affects emotions and can be used to represent how one may be feeling. For example, listening to a happy, upbeat song can lift people's spirits.

_____
_____
_____
_____

ACTIVITY 3

Smiling

_____
_____
_____
_____

IMPLEMENTATION

Write down or draw an image that expresses a memory or an event that has brought you deep joy and satisfaction. When you are feeling angry or sad, think of the memory that will make you instantly smile

_____
_____
_____
_____

OUTCOME

When a person smiles, and the muscles in their face contract, positive feedback is sent to the brain, and it reinforces feelings of happiness. Smiling will reduce the stress your body and mind may feel and generate more positive emotions within yourself.

MODULE – 5

ACTIVITY 4

Photo cards

IMPLEMENTATION

Hand out a few pictures to each participant; each participant has to choose one that makes them smile and one photo that makes them sad. Once they choose the photo, they each explain why the photo made them feel that way.

OUTCOME

Expressions are the best way to manifest our feelings, and by expressing our feelings, we can lighten the mental burden.

ACTIVITY 5

So, you think you can dance

IMPLEMENTATION

Have you ever wanted to learn how to dance? Latino? Bollywood? Hip Hop? Breakdancing? Contemporary? Ballet? Belly dance? Let loose dance?

It's never too late, and you can learn for free. All you need is YouTube and a good attitude. You can use 'Dance workouts' to help you learn moves while working out.

OUTCOME

Dance is a universal language to express ourselves. All types of dance express something; we can even relax and calm our minds by dancing.

ACTIVITY 6

Big girls do cry

IMPLEMENTATION

Ask participants to tell them anything that hurts, affects their emotions and brings them to tears. It is a sad movie, a past event, rejection, failure, fear, betrayal, loss, or any other major and minor event that automatically brings a tear to their eyes or forces them to cry.

OUTCOME

Crying too much is very uncomfortable, awkward, and embarrassing. Society makes us believe that crying signifies physical weakness in men and emotional fragility in women. But the true weakness isn't acknowledging your emotions by crying; it's hiding from them. Crying makes us

MODULE – 5

human; 9 out of 10 people feel better after doing it. It is proven to relieve stress and lower blood pressure, it's a way to remove toxins that build up when you're upset, and it boosts your mood.

ACTIVITY 7

Just Dance

IMPLEMENTATION

Ask the participants to get up and stand in front of the screen. When the music starts, everyone must mimic the dance moves.

OUTCOME

Dancing to random tunes will stuff you with excitement and provide peace of mind

ACTIVITY 8

Laughing Yoga

IMPLEMENTATION

For those who are comfortable, ask them to play a game. Start with going in a circle; then the first person says "ha" once, the second person says "ha ha" and the third "ha ha ha" and so on.

After the activity, initiate the discussion by saying: "Laughing is good for you if you find it hard to laugh sometimes; look up on YouTube or other resources to help. Try to do the exercise at least once and see how you feel afterward. You may feel silly at first, but it will be worth it due to the effect. Test it out!"

OUTCOME

Laughing brings out the feel-good hormones; it helps lift depression, increase blood flow, release stress hormones, strengthen the immune system, and help build confidence. Laughing can help release anxiety, as you cannot worry and laugh simultaneously. The body cannot differentiate between a real and a fake laugh. So, faking it causes the same positive effects.

ACTIVITY 9

Facial Expression

IMPLEMENTATION

Have three to five chairs in front of the room; ask or pick volunteers to sit in the "hot seats." Then, have them bow their heads and close their eyes. The therapist will select a situation, feeling, emotion, or expression and announce it out loud. After that, on the count of three, the "hot seat" performers will raise their heads with a facial expression that best communicates the given emotion. Tell them to freeze their faces so the group can choose who had the best expression. Switch the "hot seat" participants.

MODULE – 5

EXAMPLE

As an example of a situation or emotions, consider the following:

- You just walk into your house late at night and hear someone upstairs walking around.
- You walk to the house, and your mother has just baked fresh cookies.
- You walk into a public bathroom, and the sewer is backed up and overflowing out of the toilets.
- You wake up on your birthday, and your mother holds a gift.
- You are on the bus, and the person beside you farts loud.
- You are just about to jump on your bed and see a mouse run across your feet
- You just caught your sister stealing money out of your dad's wallet.
- You are watching a sad love movie.
- You see your friend trip on his shoes and falls
- You see someone stealing your car

OUTCOME

This activity is highly engaging and fun to do. The participants will be able to learn facial expressions and use their faces as the best tool for expressing emotions.

ACTIVITY 10

Rolling in the deep

IMPLEMENTATION

Someone will do a demonstration with a foam roller. Roll your abdomen slowly on the foam roller, going all the way down to your pelvis. Roll it on the lower back. Roll and massage the ball on the tense spot while taking deep breaths.

OUTCOME

When your body is feeling tense, you can do some rolling. The rolling will help relax your body and your mind. Just as a hot tub soothes your body and relaxes your mind, the same will be the effects of rolling. For this, all you need is a foam roller or a tennis ball.

HOME ACTIVITIES

The "Thought Expression" activities that can be done as homework are straightforward and usually consist of a revision of group/individual session activities. Following is the brief detail of home activities:

- Find music: Find a genre that makes you feel happy, whether it is rock, jazz, hip-hop, contemporary music, slow music, pop, etc. Whenever you feel down, listen to a song that will make you happy.
- Smile: Practice smiling and humming at least three days a week. When you wake up and before you go to bed, practice smiling in front of your mirror- not just with your mouth but your eyes, too. Try humming for two minutes; it will bring a smile to your face, help you feel relaxed, and promote clarity of thinking as it refreshes your mind
- Complete smiles checklist: Create and complete the checklist of things that can make you smile as best as possible.
- Learn a dance
- Therapeutic crying: If it's been a long time since you've been able to cry, you may need to make a conscious effort to get to the point where you can release your emotions through tears. Try these four things that can initiate the crying and go with it. Find a good place to cry that no one will bother you (in your bedroom, in the shower, in your car)
- Cut an onion: This will make you tear up and then let all your emotions flow as well

MODULE – 5

- Look at old pictures: Ones that bring back memories of a particular person, your family, or how much life has changed. Remember the good times you had with the people in the pictures or how much you loved a particular place.
- Watch a sad movie: When you start crying during the movie, let your thoughts turn to your situation so you can process your feelings about your own life. Example movies: Titanic, The boy in the striped Pajamas, Marley and Me, Romeo and Juliet, The Notebook, The Fault in Our Stars, Bollywood love story movies and more.
- Listen to emotional music: The right music can be the perfect way to help your emotions loom more prominent in your brain.
- Try laughing yoga:
- Smile at least three times a day for two minutes each. If you cannot hold it open, you may use your finger, a pencil, or a chopstick to keep your mouth open. It is proven to make you feel happier, even if the smile is forced.
- Try to do a rolling exercise

MODULE – 6

MODULE - 6
THOUGHT SENSORY

The objective of this instructional module is to acquaint you with the foundational notion of harnessing your senses to modulate your cognitive processes. This module aspires to educate you on strategies to deploy your senses as a viable coping mechanism when grappling with challenges like addiction, anxiety, PTSD and depressive symptoms. The ultimate ambition of employing sensory techniques is to cultivate internal tranquillity, thus alleviating the compulsion to succumb to addictive behaviours and mitigating symptoms of anxiety and depression."

THE CONCEPT

This paradigm emerged from my experiential engagement with clients/patients struggling to pivot away from destructive life patterns. Initial artistic and music therapy endeavours did not yield the anticipated transformative outcomes. The epiphany of employing all five sensory faculties as an alternative channel for mental diversion occurred. Individuals wrestling with issues including addiction, anxiety, PTSD and mood fluctuations all possess a common thread: the ability to vividly envision the circumstances when recounting their experiences. For example, those enmeshed in gambling or pornography addiction could mentally project the allure of their chosen vices. Similarly, those experiencing anxiety could mentally conjure the events triggering their unease, while those navigating mood disorders could visualize incidents that thrust them into depressive states. Remarkably, some clients reported multi-sensory experiences, including auditory and olfactory sensations.

APPLICATION

Clients/patients are consistently encouraged to identify hobbies that stimulate their senses in a fulfilling, non-harmful manner. Each of us is drawn to varying activities that resonate uniquely with us—some women derive joy from shopping, while some men find immense pleasure in sports spectating. As we probed further into the intricacies of cognitive development, it is evident that when individuals could meld their senses to evoke a quasi-real experience of well-being, they genuinely felt better. The more we integrate this sensory approach into the therapeutic process, the more positive experiences of moods and thought patterns are developed. The ultimate goal transitioned to aligning the senses in such a way that they provide a more enduring and memorable experience. For instance, if you imagine being famished, you can mentally savour an appetizing meal even if it is not physically present, especially if it's a flavour profile you have previously relished. Culinary tastes can range from hot to sweet, tailored to individual taste preferences. While we may mentally relish curry chicken and chapati, a colleague may envision a sandwich, yet another might fantasize about spaghetti. The scope of sensory imagination is boundless, although it can pose unique challenges for those unaccustomed to leveraging their sensory faculties—akin to attempting to hear a rainbow or visualize a sound.

SENSES AND THOUGHT PROCESS

Seated beside a tranquil lake, gazing at a resplendent rainbow, one can delve into a meditative state, contemplating the hues and their potential impact on one's emotional state. One could extend their gaze beyond the rainbow, focusing on the arboreal backdrop or the drifting clouds, each element contributing to a unique sense of mental serenity. Auditory stimuli, such as the rhythmic pattering of raindrops, the melodious cascade of a fountain, or the resonant crash of sea waves against rocky shores, likewise wield significant influence over our mood.

Tactile experiences also offer a rich tapestry of emotional responses. The warmth emanating from a comforting body can instigate feelings of coziness and the desire to cuddle. The gentle heat radiating from a fireplace on a frigid winter day or the tactile stimulation derived from touching varying textures, from the silky to the granular, can elicit a range of emotional reactions. It's nearly instinctive how we physically engage with potential purchases—be it produce, apparel, or other tangible goods. This tactile interaction is ingrained in our behavioural patterns. The sensation of reclining, floating on water, or simply being proximate to someone whom we can touch or embrace adds another layer to our sensory experiences.

Taste, another crucial sensory faculty, operates similarly. Our tactile interactions often precede our gustatory experiences; we feel the texture of fruits and vegetables before committing to consume them. This is why many large-scale food retailers offer sample tastings, capitalizing on our sensory-driven purchasing behaviours.

Olfactory cues also play an indispensable role in shaping our thoughts and emotions. The aroma wafting from a food court or a street-side food cart can be irresistibly compelling, driving us toward a purchase as effectively as a visually captivating commercial or an eye-catching poster. Our ability to discern between pleasing and offensive odours has a direct and potent impact on our emotional state. So, in essence, our senses are not merely passive receptors; they actively shape our internal dynamic landscape, steering us toward a range of actions and reactions.

FIVE SENSES AND THEIR IMPACT

Vision and Its Profound Influence on Thought Processes

Vision, perhaps one of the most dominant senses, has a complex yet riveting relationship with how we think, feel, and interact with our world. Here's an in-depth exploration of the twofold roles that vision plays:

1. Visual Awareness: The Conscious Engagement

When we talk about visual awareness, we're referring to the active engagement of the eye with the external environment. This form of vision serves as a gateway to a multitude of experiences, from the simple act of recognizing colours, shapes, and movements to the more complex processes of interpreting facial expressions, deciphering visual cues, and navigating spaces.

For instance, the vibrant hues of a sunset can evoke a sense of calm and contemplation, while the fast-paced visuals of an action movie can stimulate excitement or tension. Even in our day-to-day lives, our visual encounters can influence our mood, decision-making, and even long-term thinking. The layout of a store, the colour scheme in your office, or the imagery in a piece of art — these visual elements shape our immediate responses and our more profound, sustained lines of thought.

2. Non-Visual Awareness: The Unseen Realm

At the other end of the spectrum lies non-visual awareness, where the eyes are intentionally disengaged to heighten different sensory experiences. This may sound counterintuitive, but sometimes, "not seeing" can deepen our understanding of the world around us.

For example, we explored this aspect of vision at a restaurant in Toronto designed to mimic the experience of blindness. In this pitch-black setting, diners are served by visually impaired waitstaff, and the absence of visual stimuli serves to amplify the other senses to an extraordinary degree. The flavours of the food seemed to burst forth with newfound intensity, the sounds of conversation around became notably crisper, and the sense of touch became the primary means of navigation.

In these moments, the remaining senses work in overdrive to compensate for the lack of visual input, enriching your experience in a way that everyday sighted life rarely offers. This heightened state of non-visual awareness allows you to perceive nuances, details, and sensations that you might otherwise overlook.

In essence, vision acts as both a spotlight and a filter, highlighting what we should focus on while simultaneously sidelining less relevant information. Whether consciously engaged visual awareness or deliberately restricted non-visual awareness, each modality of vision offers insights, shaping our thoughts, influencing our feelings, and guiding our interactions with the world.

MODULE – 6

Hearing: A Multifaceted Sensory Experience

Hearing is an extraordinary sense that plays a vital role in interpreting and engaging with the world. It operates in two distinct dimensions, each contributing to our thought processes in unique ways:

Auditory Awareness: The Power of Sound

In its conventional form, hearing grants us auditory awareness—our ability to perceive, interpret, and respond to sound. This encompasses everything from birds chirping to the cacophony of a busy street, the melodic chords of a guitar, to the spoken words of a conversation. Every sound has the potential to evoke an emotional response, stimulate memory, or trigger a line of thought.

For instance, hearing a particular song can instantly transport us back to a specific time, place, or emotion. Similarly, the intonation or pitch of someone's voice can give us clues about their feelings or intentions, allowing us to adjust our behaviour and reactions accordingly.

Sounds, whether harmonious like music or discordant like noise, have the power to affect our mental state. Calming sounds like raindrops on a roof or waves crashing on a shore can reduce stress and promote relaxation. On the other hand, abrupt, jarring noises can evoke feelings of irritation or anxiety.

Non-Auditory Awareness: Silence as a Catalyst

The absence of sound, or what we might term "non-auditory awareness," is equally powerful. By deliberately seeking silence—perhaps by using earplugs or isolating oneself in a quiet room—our mind often transitions to internal dialogues, introspective thoughts, or meditative state. This mental space allows us to examine our inner world with greater clarity, free from external distractions.

When you quiet the auditory stimuli, your other senses become more acute, as if striving to compensate for the loss of sound. In this heightened state, you may notice subtleties in your environment or within your own body that would typically go unnoticed. This can be an essential exercise for self-awareness and mindfulness.

Moreover, this state of sensory deprivation can be a perfect setup for focused thinking or meditation. By narrowing your sensory input, you can more easily concentrate on a single word, phrase, or idea, exploring it with a depth that would be difficult to achieve in a noisier setting.

Understanding and utilizing both the auditory and non-auditory aspects of hearing can enhance our emotional well-being, cognitive functioning, and interpersonal relationships. Sound can be a mirror reflecting our inner emotional states and a window into understanding the external world. Whether we are enveloped in the rich tapestry of sounds that life offers or seeking solace in the quietude, our sense of hearing serves as an invaluable tool for navigating the complexities of our thoughts and emotions.

Touch: The Multifaceted Sensory Experience

Touch is an incredibly nuanced and complex sense that affects our thought processes, emotions, and overall well-being in obvious and subtle ways. Unlike the other senses that primarily serve as windows to the external world, touch is more intimate and deeply ingrained in our emotional and physiological makeup. Here's a more in-depth exploration:

Varieties of Touch Experiences

1. **Texture and Material**: Whether it's the silkiness of a fabric or the roughness of a wooden surface, the texture of materials can evoke specific emotional states. The tactile sensation of holding a smooth, cold stone might bring a sense of calm, while the scratchy surface of a wool sweater might cause mild irritation.
2. **Interpersonal Touch** involves the sensation you experience when you touch another person or are touched in return. A hug from a loved one can bring comfort and security, a pat on the back can signify approval, and an unwelcome touch can bring about feelings of discomfort or fear.
3. **Environmental Touch**: This includes how we interact with our surroundings. The feeling of sand between your toes, the touch of warm water in a bath, or the experience of a gentle breeze against your skin all contribute to our emotional state, either elevating our mood or affecting it adversely.
4. **Self-Touch**: This involves the sensations we feel when we touch our bodies. Whether stroking a beard thoughtfully, nervously tapping a foot, or the comforting wrap of arms around oneself, self-touch can be a powerful regulator of emotions.
5. **Instrumental Touch**: This involves a touch that serves a specific purpose, such as gripping a steering wheel, typing on a keyboard, or using a cooking utensil. These types of touch may seem mundane, but they also contribute to our sense of agency and efficacy in the world.

Emotional and Psychological Impact

1. **Comfort and Security**: Gentle, warm touches from people we trust can trigger the release of oxytocin, often referred to as the "love hormone," which fosters feelings of trust, comfort, and social bonding.
2. **Stress Reduction**: Studies have shown that human touch can lower levels of the stress hormone cortisol, leading to increased feelings of relaxation and well-being.
3. **Pain Alleviation**: Touch has been shown to release endorphins, which are natural pain relievers. That's why a mother's touch can soothe a child's scrape, or massage can feel relieving.
4. **Emotional Communication**: Sometimes words can't capture what we want to express, and touch becomes a language of its own. Whether holding a friend's hand in a moment of grief

or the celebratory high-five after a victory, touch can communicate complex emotions succinctly and powerfully.

Cognitive Implications

1. **Memory and Association**: The sense of touch is closely linked with memory. A specific texture or sensation can instantly transport us to a particular time, place, or emotional state.
2. **Decision-making**: Believe it or not, touch can influence our judgments and decisions. For instance, a product's texture or a handshake's firmness can influence our perceptions and choices.
3. **Concentration and Focus**: Fidget toys and stress balls are examples of how touch can improve concentration. The act of touching or manipulating an object can help some people focus better on tasks.
4. **Empathy and Compassion**: The act of touch fosters human connection and can make us more empathetic and compassionate. It reminds us of our shared humanity and can influence our thoughts and feelings about others.

In sum, the sense of touch is a complex and integral part of our human experience, influencing everything from our emotional state to our cognitive processes. It serves as a link between our internal and external worlds, making it a crucial focus in understanding human thought, behaviour, and well-being.

Taste: A Complex Sensory Experience

Taste is a rich, multifaceted sense beyond simply identifying flavours; it plays a pivotal role in our decision-making, emotional state, and cultural identity. Let's delve into the complexities of taste and its influence on our thought processes:

Dual Facets of Taste Experience

1. **Active Tasting**: This involves directly engaging with diverse flavours, textures, and temperatures. From the chilli pepper's spiciness to the mint's cooling sensation, vibrant tasting is a journey through a culinary landscape. It shapes our preferences, dictates our cravings, and evokes strong emotional responses. For example, the comforting taste of a childhood dish might transport you back to simpler times, filling you with nostalgia and warmth.
2. **Restrained Tasting**: On the other end of the spectrum is the art of self-control. This is a mental exercise in restraint, in which you consciously resist the pull of enticing aromas and visual temptations. It's the internal debate that occurs when you pass by a bakery exhaling the buttery scent of fresh croissants or when you're at a party, trying to avoid the allure of a decadent chocolate cake. This taste experience is less about the palate and more about willpower, self-discipline, and mental fortitude.

The Psychological Dimensions of Taste

Taste is often tied to our emotional state. A well-prepared meal can lift our spirits, while a poorly executed dish can leave us disappointed or irritated. Foods we enjoy can release dopamine, the "feel-good" neurotransmitter, reinforcing our positive association with those flavours. This is why comfort foods can be so emotionally satisfying; they're often linked to pleasant memories and feelings of security.

Social and Cultural Aspects of Taste

Taste is also a social sense, deeply embedded in cultural practices and rituals. Whether sharing a festive holiday meal, toasting champagne at a wedding, or gathering around a barbecue with friends, the foods and flavours we enjoy become part of our communal experiences. They can signify belonging, tradition, and identity.

The Cognitive Angle

Your brain plays a critical role in the experience of taste. The anticipatory phase, fueled by sight and smell, sends signals to your brain, preparing it for the food about entering your mouth. Once the food is tasted, cognitive processes such as perception, recognition, and memory come into play, helping you identify the flavour, compare it to past experiences, and decide whether it's pleasurable.

The Health Factor

Taste also affects our health. Our natural affinity for sweet, salty, and fatty foods, which are high-energy but often low-nutrient, can lead to poor dietary choices. Learning to appreciate the subtle flavours in healthier foods like vegetables and grains can shift our taste preferences and, by extension, our eating habits, contributing to better overall health.

In summary, taste is not merely a biological function but a comprehensive sensory experience that engages us on multiple levels—emotional, cognitive, social, and ethical. Understanding the complexities of taste can help us make more informed choices, enrich our culinary experiences, and deepen our appreciation for this remarkable sense.

Smell and Its Profound Influence on Thought Patterns

Smell is often considered the most evocative of the senses, with an unparalleled capacity to trigger memories, influence moods, and even guide our decisions. This olfactory sense functions in several distinct ways:

- **Diverse Olfactory Experiences**: Some people possess an innate curiosity about smells, embracing a wide variety of scents, from the invigorating aroma of freshly brewed coffee to the earthy scent of wet soil. Their olfactory palette is broad and accepting, allowing them to navigate different environments and situations easily. For these individuals, the world is a kaleidoscope of scents waiting to be explored, each imbued with its narrative and emotional undertones.

- **Selective Olfactory Engagement**: On the flip side, there are those who have specific scent tolerances or intolerances. These individuals may experience allergies, sensitivities, or personal preferences dictating their olfactory experiences. Whether it's an aversion to strong perfumes or a particular fondness for the smell of old books, these selective olfactory tendencies can profoundly shape a person's interactions with their surroundings.
- **Smell as a Trigger for Emotional States**: Scents have an extraordinary ability to elicit emotional responses. The aroma of lavender may produce a sense of calm, while the smell of freshly cut grass might evoke memories of childhood summers. Conversely, unpleasant odours can induce feelings of discomfort, irritation, or even revulsion. This emotional impact demonstrates our minds' deep psychological connections with the olfactory world.
- **Smell as a Decision-Making Factor**: Believe it or not, smell often plays an under-recognized role in our decision-making processes. Whether it's the scent of a potential partner, the aroma wafting from a restaurant, or the fresh smell of a new car, our olfactory experiences often tip the scales when making significant and mundane choices.
- **Therapeutic Applications of Smell**: Aromatherapy, a practice that uses natural plant extracts to promote well-being, is based on the idea that scents can have a powerful impact on our mental state. Essential oils like peppermint and eucalyptus are believed to invigorate the mind, while others like chamomile and rose are thought to have a calming effect.
- **Smell and Memory**: Our olfactory system is closely linked to the hippocampus, the brain's memory center. This is why certain smells can instantly transport us back to specific moments in our past, triggering a flood of vivid memories and associated emotions.
- **Cultural and Social Implications of Smell**: Our perceptions of smell are also shaped by cultural and social norms. What is considered a pleasant or unpleasant odour can vary significantly from one culture to another. In some societies, body odours are embraced as a natural part of human existence, while in others, they are masked with deodorants and perfumes.

Indeed, the sense of smell is a complex and nuanced faculty that exerts a powerful influence over our thoughts, emotions, and behaviours. Whether consciously aware of it or not, our olfactory experiences continually shape our interactions with the world, providing a rich tapestry of sensory information that our brains use to form perceptions, make decisions, and even construct our sense of self.

In summary, each of our five senses has a profound impact on how we think, feel, and interact with the world. They can either serve as gateways to a richer understanding of our surroundings or, when intentionally restricted, as catalysts for heightened sensitivity in our remaining faculties.

Strategies For Leveraging The Senses To Optimize Thought Patterns

We advocate for people to harness their senses as an innovative way to refine and enhance their mental well-being. A multi-sensory approach can be remarkably beneficial for recalibrating your thoughts and emotions as a powerful tool for self-improvement.

- **Visual Isolation Technique**: One effective method involves secluding yourself in a dark room at your workplace or in the comfort of your home. Utilize an eye mask or a folded cloth to cover your eyes, effectively blocking out all visual stimuli. This allows your other senses to come alive, sharpening your focus on the conversations around you or the internal dialogue within your mind. The aim here is to empty your mind, concentrate on a singular word phrase, or even enter a restful sleep.
- **Auditory Focus**: Often, we're oblivious to the cacophony of sounds permeating our daily lives—the hum of traffic, the clangour of construction, the murmur of conversations, and the like. We encourage you to isolate a single sound, perhaps a piece of serene music or a nature soundscape, to serve as your auditory anchor. This focused auditory experience can act like a mental cleanse, sweeping away distractions and centring your thoughts.
- **Tactile Therapy**: The sense of touch offers another avenue for mental renewal. Some clients have reported a reduction in anxiety and addictive urges through tactile engagement, such as petting an animal or rubbing a piece of jewelry. The tactile sensation of stroking a chain or twirling a "stress ring" can be a discreet but effective way to manage anxiety.
- **Sensory Comfort Objects**: For a more textured tactile experience, consider keeping sensory comfort objects close at hand. This could range from a soft blanket or stuffed animal to a silk scarf or even a set of worry beads. These items can serve as tactile anchors, offering comfort and focus when your thoughts spiral.
- **Water and Temperature Therapy**: The feeling of water can have a calming or invigorating effect on your mental state. Whether it's the soothing sensation of a warm shower, the chill of ice against your skin, or the weightlessness of floating in a pool, water can serve as a powerful mental reset button.
- **Body Care Rituals**: Engaging in self-care rituals involving lotions, creams, or oils can nourish your skin and serve as a form of tactile meditation. The very act of applying these substances can become a mindful practice, tuning you into the present moment and away from intrusive thoughts.
- **Spa Treatments**: For those who wish to take it a step further, a trip to the spa can offer a comprehensive sensory experience. Saunas, steam rooms, hot tubs, and various forms of bodywork can contribute to a profound sense of physical and mental well-being.

By consciously integrating these sensory-based strategies into your routine, you provide yourself with various tools to navigate and manage your thought patterns. Each sense can be considered a different instrument in an orchestra, and when played in harmony, they create a symphony of mental clarity, focus, and peace.

Extend the Role of Sight and Sound

MODULE – 6

- **Visual Engagements for Mental Well-being**: Many clients/patients have found using visual stimuli to be immensely beneficial in diverting their thoughts from negativity. Some find solace in leafing through old photographs of family, friends, or memorable trips, each image serving as a portal to happier times. Others find comfort in reading—song lyrics, heartfelt poems, articles, diaries, old report cards, love notes, or even engaging in research on a specific topic.
- **Artistic Endeavours and Scenic Visits**: The world of art also offers a sanctuary for some. Visiting art shows galleries or even attempting to create their art allows people to engage deeply with visual stimuli. Scenic drives through the countryside, lakeside visits, or oceanic getaways provide a natural canvas that can soothe the mind. Urban settings, too, whether a park, a restaurant with a view, a cinema, or a bustling downtown, offer their form of visual therapy.
- **Visual Boards and Social media**: Personalized visual boards, like whiteboards or corkboards, adorned with photographs, notes, or favourite sayings, serve as daily reminders of what matters most. For the digitally inclined, platforms like Facebook, LinkedIn, Instagram, and Vine offer endless visual stimuli that can serve as effective thought diverters. Video games, too, can absorb attention, offering a visually immersive experience.
- **Aquatic Therapy**: A less conventional but equally effective method involves the therapeutic observation of fish aquariums, where the varying colours and movements can captivate attention for hours, offering a peaceful diversion from turbulent thoughts.
- **Auditory Channels for Coping**: Sound also plays a significant role in influencing thought patterns. Clients have reported that listening to calming music, or even just music in general, has a profound impact on their mental state. Some have sought out specific auditory experiences like birds chirping, children's laughter, or even musical instruments' soothing sounds.
- **Sound-Based Interactions**: Interactive auditory experiences like calling hotlines, engaging in conversations with friends or family, or listening to crisis line advisors can also serve as effective coping mechanisms. These conversations provide auditory stimulation and valuable advice, suggestions, and recommendations.
- **Natural Soundscapes**: Documentaries focusing on natural settings such as oceans or forests offer a dual benefit. They provide visual engagement and a rich tapestry of natural sounds that can be incredibly calming. Alternatively, some find solace in the sounds of nature itself—be it the falling rain, a gushing waterfall, or the flow of a river.

By proactively incorporating these visual and auditory techniques into their daily lives, clients have found diverse and effective ways to manage and improve their thought processes. These methods offer a distraction and a meaningful engagement of the senses, each contributing to a more balanced and mentally enriching life experience.

Our sense of smell, often underestimated, holds potent emotional sway. Numerous clients have found comfort and balance through aromatic experiences. Some lean towards the calming fragrance of incense or scented candles, while others find solace in the aroma of potpourris or plug-in fragrances designed to neutralize odours. Household smells, such as the clean scent of pine-based floor cleaners or laundry detergents, evoke a sense of order and cleanliness. Several clients are captivated by the aroma of freshly brewed coffee or the comforting smells of various foods—freshly baked bread, aromatic curries, or simmering stews. From personal fragrances like perfumes and colognes to the simple pleasures of minty chewing gum or even the scent of nail polish, these olfactory experiences contribute to a more focused and peaceful state of mind.

When it comes to our sense of taste, the experience can be downright adventurous. Clients have explored a full spectrum of flavours: salty, sweet, sour, bitter, spicy, and some that defy easy categorization. They've embraced gastronomic adventures, dining at restaurants that offer cuisines from diverse cultures. Some have discovered new beverages, sampled an array of candies, or even embarked on quests to find the perfect cheese. Non-alcoholic options like sparkling juices and specialty virgin drinks have also been explored. The aim here is to fully engage the sense of taste, not just for the pleasure it brings, but as a means to anchor oneself in the present moment.

The Integral Role of Sensory Techniques

Our five senses—sight, smell, hearing, touch, and taste—are not just physiological mechanisms; they are gateways to our emotional and mental well-being. Each sense contributes to how we perceive and engage with the world. Incorporating sensory techniques into thought management aims to harness these senses to instigate positive thoughts and emotions while diminishing negative or disruptive ones.

By consciously engaging our senses, we can divert our minds from harmful pathways, such as those leading to addiction, anxiety, or depressive states. The ultimate goal is to achieve a tranquil state of mind that reduces the compulsion to indulge in addictive behaviours or succumb to anxiety and depression. This involves becoming fully aware of our sensory experiences: tuning in to ambient sounds, savouring the nuances of flavours, appreciating the textures of objects we touch, and thoroughly absorbing the visual and olfactory world around us. This multi-sensory awareness serves as an effective tool in guiding our thoughts towards positivity, anchoring us in the present, and thereby enhancing our overall emotional well-being.

Sensory Activities

The activities designed for the 'Thought Sensory' module are bifurcated into two primary sections: "Guided Activities Under Therapist Supervision" and "Self-led Home Activities." The session begins with a recapitulation of learnings from the previous module, followed by a detailed introduction to the current 'Thought Sensory' session and its associated activities. To ensure a smooth and compelling session, participants are advised to prepare and collect the following materials beforehand:

MODULE – 6

- **Reusable Water Bottles:** Ideal for hydration exercises and can also be used for various sound and touch exercises.
- **Food Colouring:** For activities that engage your sense of sight, often used in conjunction with water to create colourful sensory experiences.
- **Glitter and Beads:** Additional materials to augment the visual appeal of various activities.
- **Candy and Assorted Food Items:** Selected to stimulate the sense of taste, ranging from sweet and salty to sour and spicy.
- **Candles and Tea:** To incorporate the olfactory sense, aromatherapy candles and fragrant teas can be highly effective.

These materials serve as tactile stimuli and are integral to the activities that will be conducted, enabling a comprehensive exploration of the senses to modulate and enhance thought processes.

THOUGHT SENSORY – GROUP/INDIVIDUAL ACTIVITIES

The "Thought Sensory" activities are given in the following table:

ACTIVITY 1

Touch & Guess

IMPLEMENTATION

Put together a bag containing various items. Participants reach into the bag, feel the item with their hands and attempt to guess the item.

OUTCOME

This is the warm-up activity that highlights how the senses become heightened to compensate for the missing sense.

ACTIVITY 2

Taste

IMPLEMENTATION

Have the participants close their eyes. The facilitator reads the following:

"Imagine a bright yellow, juicy lemon in your hand. Visualize the lemon until you can smell its clean tartness. Now imagine cutting a thick slice from the lemon that releases a fine, fresh mist. Now, bite into the wedge of lemon and feel it."

After this, proceed to another activity.

Hand out food(s)/ candies of different flavours (sweet, salty, sour, bitter, hot) to participants and let them discuss with each other the taste, texture, sensation, and shape of each flavour.

OUTCOME

The idea behind the 'lemon' activity is to predict how strong our taste sense is. Just by imagining the lemon, one can taste it although it doesn't exist in reality.

The 2nd activity is also focused on the diversity of taste sensations.

ACTIVITY 3

What are you eating?

IMPLEMENTATION

MODULE – 6

Handout assorted candies and ask participants;

"Take a few minutes and think about what you are eating. What is the shape, texture, & flavour? Is there any unusual sensation?"

Participants may draw, write, and describe everything related to candies to each other.

_____
_____
_____
_____

OUTCOME

"What are you eating?" will elaborate on your taste and how this sense helps interpret different aspects, i.e., shape, texture, or any other unusual sensation.

_____
_____
_____
_____

ACTIVITY 4

Ice cube

_____
_____
_____

IMPLEMENTATION

Hand out pieces of ice and ask participants to hold the piece of ice in their hand, close their palms, and also close their eyes along with the palm. Now, initiate a discussion by asking the following questions:

How does it feel in your hand? Cold? Does it feel good? Can you hear the ice? Does it smell like anything? Does it take you back to a memory?

Feel the shape change in your hand and conform to fit. Rub the ice on the back of your hand, outside of your arm, and inside of your arm.

_____
_____
_____
_____

THOUGHT DEVELOPMENTAL PRACTICE

OUTCOME

This activity will link the complex thinking process with external feelings and sensations. Also, this activity will explore if a particular object brings back any memory.

ACTIVITY 5

Smell, guess, and remember

IMPLEMENTATION

Pass around three different teas in a container and have the participants guess the scents. After that, distribute candles to participants and have them describe what smell reminds them of and a memory that it brings back.

OUTCOME

This activity will activate your sense of smell and bring back memories related to specific smells

HOME ACTIVITIES

The "Thought Sensory" activities that can be done as homework are given below:

ACTIVITY 1

Water running

MODULE – 6

IMPLEMENTATION

Open YouTube or any other similar site and search for water running sounds. Listen to these sounds for 10-15 minutes or as long as you wish.

OUTCOME

Such natural sounds are stress killers and mood enhancers, providing you with much-needed peace of mind.

ACTIVITY 2

ASMR (Autonomous Sensory Median Response)

IMPLEMENTATION

Use YouTube or any other platform and search for ASMR videos/audio. Earphones are highly recommended for this job. Another alternative is to listen to relaxing, instrumental music. You can create your playlist and listen to it when you have cravings. Or create your own ASMR by tapping your fingers on different surfaces.

In short, do anything that suits you and calms you.

THOUGHT DEVELOPMENTAL PRACTICE

OUTCOME

ASMR is a relaxing tingling that starts in the scalp and back of the neck and can extend to the rest of the body. ASMR has guided mediation that decreases stress levels and increases concentration, which induces relaxation.

ACTIVITY 3

Sensory Bottle

IMPLEMENTATION

Take a water bottle, fill half of it with water, and add some food colouring. You can choose to add glitter, beads, and figurines or leave it just with coloured water. Add vegetable oil at the top. Close the cap shut.

OUTCOME

The sight of a sensory bottle stimulates the imaginary mind and helps to visualize something peculiar regarding that colourful bottle

HOME ACTIVITIES

In addition to the structured activities under the 'Thought Sensory' module, there are also several straightforward yet effective activities you can engage in at home to fine-tune your sensory experiences further and distract your mind from cravings or distress. These include:

MODULE – 6

- **Multi-Sensory Cooking Experience**: This is not just cooking; it's an experience that engages all of your senses. Immerse yourself in the visual aesthetics of the ingredients, the tactile sensations of food preparation, the aromas wafting through the air, the sounds of sizzling and chopping, and finally, the flavours that delight your palate. Consider it a 'Holistic Culinary Journey' that fully engages all five of your senses.
- **Aromatic Atmosphere**: Light a fragrant candle that emanates a scent you find both pleasing and calming. Pair this olfactory experience with soothing background music to create a tranquil ambiance.
- **Pet Therapy**: Spend quality time with your pet, whether a dog, cat, or fish. The tactile sensation of petting an animal and the unconditional love they provide can be extremely calming.
- **Texture Therapy**: Find a material or texture that you find particularly comforting—perhaps a soft blanket, a plush toy, or even a smooth stone. Gently stroke it and focus intently on how it feels against your skin, allowing this tactile interaction to occupy your thoughts and soothe your mind.

Each of these activities aims to engage one or more of your senses in a positive way, offering alternative methods for modulating your thought patterns and improving your emotional well-being.

MODULE – 7

MODULE – 7
THOUGHT IMAGINATION

The aim of this module is to elucidate the remarkable capabilities of imagination and how you can harness this innate power to actualize your life's aspirations. Furthermore, this module will differentiate between thoughts and imagination and explore the interconnectedness of these two mental faculties. A series of activities within this module are designed to specifically hone your imaginative abilities and leverage them to bring positivity into your life.

THE GATEWAY TO REALITY

Imagination isn't merely a flight of fancy; it's the cornerstone that lays the foundation for both minor and monumental events in our lives. While thoughts are involuntary cognitive processes overseen by the mind, imagination is a voluntary act of conceptualizing or visualizing scenarios that either enthuse or frighten us. By synchronizing these two crucial mental elements—thoughts and imagination—you can manifest your deepest desires and convert them into tangible realities. Although actions are typically rooted in thought, thoughts themselves have limitations—they reach a saturation point beyond which they can't extend. Imagination, however, knows no bounds. It's an expansive mental landscape that can astonish even us at times. Simply put, when thoughts hit a wall, imagination takes flight. Mastering the synergy between thoughts and imagination can give you unprecedented control over your mind and, subsequently, extraordinary outcomes in your life.

THE SIGNIFICANCE OF THOUGHT IMAGINATION

The importance of integrating thoughts with imagination is a subject of paramount significance, one that transcends mere intellectual curiosity and has direct applicability to our lives. If you've been following along with the previous modules, you've already delved into the profound role that thoughts play in shaping our realities. They serve as the blueprint of our actions, reactions,

MODULE – 7

and, indeed, the trajectory of our lives. However, thoughts alone are often insufficient for transformative change; this is where the role of imagination becomes critically important.

Imagine thoughts as the building blocks of your life, while imagination serves as the architect's vision—expansive, unrestricted, and full of potential. This vision guides the building blocks into forming structures that are not just functional but also awe-inspiring. Without imagination, thoughts can become repetitive, limited, and myopic. With imagination, however, the realm of possibility expands exponentially. It's like adding wings to the foundational blocks, allowing them to ascend and arrange themselves into formations that were previously unthinkable.

Imagination acts as a catalyst, an agent of change that reorients thought patterns from being stuck in cycles of stress, depressive states, or addictive behaviours. It creates a paradigm shift, turning your focus toward constructive, fulfilling, and positive avenues. You initiate a chain reaction once you unlock this alchemical process where imagination influences thought. Once hemmed in by limitations or negativity, mental activities now find a new avenue for expression. This mental shift inevitably leads to tangible changes in your physical world. You'll find that as your mental landscape broadens and brightens, your external circumstances mirror these internal changes.

Additionally, the concept of "Thought Imagination" transcends mere daydreaming or wishful thinking. It's a disciplined practice, almost a form of mental athleticism that requires consistent training, focus, and application. Unlike random musings, directed imagination aims to manifest specific outcomes. It's a targeted approach that combines the specificity of thought with the expansiveness of imagination to create a balanced mental framework. This framework becomes the fertile ground upon which you can cultivate a life that is not only successful by your standards but also profoundly enriching.

In summary, integrating thought with imagination is not an optional luxury but a necessary strategy for anyone looking to elevate their life's quality. This fusion of thought and imagination serves as the cornerstone for mental well-being, emotional balance, and physical actualization. It's not just about thinking outside the box; it's about realizing there was never a box to begin with. Imagination allows you to step beyond self-imposed limitations, empowering you to live a life aligned with your highest potential.

ACTIVITIES

This module on thought imagination contains two categories of activities: the first to be executed under the watchful guidance of a therapist, either in group settings or one-on-one, and the second as at-home assignments. Each session starts with a recap of the previous module, followed by an introduction to the current module on 'thought imagination,' its activities, and a round-up of the necessary materials needed for the session. This includes items like staplers, paper clips, adhesive tape, pens, charts, and paper.

GROUP/INDIVIDUAL ACTIVITIES

The "Thought Imagination" activities are given below:

ACTIVITY 1

Product/Sculpture

___

IMPLEMENTATION

Gather as many items as possible to create a new product/ sculpture, such as a stapler, paper clips, tape, pens, etc. At the end of the activity, see if you can repurpose this new product developed.

___

OUTCOME

This warm-up activity will give a 'push' to your imagination, and you will be able to convert your imagination into a practical thing.

___

ACTIVITY 2

Illusionary Image

___

IMPLEMENTATION

All the participants will be given an illusionary image. Ask them to look at the image and discuss or write what they think of that image.

___

OUTCOME

MODULE – 7

Does this image create an illusion in the brain that causes the imagination to think about the meaning behind this image?

_____
_____
_____
_____

ACTIVITY 3

Emotion

_____
_____
_____
_____

IMPLEMENTATION

Fill out a daily activity diary. This records you:
- Body care: exercise, healthy eating, rest, and sleep.
- Achievement: work, chores, and study.
- Connect friends, family, and community.
- Enjoyment: play, fun, and pleasure.

Note these on the activity page for your morning, afternoon, and evening.

_____
_____
_____
_____

OUTCOME

Keeping a record of your every small and big life detail can help you accomplish more productively.

_____
_____
_____
_____

ACTIVITY 4

What movies do you like to watch?

_____
_____
_____
_____

IMPLEMENTATION

When watching a movie, record which type of emotions and imaginations you sense. For example, when watching a comedy movie, do you feel happy? What does your brain stimulate to create this feeling? When watching a horror, does your imagination play tricks on you?

_____
_____
_____
_____

OUTCOME

This activity will help you to understand how external stimuli affect your imagination and then modulate thoughts accordingly.

_____
_____
_____
_____

ACTIVITY 5

Beach, Forest

_____
_____
_____
_____

IMPLEMENTATION

Think why people love going to the beach. Why is the water so welcoming to people who want to relax? Write down your thoughts on why the beach is welcoming to everyone. Next, write about the forest. The positive and the negative of the forest and why someone may choose to hike in the forest as relaxing rather than going to the beach.

_____
_____
_____
_____

OUTCOME

Beaches and forests are natural ways to calm the mind and induce relaxation. This simple activity will help you to unite the benefits of nature with imagination and extract maximum mental benefits.

_____
_____

MODULE – 7

ACTIVITY 6

Short Story

IMPLEMENTATION

Create a story in your mind. It can stem from a situation and fabricate the story. The person next to you will continue the story where you left off, then the next person and then the next person until the last person in the group. At the end of the story, the group should discuss and see what could have been added or taken away.

OUTCOME

This stimulates the brain and your imagination and each person in the group. A novel can be created by everyone putting their thoughts together, flowing from one person to another. This helps to divert the thoughts and keep them focused on the story created by the first person.

ACTIVITY 7

Take A Journey

IMPLEMENTATION

The therapist takes the group on a journey. Each participant needs to close their eyes, and the therapist will share a story of taking the group on a trip. Start with the transportation to the location and share details to paint the picture in the mind, like playing a movie.

THOUGHT DEVELOPMENTAL PRACTICE

OUTCOME

The outcome will keep the participants alert as they visualize in their minds this journey affecting their emotions with fears, excitement, thoughts, and feelings. Although the participants are in one room, their imagination can carry them to another part of the world.

HOME ACTIVITIES

The "Thought Imagination" activities that can be done as homework are:

ACTIVITY 1

Paintings

IMPLEMENTATION

Go to an art gallery or look up paintings online. Write down your thoughts on each painting, imagining what the story is behind each painting.

OUTCOME

After you have written down your thoughts, look up the real reason why that painting was painted and the story behind it. Compare your thoughts to the story of the painting and see if you were close to guessing the right back story.

MODULE – 7

ACTIVITY 2

The blind man and the elephant

___
___
___
___

IMPLEMENTATION

Look over the video 'The blind man and the Elephant' and write down your thoughts on this illusion and imagination of the blind man.

___
___
___
___

OUTCOME

This activity will ignite your imagination and keep pushing you to expand your imaginative powers.

___
___
___
___

ACTIVITY 3

Positive thinking

___
___
___
___

IMPLEMENTATION

Create long-term and short-term goals and write them in a journal.

___
___
___
___

OUTCOME

THOUGHT DEVELOPMENTAL PRACTICE

The brain is powerful, and if we can work towards our goals step by step and imagine the best possible scenario for ourselves, our life will improve. By writing these positive goals, you can manifest them and live more fruitful lives.

___
___
___
___

ACTIVITY 4

Memory Lane

___
___
___
___

IMPLEMENTATION

Pick photos from a vacation trip, a party, a family gathering, or another memory. After reviewing these photos, go down memory lane and write a story that happened from each of the photos.

___
___
___
___

OUTCOME

This stimulates the brain, and your imagination may grow, ringing up joyful memories.

___
___
___
___

MODULE – 7

MODULE – 8

MODULE - 8
THOUGHT TRANQUILITY

This module aims to explore the benefits of achieving a tranquil state of mind and provide practical methods for attaining such tranquillity. This session aims to equip you with various exercises designed to pacify your thoughts, bring you to a state of internal equilibrium, and reorient your thought process from negative spirals to constructive and optimistic frameworks.

A GATEWAY TO INNER PEACE

The essence of thought tranquillity is not complex but straightforward and universally applicable. It encompasses any practice, activity, or strategy that has the power to quiet your mind and soothe your senses, granting you the serenity you seek. However, it's crucial to note that while many activities might offer a temporary respite from stress or emotional turmoil, it is imperative to select those that are inherently positive and constructive. Opting for detrimental or escapist habits may provide momentary relief but could prove counterproductive in the long run, exacerbating your challenges rather than alleviating them.

METHODS

The realm of thought tranquillity is abundant with diverse techniques and activities aimed at one ultimate objective: to nurture a peaceful mind and steer it away from the storms of negativity and stress. While numerous globally recognized methods can be employed for this purpose, some popular ones include:

- Therapeutic Massage or Acupressure
- Sauna Baths
- Steam Room Experiences

- Swimming for Relaxation
- Immersion in Scenic Environments
- Core Mindfulness Training

Although the majority of these methods are well-known and self-explanatory, Core Mindfulness Training stands out as a specialized technique that merits further discussion for its unique approach to mental tranquillity.

CORE MINDFULNESS TRAINING

Core Mindfulness Training is a comprehensive strategy that advocates the profound practice of internal focus. It urges you to turn your attention inward to engage in self-observation, cultivate heightened awareness, and ultimately master the art of mind control rather than allowing your thoughts to dominate you.

This specialized training introduces you to the concept of balancing what is termed a 'reasonable mind' with an 'emotional mind' to achieve what is known as a 'wise mind.' A reasonable mind operates on facts, logic, and rationality. It promotes decisions based on empirical evidence and objective reasoning. On the other end of the spectrum is the emotional mind, which is often swayed by feelings and impulses, leading to irrational decisions that one might later regret.

The brilliance of Core Mindfulness Training lies in its ability to harmonize these two disparate aspects of human cognition. When the logical acumen of the reasonable mind collaborates with the intuitive instincts of the emotional mind, what emerges is a 'wise mind.' This balanced state embodies our inner wisdom or 'gut feelings,' providing a fertile ground for decision-making that not only aligns with factual data but also resonates with our emotional sensibilities. For instance, it's the ability to process grief healthily while carrying on one's daily responsibilities effectively.

In summary, the journey to thought tranquillity is an expedition that requires a judicious selection of positive, constructive activities and may greatly benefit from the specialized approach of Core Mindfulness Training. Achieving this balanced state of mind could be your cornerstone for a harmonious life within yourself and the world around you.

THE THREE-TIERED APPROACH

At its core, mindfulness is an exercise in attentiveness, a focused awareness that encompasses three primary levels: Observing, Describing, and Participating.

The first level, Observing, is about pure, unfiltered perception. It's the act of attentiveness devoid of interpretation or judgment. For example, when you peel or smell an orange, you're simply experiencing the scent and texture, not mentally categorizing or evaluating them. Similarly, walking outside and feeling the air on your skin without mentally noting it as 'cold' or 'warm' is an act of pure observation.

The second layer, Describing, comes after observation and adds a linguistic dimension to what you've perceived. It involves labelling your experiences with words, thus grounding them in language and making them more conscious. This can help bring you fully into the present moment, setting a barrier against the pull of emotional impulsiveness. In essence, describing acts as a bridge between raw experience and mental comprehension, allowing you to understand better and manage your emotional responses.

The third and final level is Participating, which means immersing yourself entirely in the present experience. For instance, when you are learning to drive, your attention is riveted on multiple aspects of the experience—traffic signs, speed limits, pedestrians, other vehicles, and so on. At this stage, you're not merely observing or describing; you're living the experience fully, engaging all your senses and cognitive faculties. Participating is the embodiment of 'being in the moment,' a complete synchronization of mind and action.

Each of these levels serves a unique function but together, they form a cohesive method for achieving mindful awareness, a crucial skill that can dramatically improve your quality of life.

ACTIVITIES

Regarding "Thought Tranquility," the activities designed to help you achieve this state are bifurcated into two categories: those conducted under the watchful eye of a therapist, either in a group setting or one-on-one, and those designated for individual practice at home. Each session of "Thought Tranquility" initiates with a recap of the preceding module, an orientation to the present module's goals and exercises, and a preparatory phase where necessary materials are gathered as specified by the therapist or facilitator.

Through this structured approach, the "Thought Tranquility" module aims to equip you with practical techniques that can facilitate a shift from mental chaos to serene contemplation, helping you manage and thrive amidst life's complexities.

GROUP/INDIVIDUAL ACTIVITIES

The "Thought Tranquility" activities are given below:

ACTIVITY 1

Deep breathing

_____
_____
_____
_____

IMPLEMENTATION

MODULE – 8

Ask the participants to gather in a quiet spot, preferably outdoors near nature. Now, tell them to clear all thoughts from the mind and take a deep breath in and a deep breath out. This activity can be done sitting down or lying down.

OUTCOME

This warm-up activity will clear your mind and prepare you for the remaining activities of this session.

ACTIVITY 2

Puzzle

IMPLEMENTATION

Let all participants complete a puzzle. Tell them not to think of work or school and try focusing on completing a puzzle. Try listening to calm meditation music while completing the puzzle.

OUTCOME

By doing this, your mind can find rest from your busy schedule, and there will be an improvement in cognition and visual-spatial reasoning.

ACTIVITY 3

Create a routine

IMPLEMENTATION

Tell all participants to bring out their diaries and create a routine such as exercising before work, eating a healthy lunch, reading a book chapter, going for a walk, and journaling.

OUTCOME

You can develop a sense of accomplishment and clear your mind by creating a healthy everyday routine.

HOME ACTIVITIES

The "Thought Tranquility" activities that can be done as homework are:

ACTIVITY 1

Tea and a book

IMPLEMENTATION

Take time every day at a specific time and drink a hot drink such as tea, hot chocolate, water with lemon, etc. After making yourself a hot drink, read a chapter or two from a book to relax the mind.

MODULE – 8

OUTCOME

This is the best activity to calm your mind after a stressful day or to start your day with a peaceful mind.

ACTIVITY 2

Journal

IMPLEMENTATION

Buy a journal that catches your eye, and write down all your thoughts.

OUTCOME

Doing this lets you relax and release your stressful thoughts onto a piece of paper.

ACTIVITY 3

Go away for a night

THOUGHT DEVELOPMENTAL PRACTICE

IMPLEMENTATION

Reserve a night or a full day for yourself. For this, you can book a hotel and a massage session.

OUTCOME

This can create a sense of calmness. You can make calm and positive thoughts by staying at a hotel, enjoying the hot tub, and having a massage.

ACTIVITY 4

Visit A Garden

IMPLEMENTATION

Take some time and visit a garden with a limited number of people. Sit down, feel the ground and spend some time tapping into your senses. Take note of what you hear, feel, touch and see. Describe your feelings and emotions about being in a peaceful environment.

OUTCOME

This can create a sense of calmness. By staying in a less stimulated environment, you can enjoy the peace you feel inside of your mind.

MODULE – 8

ACTIVITY 5

Forest Bathing

IMPLEMENTATION

Take some time and visit a forest, go to the woods or take a hike where there are a limited amount people. Get immersed in the forest around you. Close your eyes and try to pick up on your five senses from the environment around you. Take deep breaths, like blowing out a candle and smelling a rose. Sit down, feel the ground and spend some time tapping into your senses. Bath yourself in this environment. Describe your feelings and emotions in being in this type of place.

OUTCOME

This can create a sense of calmness. By staying in a less stimulated environment, you can enjoy the peace you feel inside your mind. You can become one with the forest.

ACTIVITY 5

Visit a waterfall

IMPLEMENTATION

THOUGHT DEVELOPMENTAL PRACTICE

Find a place where you can hear water falling. Describe what you feel and your emotions.

___

OUTCOME

This can create a sense of calmness and peace. It's an excellent attraction to the eyes and taps into the emotions. Many visual images will be created for the mind and a sense of relaxation.

___

ACTIVITY 6

Spa

___

IMPLEMENTATION

Visit a spa and share your experience. Feel the heat from the sauna, steam room, and hot tub. Describe what you feel and how it calms the mind from being in a peaceful environment.

___

OUTCOME

This can create a sense of mindfulness, what you feel and what thoughts are stimulated from being in an environment where physical toughness is most dominant.

___

ACTIVITY 7

MODULE – 8

Therapeutic Massage or Acupressure

___
___
___
___

IMPLEMENTATION

Take some time for a massage or acupressure. Describe what you felt when someone else touched you physically and put pressure on your body. What were your thoughts? Did you feel relaxed, and why?

___
___
___
___

OUTCOME

This can create a sense of relaxation. It helps the body to feel good and release toxicity. The mind can create positive feelings and negative feelings. It's a time to explore if unresolved past issues need addressing from a physical touch.

___
___
___
___

MODULE – 9

MODULE – 9
THOUGHT AMPLIFICATION

This module aims to unpack the multi-faceted concept of Thought Amplification. This term refers to the intentional magnification and development of thought patterns for constructive outcomes. Through easy-to-follow activities, this module aims to demystify the complex idea of amplifying thoughts and making them accessible to everyone.

THE SCIENCE AND ART

Traditionally, the term 'amplification' has roots in physics and engineering, denoting the increase in amplitude or strength of a signal. However, its application has transcended these fields and permeated various domains such as medicine, psychology, arts, and literature. Amplification is a universal phenomenon, transcending boundaries like age, gender, ethnicity, and professional background. It signifies the art and science of enhancing, enlarging, or elaborating upon a given element, whether a speech, a piece of writing, or a thought process.

EXPLORING

In the context of cognitive functions, Thought Amplification refers to the deliberate expansion and intensification of thought processes. For instance, our minds often dwell on hypothetical scenarios or implications that may not have a concrete basis in reality. In such cases, the amplification of thoughts can entail the embellishment, exaggeration, or even fabrication of these ideas. This isn't limited to internal dialogues; it can extend to the external expression of these thoughts, such as justifying actions based on distorted thought patterns or affecting interpersonal relationships through self-fulfilling prophecies. Thought Amplification can be both a conscious and subconscious act, guided by internal and external stimuli and influenced by emotional and rational considerations.

MODULE – 9

STRATEGIES

Amplifying your thoughts is more than a mental exercise; it's an integrated approach involving mindset, physical posture, facial expressions, and continual learning. Here are some actionable strategies:

- **Mindset Shift**: Transition from a limiting belief system characterized by thoughts like "No, I can't" to an empowering one that says, "Yes, I can." This mental reorientation can be a catalyst for positive thought amplification.
- **Posture and Physicality**: The body-mind connection is profound. Simply changing from a reclined to an upright posture can signal your brain that you are capable, thereby amplifying positive thoughts.
- **Expressive Dynamics**: Believe it or not, your arm movements, facial expressions, and hand gestures can significantly influence your thought processes. They can either dampen or amplify the mood and behavioural responses that you experience.
- **Vocalization**: Speaking your thoughts aloud, especially those you firmly believe in, can clarify ambiguities and reinforce your convictions. This verbalization acts as a form of cognitive reinforcement, solidifying and amplifying your thoughts.
- **Perpetual Learning**: Thoughts are nurtured and expanded by new information and perspectives. The act of continual learning—whether through reading, discussions, or experiences—serves to enrich and amplify your thought processes.

Adopting these strategies expands your thoughts and amplifies your entire being, setting the stage for a more improved, fulfilled life.

THOUGHT AMPLIFICATION IN SUBSTANCE ABUSE

Thought Amplification is a potent tool in cognitive functioning, capable of steering our minds toward constructive or destructive paths. Its significance becomes particularly critical when examining substance abuse or drug addiction. For individuals entrenched in addictive behaviours, Thought Amplification can serve as both the villain and the potential saviour, depending on its application.

THE DOUBLE-EDGED SWORD IN ADDICTION

Many people who engage in substance abuse initially do so to experience a euphoric state, often described as a heightened sense of pleasure, confidence, or motivation. Over time, the brain begins to associate the drug with these pleasurable experiences, thereby amplifying the desire to continue its use. This amplified thought process can quickly escalate into obsessive thinking, wherein the individual feels almost a compulsive urge to act in alignment with these dominating thoughts.

For instance, it's common for substance abusers to rationalize or justify their actions through amplified thought patterns. Phrases like "Everyone else is doing it, so why shouldn't I?" often circulate in their minds, particularly among adolescents highly susceptible to peer pressure. These rationalizations serve to distort or even negate the authentic and harmful effects of substance abuse.

THE PSYCHOLOGICAL CASCADE

Moreover, Thought Amplification can lead to a cascade of psychological reinforcement in people with an addiction. Take, for example, the standard justification among smokers: "I know smoking can lead to lung cancer, but I know many smokers who have lived long lives without any such issues." Such thoughts not only amplify existing beliefs but also introduce new, misleading thoughts that serve to sustain the addiction.

Additionally, some individuals hold amplified beliefs that stimulant substances can enhance their cognitive or physical performance. This further intensifies their psychological dependence on the substance, creating a self-perpetuating cycle of amplified thoughts that rationalize and perpetuate their addiction. The outcome? Even when faced with severe life consequences—deteriorating health, broken relationships, loss of employment, and social isolation—the amplified thoughts continue to fuel the addictive behaviour.

THE NEED FOR POSITIVE AMPLIFICATION

Given the influential role that Thought Amplification can play in sustaining addictive behaviours, there's an urgent need to redirect this cognitive tool towards positive ends. Interventions should focus on amplifying thoughts that contradict the rationale for substance abuse. Whether through cognitive behavioural therapy, motivational interviewing, or other psychological interventions, the goal should be to amplify healthier, more constructive thoughts that promote abstinence and long-term recovery.

In conclusion, while Thought Amplification has the power to sustain and exacerbate addictive behaviours, it also holds the promise of being a transformative tool for positive change. The challenge lies in harnessing this cognitive process wisely, steering it away from destructive paths and towards a life of health, happiness, and genuine fulfillment.

EXERCISES FOR THOUGHT AMPLIFICATION

The activities designed for the "Thought Amplification" module fall into two distinct groups. The first set is intended to be carried out in a guided setting, typically supervised by a qualified therapist or facilitator, and can be tailored for individual or group sessions. The second set is intended for at-home practice, serving as homework to reinforce the techniques learned during the supervised sessions. Each session starts with a recap of the material covered in the previous module. This is followed by an introduction to the current "Thought Amplification" module, its associated activities, and a rundown of any materials needed for the exercises, as specified by the therapist or facilitator.

This structured approach ensures that participants understand the theoretical framework behind Thought Amplification and gain hands-on experience applying these principles to their daily lives.

MODULE – 9

The objective is to equip individuals with the practical tools to magnify positive thoughts and minimize negative ones, fostering a more constructive and fulfilling life experience.

GROUP/INDIVIDUAL ACTIVITIES

The "Thought Amplification" activities are given below:

ACTIVITY 1

Ted Talks

_____
_____
_____
_____

IMPLEMENTATION

Put on a TED talk, either a video or audio version and ask participants to listen carefully. Participants are also instructed to write down important points in their notebooks to discuss them later.

_____
_____
_____
_____

OUTCOME

This is the warm-up activity that will help to expand your mind on different topics, and you can rethink.

_____
_____
_____
_____

ACTIVITY 2

Should I think about it, or should I say it?

_____
_____
_____
_____

IMPLEMENTATION

Write down everything that you are thinking into separate sections of "bad thoughts and good thoughts." Go over these thoughts and see if they are appropriate to say to others, such as 'I like that...' 'That's ugly...' 'He's nice...' or 'Yuck...'. If group members are comfortable, let them speak these thoughts; otherwise, do not.

OUTCOME

By splitting up the bad and good thoughts on what to say out loud and what not to say out loud, you can keep your thoughts organized and in order.

ACTIVITY 3

Reading a book

IMPLEMENTATION

Tell participants to try reading one book a month, especially those books that they find enjoyable so that when reading the book, they will be excited to learn and want to finish the book ASAP

OUTCOME

This can help grow knowledge and increase the thinking process.

MODULE – 9

HOME ACTIVITIES

The "Thought Amplification" activities that can be done as homework are:

ACTIVITY 1

Write and speak

IMPLEMENTATION

Write down your morning and night thoughts daily, then say them out loud.

OUTCOME

This will help to amplify the thoughts and enhance thought processing

ACTIVITY 2

Dream Journal

IMPLEMENTATION

Create a dream journal. In the morning, write the dream you had last night in this journal and say it out loud. Then, look up the meaning of the dream.

THOUGHT DEVELOPMENTAL PRACTICE

OUTCOME

A compelling activity that will keep you engaged and grasp a better understanding of your thinking styles

ACTIVITY 3

Talk to someone

IMPLEMENTATION

Schedule weekly to talk to someone close to you or a professional you trust about new thoughts and feelings.

OUTCOME

By having someone to communicate with, you can release stress and get helpful opinions from a trusted person

ACTIVITY 4

Think Aloud

MODULE – 9

IMPLEMENTATION

While completing a task for work or school, instead of just writing down your decision/ thought process, go to a quiet room and state out loud your thought process for this task.

OUTCOME

By thinking out loud, you can force yourself to slow down your thoughts and process your thoughts differently.

MODULE – 10

MODULE - 10
THOUGHT VALIDATION

This module aims to guide you through the process of validating your thoughts by acknowledging and embracing your emotions and feelings. This module will provide you with the tools to accept critical thoughts instead of repressing them, discern their origins and purposes, and, if warranted, act upon them to shape your lived experience. Thought validation extends beyond the mental sphere, encompassing physical, social, and spiritual dimensions. You can practice various facets of thought validation through a series of structured activities in this module.

THE ESSENCE OF THOUGHT VALIDATION

Have you ever regretted an impulsive email in a moment of emotional turbulence? Or perhaps you've uttered words in a sadness that didn't reflect your feelings? Maybe you've assented to something while emotionally charged, only to rue your decision later? Or did you want to offer emotional support to a loved one but found your emotional state to be a barrier? Validation is the art of acknowledging and accepting one's own and others' thoughts, feelings, sensations, and actions. It's a skill that can be profoundly impactful and challenging to master, but the rewards are significant in personal and relational growth. Validation is not synonymous with agreement or approval; instead, it serves as a vehicle for expressing acceptance and understanding, irrespective of whether you share the same views or feelings. It strengthens the relational bond by conveying the message that despite differences in opinions or actions, the relationship remains strong and valuable. Self-validation involves acknowledging your own internal experiences as legitimate, serving as a cornerstone for emotional well-being and effective interpersonal relations.

EXPLORING THE CONCEPT

While validation may appear straightforward, its application can be intricate. Validation does not imply that you're endorsing or fueling someone's thoughts or feelings. It's not a measure of affection or fondness. Indeed, it's possible to validate someone you don't particularly like, although it may not be your preference.

Effective communication can be particularly challenging when one is overwhelmed by emotions. For emotionally sensitive people, mastering their emotions becomes essential for effective interaction and achieving desired outcomes. Receiving validation from others can serve as a potent mechanism for managing emotions, especially for those more emotionally sensitive. Self-validation functions similarly but focuses inward, allowing individuals to manage their emotions better. This self-managed emotional regulation sets the stage for self-compassion, serving as a prerequisite.

Through practicing validation, both of yourself and others, you cultivate an environment where emotions can be safely explored, understood, and managed. This process is particularly crucial for those who experience intense emotions regularly. Learning to validate effectively can profoundly impact your emotional well-being and the quality of your interpersonal relationships.

LEVELS OF VALIDATION

Drawing upon the work of psychologist Marsha M. Linehan, the concept of validation can be understood through six distinct but interrelated levels. These levels are applicable to validating others and equally significant for self-validation.

Level 1: Be Present

The first level of validation, often termed "Being Present," is far more than a mere introduction to the practice of validation. It serves as the foundational bedrock upon which the entire structure of self-validation is built. At its core, this level is about mindfulness—a fully embodied awareness of the present moment, free from judgment or the urge to alter one's experience. Being present transcends mere physical presence; it is a deliberate, emotionally resonant engagement with oneself.

In this context, mindfulness entails a heightened awareness of your emotional states, thought processes, and physical sensations. It requires you to confront, rather than flee, the range of emotions you're experiencing, whether painful or pleasant. This act of 'staying with yourself' affirms your worth, a tacit acknowledgment that your feelings, thoughts, and experiences have intrinsic value and deserve attention.

The instinct to avoid painful emotions is a deeply rooted evolutionary mechanism designed to protect us from harm. However, in the nuanced landscapes of our emotional lives, avoidance often serves as a counterproductive strategy. It might offer temporary relief but usually exacerbates the emotional pain in the long term, leading to a cycle of suppression and escalation. Being present cuts through this cycle by encouraging emotional confrontation. It validates the concept that it's okay to feel what you're feeling, thereby reducing the secondary emotional suffering that comes from judging oneself for having 'improper' emotions.

Being present also extends to a keen awareness of one's bodily sensations. Emotions are not abstract constructs; they manifest physically in various forms—tightness in the chest, a knot in the stomach, an accelerated heartbeat, or even a sense of lightness and expansiveness. By tuning into these physical cues, you become more adept at identifying and labelling your emotional states, thus gaining a more nuanced understanding of your emotional landscape.

Being present doesn't merely serve as a form of acknowledgment; it is also a tool for building emotional resilience. The act of fully experiencing an emotion, without attempting to immediately 'fix' it, often allows the emotion to naturally peak and subside, much like a wave. This fosters a form of emotional courage—a confidence that you can survive your feelings, however intense they might be.

Self-compassion is a natural byproduct of being present. When you allow yourself the grace to experience your emotions fully, without self-judgment, you're practicing a form of self-love. This cultivates a more compassionate relationship with yourself, which is crucial for mental well-being.

Level 2: Accurate Reflection

The concept of "Accurate Reflection" serves as a linchpin in the framework of self-validation. It goes beyond the foundational aspect of merely being present in your emotional landscape. Accurate Reflection involves a comprehensive yet nuanced acknowledgment and accurate labelling of your internal states, emotions, or thoughts.

So, what exactly is Accurate Reflection? Essentially, it is the cognitive exercise of introspectively identifying, acknowledging and labelling your internal emotional or psychological state. It's akin to holding up a mental mirror to yourself and taking a hard, nonjudgmental look at what is reflected.

Understanding the importance of Accurate Reflection is fundamental to its effective practice. This level of validation is crucial for several reasons. It enhances self-awareness by enabling a clearer understanding of one's emotional and cognitive processes. It provides a structured approach to navigating complex emotional terrains by dissecting them into smaller, more digestible components. Furthermore, it establishes a sense of trust in your own experiences and judgments, serving as a bedrock for future emotional regulation and general psychological well-being.

The components of Accurate Reflection are multifaceted. It begins with identifying triggering events, which is about understanding the situation or event that led to the emotional state you find yourself in. This is often the first step in the reflective process and serves as an enlightening gateway to a deeper emotional understanding.

Alongside identifying the triggering event, recognizing the physical sensations accompanying emotional states forms another critical aspect. Sensations like a tightening chest or a churning stomach are more than physical symptoms; they are gateways to better understanding your emotional self.

Another significant element is the recognition of associated behaviours. These actions or behavioural tendencies are directly linked to your emotional state. For instance, social withdrawal is when you're feeling anxious or stressed eating. These behaviours offer valuable insights into the nature and intensity of your feelings.

Finally, labelling or cognitively naming the emotion or state comes into play. This act of labelling is not as straightforward as it may seem. Emotions can often be complex, interlinked, and layered, making it challenging to pinpoint precisely what one feels. However, naming these emotions, as complex as they may be, serves as a final validating step in the Accurate Reflection process.

Practicing Accurate Reflection involves a series of interconnected cognitive actions. First, there's the pause and observe phase, where you halt your regular stream of consciousness to introspectively assess your emotional state. This is followed by an inquiry phase, where you mentally ask yourself questions to delve deeper into your emotional experience. Then comes the crucial act of labelling your emotional state, which should be executed with as much specificity as possible. Documenting these reflections can provide additional clarity and be a valuable reference for future emotional exploration.

While practicing Accurate Reflection, it's crucial to avoid common pitfalls like overgeneralizing emotions with broad, vague labels or adding a layer of self-criticism and judgment, as these can invalidate the experience and are counterproductive to the purpose of validation.

Level 3: Guessing

In the realm of emotional intelligence and self-validation, Level 3—Educated Guessing—occupies a unique position. It bridges the clarity of accurate reflection and the ambiguity that often accompanies emotional and cognitive states. When you find yourself in a situation where your emotions or thoughts are not entirely clear or identifiable, educated guessing acts as an exploratory tool that allows you to venture deeper into understanding your internal landscape. This level is particularly vital when you experience complex, mixed emotions or when facing new or unfamiliar situations that make immediate identification of your emotional state challenging.

One of the ways to employ educated guessing is by observing your behavioural inclinations. For example, if you find yourself avoiding social interactions, an educated guess might lead you to consider whether you're experiencing social anxiety or perhaps sadness. The behaviour is an external manifestation of an internal state, offering you a clue to delve deeper into your emotional well-being.

Your body often provides clues about your emotional state before you consciously recognize them. If your heart rate increases when you think about a specific event, it might indicate stress or excitement. Similarly, a sinking feeling in your stomach might show dread or apprehension. These physical sensations can serve as starting points for educated guesses about your emotional state.

Context also plays a significant role in educated guessing. Understanding the situational factors accompanying your unclear emotional state can provide clues to identify it. For instance, if you're feeling uneasy after a heated discussion with a friend but can't quite put a finger on your emotions, considering the context can help. You might guess you're experiencing a mixture of anger, regret, and concern.

Another approach within educated guessing is to think about how most people would feel in a similar situation. While emotions are highly individual, certain universal reactions to specific situations exist. For example, most people would feel anxious before a significant life event like a job interview. You can make an educated guess about your feelings by comparing your emotional state to a generalized reaction.

Educated guessing is often an iterative process. You make an initial guess, act or think accordingly, and then observe how your emotional state evolves in response. This feedback loop can offer additional insights, confirming or refining your initial guess and helping you become more attuned to your emotional self over time.

Level 4: Validating by History

The concept of historical context as a form of validation deserves nuanced attention. This level of validation seeks to understand and legitimize your current emotional or cognitive states by tracing them back to their roots in past experiences or learned behaviours. Doing so validates what you are feeling in the moment and fosters a deeper understanding of the 'why' behind those feelings. Here's a more detailed exploration of this level:

Our emotional responses are not isolated events but are often the culmination of a series of past experiences, teachings, and conditioning. Whether it's a traumatic event from childhood or a pattern of negative reinforcement over the years, these historical contexts shape how we react to current events. Recognizing this connection allows us to give our emotions the weight and validity they deserve.

Often, our emotional triggers are linked to past experiences. Understanding this can demystify why certain situations or stimuli provoke strong emotional responses. For example, if you find yourself disproportionately anxious during confrontations, it might be linked to past experiences where confrontations led to unpleasant outcomes. Validating your feelings through this lens means acknowledging that your reaction isn't 'over the top' but rooted in a real historical context.

This level of validation is an invitation to unpack the emotional baggage that may subconsciously influence your thoughts and feelings. By explicitly acknowledging how your past has shaped your present, you can validate your current experiences as legitimate and rational reactions, even if they seem disproportionate to the current situation.

This form of validation is often used in therapeutic settings to help individuals make sense of complex emotions. Therapists may guide you to explore your past, draw connections to your present, and validate your emotional experiences as real and meaningful rather than arbitrary or irrational.

Historical validation can significantly contribute to self-compassion. When you understand that your feelings have a basis in past experiences, it's easier to offer yourself the compassion you'd extend to someone else who has lived through similar circumstances.

Validating your emotions through their historical context can also be the first step toward healing. While it doesn't change the past, it does offer a framework for understanding and, eventually, for letting go. Acknowledging the validity of your feelings and reactions paves the way for emotional growth and resilience.

Level 5: Normalizing

Normalization in the context of validation serves as a corrective lens through which we can reframe our emotional experiences. For individuals with heightened emotional sensitivity, emotions can often feel overwhelming, "abnormal," or even "wrong." These perceptions can exacerbate feelings of isolation and amplify self-critical thoughts. Therefore, the concept of normalization serves as a crucial component of self-validation.

The first step in normalizing emotions is to acknowledge that emotions are universal experiences. From joy to sorrow, from confidence to insecurity—everyone, regardless of background or circumstances, undergoes a range of emotional states. The very fact that emotions are ubiquitous across cultures and societies attests to their normalcy.

Emotions are not inherently good or bad; they are part of the rich tapestry of human experience. Labelling certain emotions as 'abnormal' or 'undesirable' is a disservice to our emotional well-being. Every emotion has a role, whether the protective role of fear in dangerous situations or the bonding role of love in relationships. Recognizing this can alleviate the self-imposed pressure only to feel 'acceptable' emotions, thereby validating the full spectrum of your emotional experiences as normal.

Understanding that emotions are often context-dependent can also aid in their normalization. For example, feeling anxious before a big presentation or feeling euphoric after achieving a hard-fought goal is not just normal but expected. Acknowledging the contextual cues that trigger specific emotional responses can help validate those emotions as appropriate and expected reactions to particular situations.

Social and cultural norms often dictate what is considered 'acceptable' emotional expression, which can lead to self-stigmatization. The process of normalization involves challenging these socially constructed narratives. It means giving yourself permission to feel, irrespective of societal expectations or judgments, and acknowledging that your emotional experience is valid simply because it is human.

Self-compassion is an invaluable tool in the normalization process. Treating yourself with the same kindness and understanding as you would a good friend facilitates a more accepting emotional environment for yourself. This involves recognizing that you, like everyone else, are deserving of experiencing a broad array of emotions without judgment.

Level 6: Radical Genuineness

As the term suggests, radical genuineness is about embodying an unfiltered, authentic version of yourself. It's a form of self-validation that transcends the superficial layers of social expectations, self-criticism, and the personas we often adopt to navigate the world. But what does it mean to be "radically genuine," especially in the context of self-validation?

Being radically genuine requires you to shed any masks or facades you wear to fit societal norms or expectations. This is not about mere transparency but a profound form of honesty with yourself. It involves acknowledging your desires, fears, strengths, and vulnerabilities without judgment.

One of the most challenging aspects of radical genuineness is the courage it takes to confront your complexities and contradictions. It's about facing your shortcomings without self-flagellation and acknowledging your virtues without arrogance. This balanced perspective helps foster a harmonious relationship with oneself, the cornerstone of self-validation.

A significant aspect of radical genuineness is separating your core self from your actions or behaviours. While your actions may be subject to judgment based on societal norms or your moral compass, they are not the sum total of who you are. For instance, making a mistake does not make you a failure. Radical genuineness allows you to validate your worth beyond the scope of your actions, ensuring that your self-validation is not contingent on external validation or achievement.

Being radically genuine also involves emotional sincerity, allowing yourself to feel your emotions in their purest form. This is not about indulging every emotion that arises but about giving yourself the space to feel, understand, and then thoughtfully react to your emotional state. This sincere engagement with your emotions validates your emotional experiences as meaningful and worthy of attention.

Radical genuineness strives to align your internal emotional landscape and your external actions. When these are in harmony, the need for external validation diminishes. You validate yourself by living authentically, which inherently supports your mental and emotional well-being.

Radical genuineness is closely linked to self-compassion. By being genuine, you create an internal environment where compassion can flourish. You become kinder to yourself, recognizing that you, like everyone else, deserve love, respect, and understanding, regardless of your imperfections.

Embracing radical genuineness is not a one-time event but a lifelong journey of self-discovery and self-validation. It is a continuous process that evolves as you face new challenges and accumulate new experiences.

By integrating radical genuineness into your approach to self-validation, you not only affirm your worth but also empower yourself to live a more fulfilling, authentic life. It sets the foundation upon which you can build healthier relationships, not just with others but, most importantly, with yourself.

By incorporating these six levels into your self-validation practice, you cultivate a more nuanced, comprehensive understanding of your emotional landscape, empowering you to navigate it with greater self-compassion and authenticity.

The Crucial Role of Validation

Emotional Regulation Through Validation

Validation serves as a potent tool for emotional regulation. When people feel heard and understood, it often has a calming effect that seems to reduce emotional distress. Some theories suggest that the fear of being isolated or not fitting in stokes panic and anxiety. This fear harks back to our primitive instincts, where belonging to a group was crucial for survival. Whether it's evolutionary biology or psychology at play, validation undeniably helps dampen emotional turbulence.

Identity Formation and Self-Clarity

Validation acts as a mirror reflecting your thoughts, values, and choices, allowing you a clearer vision of your own identity. When another individual validates you, it illuminates the contours of your personality and behavioural patterns. This newfound clarity can be invaluable in personal growth and self-understanding.

The Cement of Relationships

Validation plays a pivotal role in relationship-building. Evidence suggests that the feeling of connectedness is chemically induced when one experiences validation. This chemical reinforcement strengthens bonds and deepens relationships, making validation a cornerstone of interpersonal interactions.

Facilitating Effective Communication and Mutual Understanding

The limitations of our perceptions and experiences bind us. Two individuals may witness the same event yet interpret it differently. Validation offers a gateway to mutual understanding, enabling more effective communication. It allows us to see from another's viewpoint, broadening our perspective and enhancing empathetic connections.

Fostering Resilience and Perseverance

When confronted with daunting challenges, the simple act of acknowledging the difficulty can act as a catalyst for perseverance. Validation can replenish dwindling reserves of willpower and resilience, empowering individuals to persist in their efforts despite setbacks.

Invalidation

Contrary to validation, invalidation negates or dismisses someone's experience or feelings and exists as its antithesis. Invalidation extends across various dimensions—emotional, spiritual, physical, and verbal—and can have detrimental effects. It can undermine self-esteem, disrupt emotional regulation, and even fracture relationships. Thus, understanding the profound impact of validation and its opposite, invalidation, is crucial for our relationships' well-being and health.

Categories of Invalidation

Emotional Invalidation

Emotional invalidation occurs when one's thoughts or emotions are disregarded, belittled, or outright dismissed. This can be especially damaging for individuals who are already emotionally sensitive, making them feel alienated and impairing their ability to form a coherent sense of identity. Emotional invalidation can exacerbate mental health issues, including depression and anxiety, and some experts consider it a key factor contributing to emotional disorders. While most people would never intentionally invalidate another, it can happen unintentionally, often when someone is trying to help but misunderstands the concept of validation. Regarding self-invalidation, some people may feel they deserve to be invalidated. However, it's crucial to remember that validation isn't an endorsement of an emotion or thought; it's merely an acknowledgment of its existence.

Verbal Invalidation

Verbal invalidation takes many forms and often comes from well-meaning individuals who may misunderstand the nature of emotional closeness or the principle of validation. Some common instances include:

- **Presumptive Familiarity**: Some people equate emotional closeness with knowing what the other person feels without asking, leading to presumptions that can be invalidating.
- **Misconceptions About Validation**: Some invalidate others because they think validation equates to agreement. However, one can acknowledge another's feelings without necessarily agreeing with their viewpoint.

- **Problem-Solving Instincts**: In an attempt to alleviate your emotional pain, people might offer solutions like, "Don't be sad; how about some ice cream?" This well-intended act can invalidate your emotions.
- **Fear of Causing Pain**: Sometimes, people might lie or withhold their true thoughts to spare their feelings, but this can be invalidating.
- **Overzealous Support**: Out of a desire for your success, some may push you towards choices that aren't authentic to you. For example, encouraging friendships with people you don't naturally bond with for potential future advantages.

Nonverbal Invalidation

Nonverbal cues can be potent forms of invalidation. Actions like eye-rolling, incessant checking of a watch, or focusing on a phone during a conversation send a clear message of disinterest or dismissal, whether intended or not. Self-invalidation can also be nonverbal, manifesting in behaviours like overworking or excessive shopping, which serve to distract from one's emotional and mental state.

Understanding these different forms of invalidation, both from others and from oneself, is vital for emotional well-being and healthy interpersonal relationships. By being aware of these, one can strive for more genuine, validating internal and external interactions.

Methods of Invalidation

Blaming

Blaming is an overt form of invalidation where the individual's feelings or actions are attributed solely to their shortcomings or emotional state. Phrases such as "You're always the crybaby, ruining every holiday" or "Why didn't you fill the car with gas? You never think things through" are typical examples. This form of invalidation dismisses the individual's feelings and places the onus entirely on them, making it difficult for them to assert their emotional reality. It's important to note that blaming differs from taking responsibility; the latter involves acknowledging one's actions without necessarily dismissing or belittling them.

Hoovering

Hoovering refers to the act of sucking up or dismissing feelings that make one uncomfortable, often to avoid vulnerability or conflict. Examples include downplaying an essential issue by saying, "It's not a big deal," or offering insincere compliments like, "You did a great job," when the performance was subpar. Hoovering can also manifest as denying one's own needs or difficulties. For instance, agreeing to a task by saying, "No problem, I can do that," even when feeling overwhelmed, is a form of self-invalidation through hoovering.

Judging

Invalidation through judgment happens when one's thoughts or feelings are labelled extreme or absurd. Phrases like "You're so overreacting" or "That's a ridiculous thought" invalidate by demeaning the emotional experience. Ridicule takes this further, using sarcasm or irony to belittle the individual. An example would be, "Here we go again, crying over nothing. Might as well cry because the grass is growing."

Denying

Denial as a form of invalidation occurs when one's feelings or experiences are flatly rejected. Statements like "You're not angry; I know how you act when you're angry" or "You've eaten a lot, you can't be hungry" negate the individual's self-reported state, implying that they are either lying or misguided about their feelings.

Minimizing

Minimizing involves downplaying the significance of one's emotions or experiences, usually with the intent of comforting but with the effect of invalidating. Phrases like "Don't worry, it's nothing. You're just losing sleep over trivial matters" may be well-intended, but they dismiss the emotional weight of the experience for the individual.

Understanding these different ways of invalidation is crucial for emotional well-being. Each form can have a lasting impact on self-esteem, emotional health, and the quality of interpersonal relationships. By becoming aware of these tactics, whether used by oneself or others, one can strive for more authentic, validating interactions.

Embrace Validation Over Invalidation

Validation is not about endorsing or agreeing with someone's thoughts or feelings but acknowledging and understanding them. This seemingly simple act has profound implications. When we validate someone else's emotional experience, it's like using emotional glue in the relationship, strengthening the bonds of understanding and respect. The same applies to self-validation, which involves recognizing and affirming your own emotional experiences.

Self-validation is more than just self-assurance or self-belief; it's an acknowledgment of your own emotional experience. This doesn't imply that you always agree with your thoughts or consider your emotions to be rational. It's entirely possible, even likely, that you'll have thoughts and emotions that neither align with your core values nor stand up to rational scrutiny. The key is not to fight or judge these experiences but to accept them. Doing so can decrease emotional distress and offer valuable insights into your inner self.

The Intersection of Mindfulness and Validation

Understanding and practicing validation is intrinsically linked with the concept of mindfulness. Being mindful means being acutely aware of your thoughts and feelings without judgment. It's a prerequisite to validation because you must first recognize your internal experiences and then acknowledge them. Whether it's your experience or someone else's, the essence of validation starts with being mindful of the present moment.

Emotional Management Through Validation

Validating your thoughts and feelings can be an effective way to manage emotions. It reduces emotional turmoil and contributes to a more grounded sense of self. Through self-validation, you find the wisdom to better deal with complex emotions. This leads to a more stable identity and improved emotional coping skills.

Applying Levels of Validation to Self-Validation

When we talk about self-validation, it's beneficial to apply the six levels of validation conceptualized by Marsha M. Linehan. These levels, ranging from being present with your emotions to radical genuineness, serve as a comprehensive framework for understanding how to validate others and yourself. These levels guide you through the process of acknowledging, understanding, and accepting your internal experiences, thus facilitating a more holistic emotional well-being.

Activities

Activities designed to practice thought validation are categorized into two main types: those carried out under a therapist's guidance and those practiced at home. Each thought validation session begins with a recap of the previous session, followed by an introduction to the focus of the current session and its corresponding activities. Participants will also be given a list of required materials in preparation for the activities.

In essence, the journey from invalidation to validation is both crucial and transformative. It fosters better emotional health, enriches relationships, and paves the way for a more authentically lived life.

GROUP/INDIVIDUAL ACTIVITIES

The "Thought Validation" activities are given in the following table:

ACTIVITY 1

Meditate

_____
_____
_____
_____

IMPLEMENTATION

THOUGHT DEVELOPMENTAL PRACTICE

Meditate on a positive affirmation word or statement. Have a weekly quote displayed on your fridge, washroom mirror, and the wall in your living room. Anywhere visible to the eyes, you can read it and meditate on it every day for a week. Preference is a green area or outdoor place for this activity. If in a group, practice the concept.

OUTCOME

Meditation will help you to stay focused throughout the day. This will also relieve stress and uplift your mood.

ACTIVITY 2

About Me activity sheet

IMPLEMENTATION

Complete the given sentences:

- I was happy when…
- Something that my friends like about me is…
- I'm proud of…
- My family was delighted when I…
- In school or work, I am good at…
- Something that makes me unique is…

MODULE – 10

OUTCOME

This "About me activity sheet" can help you to self-validate your emotions, feelings, and thoughts. Also, it will point out your qualities and strength

ACTIVITY 3

Volunteering

IMPLEMENTATION

Create a goal to join community service and volunteer at any place offering relevant opportunities, for example, local soup kitchens, community centers, shelter homes, etc. Discuss your plans and how you would implement them with the group.

OUTCOME

By putting yourself out into a community that needs help, you show others that you care about them and accept them the way they are. This also helps with self-validation because it provides a healthy boost to self-confidence, self-esteem, and life satisfaction. It will encourage others to refocus their thoughts with validating self-value and self-worth.

THOUGHT DEVELOPMENTAL PRACTICE

ACTIVITY 4

Positive thinking

_____
_____
_____
_____

IMPLEMENTATION

Write down your thoughts and feelings about yourself, your job, friendships, etc. Writing everything down helps you uncover your most authentic self; there is nothing wrong with what you feel or think.

_____
_____
_____
_____

OUTCOME

This activity is another way to learn self-validation and helps acknowledge your thoughts.

_____
_____
_____
_____

HOME ACTIVITIES

The "Thought Validation" activities that can be done as homework are:

ACTIVITY 1

Self-love

_____
_____
_____
_____

IMPLEMENTATION

Look at yourself in the mirror and write down everything you love and hate about yourself. Then, write down why you dislike those things about yourself and how you can make yourself love those things that you dislike. You need to learn to love everything about yourself.

MODULE – 10

OUTCOME

This activity is intended to get your full attention and create a comfortable environment.

ACTIVITY 2

Social Media

IMPLEMENTATION

Delete or close your social media accounts and replace the time you spend on your phone with something more productive, such as journaling, reading, or going for a walk. When you replace social media with positive habits, you can change your feelings and thoughts about your self-image.

OUTCOME

Social media is often linked with depression, low mood, and bad self-image. You can empty your mind and fill it with productive stuff by deleting social media.

ACTIVITY 3

Achievements

_____
_____
_____
_____

IMPLEMENTATION

Collect past achievements and awards and put them in a booklet/ scrapbook/ binder. By this, you can organize everything in one place and go through memories to see everything you have accomplished.

_____
_____
_____
_____

OUTCOME

You can use this collection to think about ways to help you achieve similar accomplishments in the future.

_____
_____
_____
_____

ACTIVITY 4

Validate others

_____
_____
_____
_____

IMPLEMENTATION

Go out for coffee with your friends or family members, and make sure to make them feel validated. Pay attention to what they are talking about or want to express. Ask questions and make them feel important.

_____
_____
_____
_____

MODULE – 10

OUTCOME

Validation shows the other person that they are important. Whether the person being validated is a child, spouse, parent, friend, or employee, validation communicates that they are essential to you and you care about their thoughts, feelings, and experiences.

_____
_____
_____
_____

MODULE – 11

MODULE – 11
THOUGHT EXAMINATION

The aim of this module is multi-layered. It guides you to understand the contours and nuances of your thought patterns and helps you delve into the origins and practical ramifications of these thoughts. In essence, you will learn to distinguish between various thoughts, such as positive and negative or beneficial and futile, providing you with the tools to navigate the intricate maze of your cognitive processes.

While the scientific community continues to debate the precise definition and mechanics of 'thoughts,' for the purpose of this module, let's consider a more user-friendly definition. A thought can be any idea or mental picture that materializes in response to your interactions with the world. Thoughts are not just reactions, but they also shape our perception of the world. They are cyclical in nature; one thought leads to another, making it a complex yet integral part of human cognition.

Even if the construct of 'thought' remains elusive, that doesn't mean you can't scrutinize it. A closer look into your thought process reveals patterns and recurring themes. These patterns can be particularly indicating, helping you understand your preoccupations, worries, and focus. Questions you might ask yourself include:

- Are my thoughts clustered around a specific topic or concern?
- What is it about these thoughts that disturb or unsettle me?
- If these thoughts were accurate, what implications would they have for my perceptions of myself, others, and the world?

Components of Mental State Examination

To take thought examination a step further, let's delve into a structured approach known as the "Mental State Examination." This comprehensive evaluation includes:

Observation of Thought Patterns:

Pay attention to your thoughts' frequency, content, and emotional tone. Are they primarily positive or negative? Do they relate to a particular life aspect like work, relationships, or self-worth?

Identifying Underlying Themes:

Look for recurring themes or common threads that run through your thoughts. Are they generally anxious thoughts about the future, retrospective thoughts about past mistakes, or perhaps hopeful thoughts about opportunities?

Understanding Emotional Resonance:

Examine the emotions that accompany these thoughts. Do they evoke happiness, anxiety, sadness, or excitement? Understanding the emotional component can offer insights into your emotional health.

Evaluating Real-World Impacts:

Consider the practical implications of your thought patterns. Do they motivate you to take positive actions or lead to procrastination, anxiety, or other counterproductive behaviours?

Assessing Rationality and Logic:

Scrutinize the rationality of your thoughts. Are they based on facts, assumptions, or misconceptions? Understanding this can help you weed out irrational fears and expectations.

You can better grasp your cognitive landscape by employing the Mental State Examination approach. You'll be better equipped to manage your thoughts constructively, improving your mental health and overall quality of life.

Practical Steps for Thought Examination

To make this process more actionable, here are some steps you can follow:

1. **Journaling**: Keep a thought diary where you jot down your thoughts as they come. Later, you can assess them to identify patterns or triggers.
2. **Mindfulness Meditation**: This practice involves paying focused attention to your thoughts without judging them, allowing you a clearer view of your thought processes.
3. **CBT Techniques**: Cognitive Behavioral Therapy provides practical techniques like 'thought challenging,' where you learn to identify and challenge harmful thought patterns.
4. **Consult with a Professional**: An external perspective can sometimes provide invaluable insights into your thinking. A trained psychologist can guide you through more formalized thought examination methods.

Practical Application in Daily Life

Once you've examined your thoughts, the next step is to apply your insights. Understanding that you have a tendency to think negatively about work, for example, allows you to counteract those thoughts with more rational, positive affirmations. Identifying a recurring worry about health could motivate you to make lifestyle changes or consult a medical professional for peace of mind.

MENTAL STATE EXAMINATION

The Mental State Examination (MSE) serves as a structured method for evaluating an individual's current psychological state. Essentially, it offers a comprehensive "snapshot" of a person's mental well-being at a specific moment. While many people informally engage in similar observations in everyday interactions, a formal MSE is crucial for making more definitive assessments of a person's mental health and determining whether further psychiatric evaluation is warranted. It's critical to contextualize these observations within the individual's developmental stage and age-appropriate behaviours. In cases where suicidal or homicidal ideation is evident, immediate referral to a qualified mental health specialist is imperative for risk assessment.

Domains of Assessment

The MSE typically delves into multiple domains to paint a complete picture of a person's mental state. Below are the key areas:

1. **Appearance**
   The outward appearance of an individual can offer valuable insights into their self-care, lifestyle choices, and general well-being.

   - Notable Features
   - Attire
   - Personal Grooming
   - Hygienic Practices

2. **Behaviour**
   The MSE extends beyond mere actions to include non-verbal cues, which can be instrumental in understanding a person's emotional state and general demeanour.

   - Facial Expressions
   - Body Language and Gestures
   - Posture
   - Eye Engagement
   - Reactions to the Assessment
   - Social Interaction and Rapport
   - State of Arousal (e.g., calm vs. agitated)
   - Manifestations of Anxiety or Aggressiveness
   - Psychomotor Behavior and Movement (e.g., hyperactive vs. hypoactive)
   - Anomalies (e.g., tremors or other involuntary movements)

3. **Mood and Affect**
   The relationship between mood and affect can be likened to that between climate (mood) and weather (affect), where affect is immediate, and mood is more enduring.
   - **Affect**
     - Range (e.g., restricted, expansive)
     - Congruence (e.g., appropriate vs. incongruent)
     - Stability (e.g., steady vs. fluctuating)
   - **Mood**
     - Emotional State (e.g., ecstatic, depressed)
     - Irritability Levels (e.g., explosive, calm)
     - Stability

4. **Speech**
   A person's manner of speaking can offer valuable clues into their mental state and is often indicative of underlying mood or anxiety disorders, schizophrenia, or other mental health conditions.
   - Rate of Speech (e.g., fast, pressured, slow)
   - Volume (e.g., loud, moderate, soft)
   - Tone (e.g., monotonous, tremulous)
   - Verbosity (e.g., minimalistic, loquacious)
   - Conversational Fluidity

5. **Thought Process and Content**
   The quality and form of an individual's thoughts are assessed to understand their cognitive function better.
   - **Content**
     - Delusional Thoughts (false beliefs held despite evidence to the contrary)
     - Overvalued Ideas (irrational beliefs, e.g., a person with anorexia considering themselves overweight)
     - Preoccupations or Fixations
     - Depressive Thought Patterns
     - Ideations of Self-Harm or Violence
     - Obsessive Thoughts (unwanted, repetitive thoughts often accompanied by compulsive behaviours)
     - Anxiety Levels (generalized or specific, e.g., phobias)
   - **Thought Process**
     - Logical
     - Goal-directed
     - Sequential order

6. **Cognition**
   Cognition refers to the individual's capacity for information processing, which can be highly indicative of underlying mental health conditions, especially among adults.
   - **Level of Consciousness**: Alertness, drowsiness, intoxication, or stupor.
   - **Orientation to Reality**: Awareness of time, place, and personal identity.
   - **Memory Function**: Evaluation of immediate, short-term, and long-term memory, including recollection of recent and past events.
   - **Literacy and Arithmetic Skills**: Basic understanding of reading, writing, and arithmetic operations.
   - **Visuospatial Processing**: Ability to perform tasks like copying a diagram or drawing an object.
   - **Attention and Concentration**: Observations on distractibility and performance on mentally demanding tasks (e.g., serial sevens test).
   - **General Knowledge**: Assessment of general education and awareness.
   - **Language Skills**: Naming objects and ability to follow instructions.
   - **Abstract Thinking**: Understanding abstract concepts, such as identifying similarities between different objects or situations.

7. **Perception**
   Evaluating perceptual disturbances is vital for identifying severe mental health conditions like psychosis, severe anxiety, mood disorders, or issues related to trauma or substance abuse.
   - **Dissociative Symptoms**:
     - Derealization: Sensing that the environment is unreal.
     - Depersonalization: Feeling of detachment from oneself.
   - **Illusions**: Misinterpretation of sensory experiences while recognizing that others do not share these.
   - **Hallucinations**:
     - Sensory experiences that the individual cannot distinguish from reality.
     - It may involve any sensory modality, although auditory hallucinations are most common.
     - In children, internal "voices" offering commentary or self-talk are common.
     - Command hallucinations warrant immediate attention.
     - The emotional impact of the hallucinations, such as associated fear or distress, should be noted.

8. **Insight & Judgment**: These dimensions are crucial for prioritizing psychiatric cases and making informed decisions regarding the individual's safety and treatment options.
   - **Insight**:

- Recognition of potential mental health issues.
- Awareness and willingness to engage with treatment options.
- Capacity to identify events that might be pathological, like hallucinations or suicidal ideations.
- **Judgment**:
    - Refers to the individual's general problem-solving abilities.
    - You are evaluated through exploration of recent decision-making or by posing hypothetical situations that require judgment (e.g., what actions would you take if you noticed smoke emanating from a building?).

The Mental State Examination serves as a comprehensive tool for clinicians to assess an individual's mental and emotional well-being. It aids in diagnosis, treatment planning, and ongoing management, providing a nuanced understanding of the patient's psychological state. Observing anomalies or peculiarities during a Mental State Examination (MSE) often signals a need for a more specialized mental health evaluation, particularly if there are disruptions in perception or thought processes. A comprehensive review of the domains discussed above will guide clinicians in determining whether that involves obtaining a second opinion from a specialist or initiating a direct mental health referral. It is crucial to emphasize that in any situation where there is evidence of immediate suicidal or homicidal ideation, immediate risk assessment by a qualified mental health professional is mandatory.

Activities of Thought Examination

The exercises associated with the thought examination module are categorized into two types: those meant to be conducted under the guidance of a mental health therapist—either individually or in group settings—and those designed to be carried out at home. Each session commences with a review of the material covered in the preceding module to ensure continuity and retention. Subsequently, the current module—focused on thought examination—is introduced. Before starting the session's activities, participants are instructed to assemble all necessary materials to minimize interruptions during the exercise period.

These activities aim to equip individuals with the tools and techniques required to scrutinize their thought patterns. Whether you are working under the supervision of a therapist or practicing these exercises at home, the intention remains the same: to delve deeper into your cognitive processes and understand their origins, patterns, and practical implications. This methodical examination will help you distinguish between constructive thoughts and counterproductive thoughts, facilitating a more harmonious and effective mental landscape.

GROUP/INDIVIDUAL ACTIVITIES

The "Thought Examination" activities are given below:

ACTIVITY 1

THOUGHT DEVELOPMENTAL PRACTICE

Brainstorming

IMPLEMENTATION

What is a thought? No complex explanations are needed; just say what comes to your mind upon hearing "What is thought?"

OUTCOME

This warm-up activity will create a relaxed, comfortable, and safer environment to enhance engagement in the session and where people feel compelled to free their minds and move away from traditional and professional approaches.

ACTIVITY 2

Thoughts Vs. Dreams

IMPLEMENTATION

To explain this activity, a video highlighting the distinct characteristics of thought and a dream will be shown.

DISCUSSION

MODULE – 11

A thought can be better understood by comparing it to a dream. Thought is the opposite of a dream (the one you do, and one just happens). A thought requires action to come true or become a reality, i.e., we put thought into action or motion, and it becomes a reality; for example, if you have a thought of going to a restaurant to have dinner, you go to a restaurant and have dinner. Also, note down what steps you have taken for this decision.

_____
_____
_____
_____

OUTCOME

Both thoughts and dreams operate from the same place, from within your spirit, soul, and your mind. Understanding the difference between dreams and thoughts will help you recognize what you want in life.

_____
_____
_____
_____

ACTIVITY 3

Thoughts Vs. Feelings

_____
_____
_____
_____

IMPLEMENTATION

A discussion that highlights the distinct characteristics of thoughts and feelings and how they affect the emotions.

_____
_____
_____
_____

OUTCOME

Both thoughts and feelings operate from the same place, from within the mind. Understanding the difference between thoughts and feelings will help to recognize mood swings, anxiety, PTSD and cravings.

THOUGHT DEVELOPMENTAL PRACTICE

ACTIVITY 4

Reflection

IMPLEMENTATION

Participants will be asked to reflect on the following questions and provided a notebook and pen to jot down ideas. Participants will then be asked to share their thoughts if they are comfortable.

DISCUSSION

1: What is the difference between a good thought and a wrong thought?

2: How do you know a thought is good or bad for you?

3: What kinds of things/ people/ experiences contribute to good thoughts and bad thoughts?

4: What kind of things pull you down or bring you to a low mood (depressed, anxious, stressed)?
5: What kinds of things lift you or bring you to an elevated place (joyful, peaceful)?

To help you better understand if a thought is good or bad (for you), think about the consequence(s) attached to the thought. If the result that comes after the thought is wrong, then it is not a good thought. Think about a good thought you recently had and produced a good result. Encourage the group to share.

OUTCOME

MODULE – 11

This is the main activity that will provide a detailed reflection and examination of your thoughts, and you can separate good thoughts from bad ones.

_____
_____
_____
_____

ACTIVITY 5

Large Visual Picture of a Pit (If time doesn't allow for the above activity, the group will be encouraged to do this as homework)

_____
_____
_____
_____

IMPLEMENTATION

The picture of the pit will have three positions/ spots identified – the top of the pit are you looking over, the middle of the pit is sinking, and the bottom of the pit is the position of being stuck. The group will identify thoughts associated with each specific position/ spot, be encouraged to write them down and take turns posting them in the appropriate spot.

_____
_____
_____
_____

DISCUSSION

Group discussion: The mountain will also have three spots. The first spot is looking up (positive outlook), climbing up, and reaching the top (peace, joy, feeling fulfilled). Again, the group will identify thoughts associated with each spot, write them down, and then post them on a picture.

_____
_____
_____
_____

OUTCOME

It is a group activity where the slippery slope presents bad thoughts (here, we bury ourselves), and the mountain offers a climb to good thoughts (here, we elevate ourselves to greater heights).

THOUGHT DEVELOPMENTAL PRACTICE

HOME ACTIVITIES

As homework, keep a journal and every day write down your first thought in the morning and your last thought at night. Besides, some more activities are assigned as home activities, and these activities are:

ACTIVITY 1

Reading

IMPLEMENTATION

Read a book and write down your ideas about this book, such as thoughts on why the author wrote this book, the negative and positive outcomes from this book, and how this book made you feel; in short, write every big and small thought you have while reading the book. Now, read over the thoughts you have to write down and examine why these thoughts develop.

OUTCOME

Keep you engaged and further explore the complicated world of "thoughts and emotions."

ACTIVITY 2

Crumble Bad thoughts

MODULE – 11

IMPLEMENTATION

Write down these bad thoughts coming into your mind and examine how these thoughts came about, maybe through movies, people, music, or social media. When you discover the source of these bad thoughts, try not watching those specific movies, hanging around negative people, listening to negative songs, or looking at negative social media posts. After you write these bad thoughts down, crumble the paper and throw it into the trash can.

We usually ask ourselves, "How did I get here (with a bad thought) and "How do I move out of here." The exit point is usually somewhere else. Think about the 'door' you enter when you have a terrible thought and try to understand that it is not the same door you will take to escape that thought. In other words, the person around you who is triggering bad thoughts will not be the same person who pulls you out of those thoughts. Whatever site you visit on the internet that triggers terrible thoughts will not be the same site that will allow you to come out of that negative thought pattern.

OUTCOME

Most bad thoughts are triggered by something you see or hear. The easiest thing to do is to eliminate what is good or not good for you, i.e., to stop listening to the news and avoid certain people or things triggering bad thoughts. But it is not as simple as it seems to be. We have more difficulty separating ourselves from what is wrong or not good for us. For example, unhealthy foods such as burgers and fries, social media sites that are damaging your self-esteem, drug addiction, etc.

ACTIVITY 3

Sticky notes

THOUGHT DEVELOPMENTAL PRACTICE

IMPLEMENTATION

Create positive sticky notes and post them all over your house and workplace. Positive sticky notes include "You look amazing," "You are going to do great things today," etc. After looking at these sticky notes, examine your thoughts connected. If a bad thought comes right after reading your encouraging sticky notes, write down how you feel and what you can do to make yourself happier today.

OUTCOME

By looking at these positive sticky notes, you are encouraging yourself that today will be a great day, and eventually, you will reshape your future for the better

POINTS TO REMEMBER

It takes some physical effort to bring the thought to life. The work behind the scenes (behind a thought) has a lot to do with the finished product (what is seen), i.e. If you decide to sell water as a business, you will have to think about the steps you need to take to make the business successful and then put the steps into action to become successful. Some steps may include researching the types of water that people buy, and that sell well, then need to buy enough product to make a profit, followed by a need to figure out how to market a product or make it appealing to people so they can buy it and make your business successful.

MODULE – 11

MODULE – 12

Module – 12
THOUGHT EXPECTATIONS

The objective of this module is to cultivate a heightened awareness of your thoughts, specifically focusing on the expectations you set for yourself. Additionally, you'll gain insights into the expectations others hold for you and learn effective strategies for responding to these external expectations. Ultimately, this module aims to equip you with the tools to make well-informed decisions, empowering you to control your thought processes and shape your future more effectively.

Understanding Thought Expectations

The term "thought expectations" may sound esoteric, but it is essentially a straightforward concept encapsulating your expectations and the subsequent decisions these expectations drive you to make. An expectation is a belief or anticipation that you, or someone else, will or should achieve a particular outcome—be it academic success, a job promotion, or landing your dream job. These expectations serve as motivational catalysts, propelling you toward future achievements.

While you may strive to meet your expectations or those imposed upon you by others, it's essential to acknowledge that not all efforts will yield favourable results. Sometimes, experiences may disappoint, and decisions may fall short of being prudent. However, the salient point is the act of trying. The ongoing endeavour to meet expectations—even when met with setbacks—serves as a learning opportunity. These 'unfavourable' experiences are not failures; instead, they are gateways to new expectations and the foundation for making more informed, calculated decisions in the future.

Activities of Thought Expectations

MODULE – 12

This module on thought expectations is designed to be straightforward and user-friendly, featuring uncomplicated yet impactful activities. The activities can be done individually or in a group setting under the supervision of your therapist. As with previous modules, each session will commence with a recap of the last module's key takeaways. This will be followed by a brief introduction to the current module's focus—Thought Expectations.

Before diving into the activities, you'll be guided to assemble all necessary materials to ensure a smooth and uninterrupted session. The materials you'll need are relatively basic: charts, pencils, and coloured markers.

GROUP ACTIVITIES

The activities for the "Thought Expectation" module are given below:

ACTIVITY 1

'Expectations' Chart

_____
_____
_____
_____

IMPLEMENTATION

Take a chart and write 'Expectations' as the main heading. Then, draw three columns on the chart with the headings "You," "Others," and "Goals." On the "You" side, state things that you expect of yourself; on the "Others" column, write down things that others expect of you. By writing down what you want versus what others want for you, you can get a clear idea of your life goals that will allow you to achieve what you want for yourself. Write down the gathered ideas in the "Goal" section.

_____
_____
_____
_____

OUTCOME

This is the warm-up activity that will open up your mind and prepare you for the coming activities.

_____
_____
_____
_____

ACTIVITY 2

Feedback analysis (30 mins)

_____
_____
_____
_____

IMPLEMENTATION

Think about the times when you have to make important decisions. Write down your decisions and also write why you chose this decision. Also, note down what steps you have taken for this decision.

_____
_____
_____
_____

OUTCOME

You can use these 'feedback' notes to improve your decision-making skills for future decisions.

_____
_____
_____
_____

ACTIVITY 3

Create a bucket list

_____
_____
_____
_____

IMPLEMENTATION

Create a bucket list and write down the most important goals that you want to accomplish in your lifetime. This will take a maximum of 15 minutes to think about the important goals and write them down.

_____
_____
_____
_____

MODULE – 12

OUTCOME

This will keep you focused and help you accomplish a little task that will lead to crossing things off your bucket list.

_____
_____
_____
_____

ACTIVITY 4

Grounding Techniques

_____
_____
_____
_____

IMPLEMENTATION

Practice grounding techniques to deal with the burden and stress caused by expectations you have from yourself or others have from you. Select grounding techniques that can help calm you down, such as taking deep breaths, counting to ten, spending time in nature, dancing, walking, painting, or anything that captures your whole attention and provides relaxation.

_____
_____
_____
_____

OUTCOME

Grounding techniques will redirect your thoughts and bring mental tranquillity. These simple techniques are highly effective and can be done in 10 minutes.

_____
_____
_____
_____

ACTIVITY 5

Expectations of others (10 minutes)

_____
_____

THOUGHT DEVELOPMENTAL PRACTICE

IMPLEMENTATION

Your therapist will provide you with specific videos, links, or relevant material; you have to review them. After that, write down your thoughts on the content you watched and figure out what you learned. You can discuss this activity with each other, too.

OUTCOME

This will take a maximum of 30 minutes to write down and discuss with others. And in the end, you will learn how to deal with the expectations of others.

HOME ACTIVITIES

You can revise activities you perform during the sessions with the same procedure for home activities. For example, you can complete the following activities at home by yourself:

- Expectations chart
- Grounding techniques

Moreover, you will review the activities "Feedback Analysis" and "Bucket List" and use the activity notes to ponder them further. You can place these notes on the wall in your home or workplace where you spend most of your time. You can get help from these notes and add new notes explaining your progress or make revisions to them. Besides, you can implement the following specific activity as your "Thought Expectations" home:

Activity-1: Quotes

Look over expectation quotes on the internet or any other available sources, print them off, and place them in your workplace or home on your fridge. These quotes will reset your mindset, force you to think more precisely and understand that you need to think of yourself and not what others think about you.

Activity -2: Self-awareness

MODULE – 12

Sit in a silent corner and start observing your thoughts. Give special attention to those thoughts that are focused on your expectations or the expectations others have of you. You can also write them down for your ease. This type of meditation also helps you to become aware of your personality traits, behaviours, or feeling of yourself. You will also learn to tune into those feelings and thoughts and evaluate yourself accordingly.

REFERENCES

Albert, P. R., & Benkelfat, C. (2013). The neurobiology of depression—revisiting the serotonin hypothesis. I. Cellular and molecular mechanisms. *Philosophical Transactions of the Royal Society B: Biological Sciences, 368*(1615), 20120535.

American Psychiatric Association. (2013). Diagnostic and statistical manual of mental disorders (5th ed.). Washington, DC: Author.

Baddeley, A. (1995). Working memory. In M. S. Gazzaniga (Ed.), *The Cognitive Neurosciences* (pp. 755-764), Cambridge, MA: MIT Press.

Bandelow, B., & Michaelis, S. (2015). Epidemiology of anxiety disorders in the 21st century. Dialogues in Clinical Neuroscience, 17(3), 327-335.

Bandura, A. (1991). Social cognitive theory of self-regulation. Organizational Behavior and Human Decision Processes, 50(2), 248-287.

Barlow, D. H. (1986). Causes of sexual dysfunction: The role of anxiety and cognitive interference. *Journal of consulting and clinical psychology, 54*(2), 140.

Brewin, C. R., Andrews, B., & Valentine, J. D. (2000). Meta-analysis of risk factors for posttraumatic stress disorder in trauma-exposed adults. Journal of Consulting and Clinical Psychology, 68(5), 748-766.

Briere, J. (1992). Methodological issues in the study of sexual abuse effects. *Journal of consulting and clinical psychology, 60*(2), 196.

Burhan, R., & Moradzadeh, J. (2020). Neurotransmitter dopamine (DA) and its role in the development of social media addiction. *Journal of Neurology & Neurophysiology, 11*(7), 1-2.

Cacioppo, J. T., & Petty, R. E. (1980). Persuasiveness of Communication is Affected by Exposure Frequency and Message Quality: A Theoretical and Empirical Analysis of Persisting Attitude Change. In J. H. Leigh & C. R. Martin (Eds.), *Current Issues and Research in Advertising*, (pp. 97-122). Ann Arbor: University of Michigan.

REFERENCES

Cacioppo, J. T., & Petty, R. E. (1981). Social Psychological Procedures for Cognitive Response Assessment: The Thought Listing Technique. In T. Merluzzi, C. Glass, and M. Genest (Eds.), *Cognitive Assessment* (pp. 309-342). New York: Guilford.

Campana, B., Brasiel, P. G., de Aguiar, A. S., & Dutra, S. C. P. L. (2019). Obesity and food addiction: similarities to drug addiction. *Obesity Medicine, 16*, 100136.

Clark, D. A., & Beck, A. T. (2010). Cognitive therapy of anxiety disorders: Science and practice. New York, NY: Guilford Press.

Corrigan, P. W., & Watson, A. C. (2002). Understanding the impact of stigma on people with mental illness. World Psychiatry, 1(1), 16-20.

Degenhardt, L., & Hall, W. (2012). Extent of illicit drug use and dependence, and their contribution to the global burden of disease. The Lancet, 379(9810), 55-70.

Di Chiara, G. (1995). The role of dopamine in drug abuse viewed from the perspective of its role in motivation. *Drug and alcohol dependence, 38*(2), 95-137.

Dweck, C. S. (2006). Mindset: The new psychology of success. New York, NY: Random House.

Eiser, C. (1991). Psychological effects of chronic disease. *Annual progress in child psychiatry and child development, 77*, 434-450.

Fang, H., Tu, S., Sheng, J., & Shao, A. (2019). Depression in sleep disturbance: a review on a bidirectional relationship, mechanisms and treatment. *Journal of cellular and molecular medicine, 23*(4), 2324-2332.

Fazio, R. H., & Zanna, M. P. (1978). Attitudinal Qualities Relating to the Strength of the Attitude-Behavior Relationship. *Journal of Experimental Social Psychology*, 14, 398-408.

Felitti, V. J., Anda, R. F., Nordenberg, D., Williamson, D. F., Spitz, A. M., Edwards, V., ... & Marks, J. S. (1998). Relationship of childhood abuse and household dysfunction to many of the leading causes of death in adults: The Adverse Childhood Experiences (ACE) Study. American Journal of Preventive Medicine, 14(4), 245-258.

Finlay-Jones, R., & Brown, G. W. (1981). Types of stressful life event and the onset of anxiety and depressive disorders. *Psychological medicine, 11*(4), 803-815.

Fishbein, M., & Ajzen, I. (1975). *Belief, Attitude, Intention, and Behavior: An Introduction to Theory and Research.* Reading, MA: Addison-Wesley.

Follingstad, D. R., Rutledge, L. L., Berg, B. J., Hause, E. S., & Polek, D. S. (1990). The role of emotional abuse in physically abusive relationships. Journal of Family Violence, 5(2), 107-120.

Fusar-Poli, P., de Pablo, G. S., Correll, C. U., Meyer-Lindenberg, A., Millan, M. J., Borgwardt, S., ... & Arango, C. (2020). Prevention of psychosis: advances in detection, prognosis, and intervention. *JAMA psychiatry, 77*(7), 755-765.

Gil, K. M., Williams, D. A., Keefe, F. J., & Beckham, J. C. (1990). The relationship of negative thoughts to pain and psychological distress. *Behavior Therapy, 21*(3), 349-362.

Goldstein, R. Z., & Volkow, N. D. (2011). Dysfunction of the prefrontal cortex in addiction: neuroimaging findings and clinical implications. *Nature Reviews Neuroscience, 12*(11), 652-669.

Gomes-Schwartz, B., Horowitz, J. M., & Cardarelli, A. P. (1990). *Child sexual abuse: The initial effects*. Sage Publications, Inc.

Greenwald, A. G. (1968). Cognitive Learning, Cognitive Response Persuasion, and Attitude Change. In A. G. Greenwald, T. C. Brock & T. M. Ostrom (Eds.), *Psychological Foundations of Attitudes*. New York: Academic Press.

Guasp, M., Giné-Servén, E., Maudes, E., Rosa-Justicia, M., Martínez-Hernández, E., Boix-Quintana, E., ... & Dalmau, J. (2021). Clinical, neuroimmunologic, and CSF investigations in first episode psychosis. *Neurology, 97*(1), e61-e75.

Hamby, S., & Grych, J. (2013). The Web of Violence: Exploring Connections Among Different Forms of Interpersonal Violence and Abuse. Springer Science & Business Media.

Herman, J. L. (2015). Trauma and recovery: The aftermath of violence--from domestic abuse to political terror. Basic Books.

Hiemstra, R. (2001). Uses and benefits of journal writing. *New directions for adult and continuing education, 2001*(90), 19.

Hofmann, S. G., Asnaani, A., Vonk, I. J., Sawyer, A. T., & Fang, A. (2012). The efficacy of cognitive behavioral therapy: A review of meta-analyses. *Cognitive Therapy and Research, 36*(5), 427-440.

Howes, O. D., & Kapur, S. (2009). The dopamine hypothesis of schizophrenia: version III—The final common pathway. *Schizophrenia Bulletin, 35*(3), 549-562.

Hyman, S. E., Malenka, R. C., & Nestler, E. J. (2006). Neural mechanisms of addiction: the role of reward-related learning and memory. *Annual Review of Neuroscience, 29*, 565-598.

Im, S., & Follette, V. M. (2016). Rumination and mindfulness related to multiple types of trauma exposure. *Translational Issues in Psychological Science, 2*(4), 395.

James, William. (1910). *The Principles of Psychology*. New York, NY: Holt.

REFERENCES

Jha, M. K., Qamar, A., Vaduganathan, M., Charney, D. S., & Murrough, J. W. (2019). Screening and management of depression in patients with cardiovascular disease: JACC state-of-the-art review. *Journal of the American College of Cardiology*, *73*(14), 1827-1845.

Kalaf, J., Coutinho, E. S. F., Vilete, L. M. P., Luz, M. P., Berger, W., Mendlowicz, M., ... & Figueira, I. (2017). Sexual trauma is more strongly associated with tonic immobility than other types of trauma–A population based study. *Journal of affective disorders*, *215*, 71-76.

Katz, J., & Arias, I. (1999). Psychological abuse and depressive symptoms in dating women: Do different types of abuse have differential effects?. *Journal of family Violence*, *14*(3), 281-295.

Kaźmierczak, M., & Nicola, S. M. (2022). The Arousal-motor Hypothesis of Dopamine Function: Evidence that Dopamine Facilitates Reward Seeking in Part by Maintaining Arousal. *Neuroscience*, *499*, 64-103.

Keenan, A., & Newton, T. J. (1985). Stressful events, stressors and psychological strains in young professional engineers. *Journal of Occupational Behaviour*, *6*(2), 151-156.

Kendall-Tackett, K. (2002). The health effects of childhood abuse: four pathways by which abuse can influence health. *Child abuse & neglect*, *26*(6-7), 715-729.

Kessler, R. C., Berglund, P., Demler, O., Jin, R., & Walters, E. E. (2005). Lifetime prevalence and age-of-onset distributions of DSM-IV disorders in the National Comorbidity Survey Replication (NCS-R). Archives of General Psychiatry, 62(6), 593-602.

Kira, I., Lewandowski, L., Somers, C. L., Yoon, J. S., & Chiodo, L. (2012). The effects of trauma types, cumulative trauma, and PTSD on IQ in two highly traumatized adolescent groups. *Psychological Trauma: Theory, Research, Practice, and Policy*, *4*(1), 128.

Kirkegaard Thomsen, D. (2006). The association between rumination and negative affect: A review. *Cognition and Emotion*, *20*(8), 1216-1235.

Koob, G. F., & Volkow, N. D. (2010). Neurocircuitry of addiction. *Neuropsychopharmacology*, *35*(1), 217-238.

Kreek, M. J., Nielsen, D. A., & LaForge, K. S. (2004). Genes associated with addiction. *Neuromolecular medicine*, *5*(1), 85-108.

Kross, E., Ayduk, O., & Mischel, W. (2005). When asking "why" does not hurt: Distinguishing rumination from reflective processing of negative emotions. Psychological Science, 16(9), 709-715.

Krystal, H. (1978). Trauma and affects. *The psychoanalytic study of the child, 33*(1), 81-116.

Law, K. C., & Tucker, R. P. (2018). Repetitive negative thinking and suicide: a burgeoning literature with need for further exploration. *Current opinion in psychology, 22*, 68-72.

Le Foll, B., Collo, G., Rabiner, E. A., Boileau, I., Pich, E. M., & Sokoloff, P. (2014). Dopamine D3 receptor ligands for drug addiction treatment: update on recent findings. *Progress in brain research, 211*, 255-275.

Levitt, E. E. (2015). *The psychology of anxiety*. Routledge.

Liem, R., & Liem, J. H. (1988). Psychological effects of unemployment on workers and their families. *Journal of social issues, 44*(4), 87-105.

Maddi, S. R. (2004). Hardiness: An operationalization of existential courage. Journal of Humanistic Psychology, 44(3), 279-298.

Magruder, K. M., Kassam-Adams, N., Thoresen, S., & Olff, M. (2016). Prevention and public health approaches to trauma and traumatic stress: a rationale and a call to action. European Journal of Psychotraumatology, 7(1), 29715.

Mangan, B. (1993). Taking phenomenology seriously: The "fringe" and its implications for cognitive research. *Consciousness and Cognition* 2, 89-108.

Martin, J., Raby, K. L., Labella, M. H., & Roisman, G. I. (2017). Childhood abuse and neglect, attachment states of mind, and non-suicidal self-injury. *Attachment & human development, 19*(5), 425-446.

McCutcheon, R. A., Marques, T. R., & Howes, O. D. (2020). Schizophrenia—an overview. *JAMA psychiatry, 77*(2), 201-210.

McEwen, B. S. (2007). Physiology and neurobiology of stress and adaptation: central role of the brain. *Physiological Reviews, 87*(3), 873-904.

McGrath, J., Saha, S., Chant, D., & Welham, J. (2008). Schizophrenia: A concise overview of incidence, prevalence, and mortality. Epidemiologic Reviews, 30(1), 67-76.

Metzger, R. L., Miller, M. L., Cohen, M., Sofka, M., & Borkovec, T. D. (1990). Worry changes decisionf making: The effect of negative thoughts on cognitive processing. *Journal of Clinical Psychology, 46*(1), 78-88.

Monroe, S. M., & Slavich, G. M. (2016). Psychological stressors: overview. *Stress: Concepts, cognition, emotion, and behavior*, 109-115.

Mullen, S. (2018). Major depressive disorder in children and adolescents. *Mental Health Clinician, 8*(6), 275-283.

REFERENCES

Ng, H. T. H., Zhang, C. Q., Phipps, D., Zhang, R., & Hamilton, K. (2022). Effects of anxiety and sleep on academic engagement among university students. *Australian Psychologist, 57*(1), 57-64.

Olfson, M., Blanco, C., & Marcus, S. C. (2016). Treatment of adult depression in the United States. JAMA Internal Medicine, 176(10), 1482-1491.

Oliver, D., Reilly, T. J., Baccaredda Boy, O., Petros, N., Davies, C., Borgwardt, S., ... & Fusar-Poli, P. (2020). What causes the onset of psychosis in individuals at clinical high risk? A meta-analysis of risk and protective factors. *Schizophrenia bulletin, 46*(1), 110-120.

Orsolini, L., Latini, R., Pompili, M., Serafini, G., Volpe, U., Vellante, F., ... & De Berardis, D. (2020). Understanding the complex of suicide in depression: from research to clinics. *Psychiatry investigation, 17*(3), 207.

Ouimette, P. E., & Brown, P. J. (2003). *Trauma and substance abuse: Causes, consequences, and treatment of comorbid disorders*. American Psychological Association.

Papageorgiou, C., & Wells, A. (2003). An empirical test of a clinical metacognitive model of rumination and depression. Cognitive Therapy and Research, 27(3), 261-273.

Pettorruso, M., Zoratto, F., Miuli, A., De Risio, L., Santorelli, M., Pierotti, A., ... & di Giannantonio, M. (2020). Exploring dopaminergic transmission in gambling addiction: A systematic translational review. *Neuroscience & Biobehavioral Reviews, 119*, 481-511

Petty, R. E.& Bri±ol, P. (February, 2000). *Implications of Self-Validation Theory for Resistance to Persuasion*. Paper presented in the first annual meeting of the Society for Personality and Social Psychology. Nashville, Tennessee.

Petty, R. E., & Cacioppo, J. T. (1986). *Communication and Persuasion: Central and Peripheral Routes to Attitude Change*. New York: Springer/Verlag.

Petty, R. E., & Cacioppo, J. T.(1983). Central and Peripheral Routes to Persuasion: Application to Advertising. In L. Percy & A. Woodside (Eds.), *Advertising and Consumer Psychology* (pp. 3-23). Lexington, MA: D. C. Heath.

Petty, R. E., & Krosnick, J. A. (Eds.) (1995). *Attitude Strength: Antecedents and Consequences*. Mahwah, NJ: Erlbaum.

Petty, R. E., Bri±ol, P., & Tormala, Z. L. (2002). "Thought Confidence as a Determinant of Persuasion: The Self-Validation Hypothesis." *Journal of Personality and Social Psychology*, 82, 722-741.

Petty, R. E., Ostrom, T. M., & Brock, T. C. (1981). Historical Foundations of the Cognitive Response Approach to Attitudes and Persuasion. In R. Petty, T. Ostrom, and T. Brock (Eds.), *Cognitive Responses in Persuasion* (pp. 5-29). Hillsdale, NJ: Erlbaum.

Postmus, J. L., Plummer, S. B., McMahon, S., Murshid, N. S., & Kim, M. S. (2012). Understanding economic abuse in the lives of survivors. Journal of Interpersonal Violence, 27(3), 411-430.

Robinson, T. E., & Berridge, K. C. (2008). Review. The incentive sensitization theory of addiction: some current issues. *Philosophical Transactions of the Royal Society of London. Series B, Biological Sciences, 363*(1507), 3137-3146.

Rowland, T. A., & Marwaha, S. (2018). Epidemiology and risk factors for bipolar disorder. *Therapeutic advances in psychopharmacology, 8*(9), 251-269.

Scharf, M. (2007). Long-term effects of trauma: Psychosocial functioning of the second and third generation of Holocaust survivors. *Development and psychopathology, 19*(2), 603-622.

Schneiderman, Ben. (2000). The limits of speech recognition. *Communications of the ACM,* 43:9, 63-65.

Scholl, L., Seth, P., Kariisa, M., Wilson, N., & Baldwin, G. (2018). Drug and Opioid-Involved Overdose Deaths—United States, 2013–2017. Morbidity and Mortality Weekly Report, 67(5152), 1419-1427.

Schultz, W. (2015). Neuronal reward and decision signals: from theories to data. *Physiological Reviews, 95*(3), 853-951.

Selden, J. and Selden, A. (1995). Unpacking the logic of mathematical statements. *Educational Studies in Mathematics* 29, 123-151.

Seligman, M. E. P. (1991). Learned optimism: How to change your mind and your life. New York, NY: Knopf.

Serido, J., Almeida, D. M., & Wethington, E. (2004). Chronic stressors and daily hassles: Unique and interactive relationships with psychological distress. *Journal of health and social behavior, 45*(1), 17-33.

Shavitt, S. & Brock, T. C. (1986). Delayed Recall of Copytest Responses: The Temporal Stability of Listed Thoughts. *Journal of Advertising*, 19, 4, 6-17.

Shri, R. (2010). Anxiety: causes and management. *The Journal of Behavioral Science, 5*(1), 100-118.

Sit, D., Rothschild, A. J., & Wisner, K. L. (2015). A review of postpartum psychosis. Journal of Women's Health, 15(4), 352-368.

REFERENCES

Slomian, J., Honvo, G., Emonts, P., Reginster, J. Y., & Bruyère, O. (2019). Consequences of maternal postpartum depression: A systematic review of maternal and infant outcomes. *Women's Health, 15*, 1745506519844044.

Slopen, N., Shonkoff, J. P., Albert, M. A., Yoshikawa, H., Jacobs, A., Stoltz, R., & Williams, D. R. (2016). Racial disparities in child adversity in the US: Interactions with family immigration history and income. American Journal of Preventive Medicine, 50(1), 47-56.

Sternberg, R. J. (2009). Cognitive psychology (5th ed.). Wadsworth Cengage Learning.

Substance Abuse and Mental Health Services Administration. (2014). SAMHSA's Concept of Trauma and Guidance for a Trauma-Informed Approach. Rockville, MD: Substance Abuse and Mental Health Services Administration.

Tedeschi, R. G., & Calhoun, L. G. (2004). Posttraumatic growth: Conceptual foundations and empirical evidence. Psychological Inquiry, 15(1), 1-18.

Ullman, S. E., & Peter-Hagene, L. (2016). Longitudinal relationships of social reactions, PTSD, and revictimization in sexual assault survivors. Journal of Interpersonal Violence, 31(6), 1074-1094.

Vafapoor, H., Zakiei, A., Hatamian, P., & Bagheri, A. (2018). Correlation of sleep quality with emotional regulation and repetitive negative thoughts: A casual model in pregnant women. *Journal of Kermanshah University of Medical Sciences, 22*(3).

Vafapoor, H., Zakiei, A., Hatamian, P., & Bagheri, A. (2018). Correlation of sleep quality with emotional regulation and repetitive negative thoughts: A casual model in pregnant women. *Journal of Kermanshah University of Medical Sciences, 22*(3).

Van der Kolk, B. A. (2003). *Psychological trauma*. American Psychiatric Pub.

Volkow, N. D., Fowler, J. S., & Wang, G. J. (2002). Role of dopamine in drug reinforcement and addiction in humans: results from imaging studies. *Behavioural pharmacology, 13*(5), 355-366.

Van der Kolk, B. A. (2014). The body keeps the score: Brain, mind, and body in the healing of trauma. Viking.

Volkow, N. D., Koob, G. F., & McLellan, A. T. (2016). Neurobiologic advances from the brain disease model of addiction. *New England Journal of Medicine, 374*(4), 363-371.

Walker, B. L., & Holt, M. D. (2019). Signs of Psychosis Leading to a Diagnosis of Progressive Multifocal Leukoencephalopathy: A Case Report. *Journal of Maine Medical Center, 1*(1), 11.

Walker, E. R., McGee, R. E., & Druss, B. G. (2015). Mortality in mental disorders and global disease burden implications: a systematic review and meta-analysis. JAMA Psychiatry, 72(4), 334-341.

Wegman, H. L., & Stetler, C. (2009). A meta-analytic review of the effects of childhood abuse on medical outcomes in adulthood. *Psychosomatic medicine*, *71*(8), 805-812.

Wenzlaff, R. M., Wegner, D. M., & Roper, D. W. (1988). Depression and mental control: the resurgence of unwanted negative thoughts. *Journal of Personality and social psychology*, *55*(6), 882.

Wise, R. A., & Robble, M. A. (2020). Dopamine and addiction. *Annual review of psychology*, *71*, 79-106.

Wright, P. L. (1981). Cognitive Responses to Mass Media Advocacy. In R. E. Petty, T. M. Ostrom, & T. C. Brock (Eds.), *Cognitive Responses in Persuasion* (pp. 263-282). Hillsdale, NJ: Lawrence Erlbaum Associates.

Wright, P. L.(1973). The Cognitive Processes Mediating Acceptance of Advertising. *Journal of Marketing Research*, 10, 53-62.

Yonkers, K. A., Wisner, K. L., Stewart, D. E., Oberlander, T. F., Dell, D. L., Stotland, N., Ramin, S., Chaudron, L., & Lockwood, C. (2009). The management of depression during pregnancy: a report from the American Psychiatric Association and the American College of Obstetricians and Gynecologists. *General hospital psychiatry*, *31*(5), 403–413. https://doi.org/10.1016/j.genhosppsych.2009.04.003

www.ingramcontent.com/pod-product-compliance
Lightning Source LLC
Chambersburg PA
CBHW060538010526
44119CB00052B/746